The Baseball Coaching Bible

Jerry Kindall
John Winkin

Editors

Human Kinetics

Library of Congress Cataloging-in-Publication Data

The baseball coaching bible / Jerry Kindall, John Winkin, editors.
    p. cm.
    ISBN 0-7360-0161-1
    1. Baseball—Coaching. 2. Baseball—Training. I. Kindall, Jerry. II. Winkin, John.
GV875.5 .B38 1999
796.357'07'7—dc21   99-052257
ISBN 0-7360-3331-9

Developmental Editor: Kent Reel; **Assistant Editor:** Kim Thoren; **Copyeditor:** Bob Replinger; **Proofreader:** Sue Fetters; **Graphic Designer:** Robert Reuther; **Graphic Artist:** Kim Maxey; **Cover Designer:** Jack Davis; **Photographer (cover):** © 1999 Bahr Vermeer Haecker Architects in Association with Lamp Rynearson and Associates and HNTB Architects; **Illustrator:** Keith Blomberg; **Printer:** United Graphics.

On the cover: A centerfield view of Rosenblatt Stadium in Omaha, Nebraska, site of the NCAA Division I College World Series. Opened in 1948, the stadium was significantly expanded and improved through the 1990s. Many of the coaches who contributed to *The Baseball Coaching Bible* have been frequent visitors—and winners—with their teams at this special ballpark.

Human Kinetics books are available at special discounts for bulk purchase. Special editions or book excerpts can also be created to specification. For details, contact the Special Sales Manager at Human Kinetics.

Printed in the United States of America   10 9 8 7 6 5 4 3 2 1

Human Kinetics
Web site: http://www.humankinetics.com/

United States: Human Kinetics
P.O. Box 5076
Champaign, IL 61825-5076
1-800-747-4457
e-mail: humank@hkusa.com

Canada: Human Kinetics
475 Devonshire Road Unit 100
Windsor, ON N8Y 2L5
1-800-465-7301 (in Canada only)
e-mail: humank@hkcanada.com

Europe: Human Kinetics, P.O. Box IW14
Leeds LS16 6TR, United Kingdom
+44 (0)113-278 1708
e-mail: humank@hkeurope.com

Australia: Human Kinetics
57A Price Avenue
Lower Mitcham, South Australia 5062
(08) 82771555
e-mail: humank@hkaustralia.com

New Zealand: Human Kinetics
P.O. Box 105-231, Auckland Central
09-523-3462
e-mail: humank@hknewz.com

To baseball coaches everywhere

CONTENTS

FOREWORD

In baseball there is a saying that the more you learn and understand the game, the more you will appreciate and enjoy it.

Who enjoys baseball the most? Is it the players who compete in the field who have the opportunity to be involved with all the big and little parts that make up the whole game? Is it the fans who observe the game as it develops before them between two teams of talented players? Or, is it the coaches who participate in and observe the competition, and also analyze, teach, and transmit the legacy of the game to their players?

Having experienced the game in each of these three roles, I believe that coaches have the ultimate opportunity to enjoy the great game of baseball. But to do so requires an investment of time and energy, a thirst for knowledge, and the willingness and ability to communicate.

As you read *The Baseball Coaching Bible*, you will be struck by how deeply each of the contributing coaches immersed themselves into their respective chapters in covering every facet of the game. You will also be impressed by the genuine respect and love each author has for the game, as well as their sense of responsibility to share what they have learned for the benefit of others.

In the Introduction, Dave Keilitz writes about the very special opportunity we have to positively influence the players we coach. The rest of the book is filled with the wisdom and passion of coaches who have made the most of that opportunity, in their own unique ways. Relish this direct access and draw all you can from these great baseball minds.

If you are a veteran coach you will connect with many of the insights and stories in the pages that follow. You have shared many of the same pleasures of the game, and yet will be encouraged to find that many more lie ahead for you to enjoy. If you are a beginning or less experienced coach, you will get an up-close look at what is in store as you learn and assume the important challenges and responsibilities of your role. This book will prepare you to handle them. And, no matter how much or how little experience you have, continuing the learning process will always be a key part of your baseball success.

Successful programs are built piece by piece to form a strong, complete whole. Any missing pieces decrease your chances to win. *The Baseball Coaching Bible* provides both an in-depth analysis of each critical piece and the blueprints of architects who so masterfully built their own winning baseball programs.

The title of this book prompts to high expectations. As you read it, you will find that the *Bible* delivers in every respect. It will become your baseball *Gospel*!

Tony LaRussa
St. Louis Cardinals

INTRODUCTION

Building Baseball's Future

Dave Keilitz

When I was baseball coach at Central Michigan University I often taught a psychology of coaching class. Sometime during the semester I would give the students the following assignment: I would ask them to think of the person other than a family member or relative whom they considered to have the most influence on their life. After a great deal of thought they were to write on a sheet of paper that person's name, the person's relationship to them, and why they choose that individual. I asked them to hand in the assignment in the next class period.

One might imagine the wide range of responses that could come from such an exercise—a best friend, a teacher, a member of the clergy, or an employer. But invariably, the most common response, by far, was a coach they had somewhere along the way. The responses ranged from Little League coaches to college coaches. It is true that most of these students were physical education majors or minors, or were student-athletes, and had more exposure to athletics and coaches than most other students. The fact remains, however, that among all the people who may have been instrumental in their lives, an overwhelming number named a former coach as the person who had the greatest positive impact on them.

This brings into focus the awesome responsibility that goes with coaching. At the same time it indicates what an honor and privilege it can and should be to hold the position. Some people feel that coaches should be all things to all people. Although that isn't possible, we know that coaches are called upon to be role models and to influence positively the lives of young people. Of all the duties and responsibilities that coaches have, I wish to focus on two areas of coaching responsibility. One is a coach's responsibility to his players, and the second is a coach's responsibility to the game itself.

The first of these is that a coach must be responsible to his players. Young people are impressionable. They will be watching your every move. They want to walk the way you walk, talk the way you talk, and act the way you act. It is said that a team takes on the attitude and characteristics of its coach, and I believe that is true. If you expect to have a classy program, then you must act with class and dignity. If the coach acts as a jerk, then the team will act the same way. When people see the trash talking and disgraceful behavior of some players and coaches on our diamonds, courts, and fields today, they must question the value and the future of athletics. Fortunately, to date it appears that such behavior is less prevalent in baseball than in other sports.

A coach is expected to instill the best in his players. We take a young person with a certain skill level, and a particular level of intellectual, social, and emotional development, and work to raise all of these to a higher level during the time we have with him. We want to win because winning is normally better for the athlete, the school, the community, and certainly ourselves. But winning is more than just outscoring the opponent. Winning is also helping the people we coach become better in all the areas I've mentioned. Have we taken our players from the level at which we received them and made them better in all areas of their lives? The great coaches I know have been able to do that.

To have this type of responsibility is what makes coaching a privilege and a special profession—a profession to be proud of, to protect and honor, and to share. This brings me to my second point, which is your responsibility as a coach to uphold, preserve, and strive to make our game even greater than it presently is.

When I first started in coaching at Central Michigan University, like every young coach I was eager to learn everything about the game. Sixty miles down the road in East Lansing, at Michigan State University, was one of the best and most respected coaches in the game, Danny Litwhiler. It took some time for me to work up the courage to call Coach Litwhiler, introduce myself, and ask if I could come down and talk baseball with him. To my delight (and relief) he was most kind and said that he would be happy to do so. I made that trip a couple of days later, and for years thereafter we continued to meet and talk baseball—in his office, in my office, in the dugout before our teams would play each other, and in the stands of some ballpark where we might be recruiting the same ballplayer. I will never forget how much I learned from him and will be forever thankful for his kindness and willingness to share his great knowledge of the game.

This book contains the thoughts, ideals, and philosophies of some of the top baseball people in the world. All of them are, or soon will be, American Baseball Coaches Association Hall of Famers. Collectively they have several hundred years of coaching experience. They have established themselves as outstanding baseball coaches, earning thousands of wins and many conference and national championships. But these men represent much more than just victories and championships; they represent everything that is good in athletics. It has been said that the key leadership function for a coach is getting his players to commit to something bigger than themselves. Great coaches are able to accomplish that, but they also do something else. They commit to the game itself and realize that the game is bigger than they are. Like Danny Litwhiler, they give to others so the game continues to grow and improve. They speak at clinics. They write articles and books. They sit in hotel lobbies at conventions and clinics and discuss with young coaches the curveball, the hit-and-run, the double play. They respect the tradition of the game and look to promote the continued growth, development, and betterment of it.

In my almost 30 years of attending the ABCA convention and working with baseball coaches around the country as a coach, athletic director, and as executive director of the ABCA, I find that most of the great ones have been willing to give back. They realize they do not own the game. They know that they became good at what they do because they too learned from others who were willing to share with them. It is the duty and the responsibility of coaches to do this.

Coaching is a great profession. Although at times it is extremely difficult and often frustrating, few jobs are as rewarding. At one time or another, most coaches have probably been asked, "What was your best moment as a coach?" Most people who ask that question are thinking of all your victories, your championships, your Coach of the Year awards. Well, photos and articles fade with time, trophies and plaques gather dust, and fans soon forget your outstanding accomplishments. But forever some moments will shine, most with what you have given your players and the game. One such moment is when a young man who has just played his last game with you as his coach comes up, extends his hand, and simply says, "Thanks, Coach." For three or four years you have worked closely with this person. You have shared your skills, knowledge, and expertise with him. You have given him the devil, and you've put your arm around him. You have leaped for joy with him over great accomplishments, and you've felt pain together over major disappointments. But when it's over and he comes up and says, "Thanks, Coach," that's enough. You know that his thank-you is an expression of appreciation, admiration, respect, and love. It's about all the time you have spent together. You know that nothing is greater than that thank-you. You know that you have done your job.

That is much of what it's all about—past, present, and future. And someday when a former player of yours, or a young coach you've helped along the way, is asked who influenced his life, he will state your name.

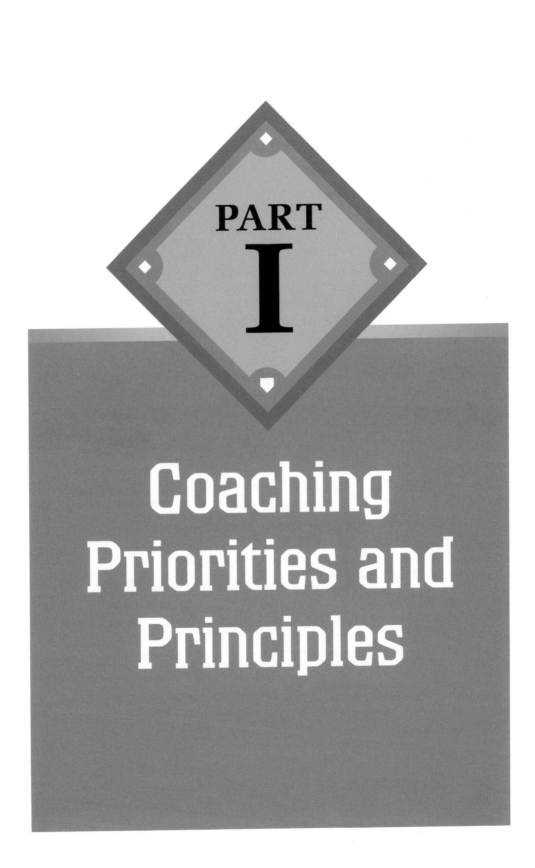

PART I

Coaching Priorities and Principles

CHAPTER ONE

Sharing a Love for the Game

John Scolinos

The most meaningful of all team games is baseball! After coaching baseball for over 50 years, I have come to believe it is the game that most closely parallels everyday life. The lessons learned by playing and coaching baseball apply directly to successful living. Fans, too, can benefit by observing how players react in learning situations.

Table 1.1 illustrates eight life lessons inherent in playing and coaching baseball.

TABLE 1.1

Life's Lessons in Baseball

Life Lesson	Example in baseball
Handling failure	Striking out Making an error Walking a batter Losing a game
Handling fear	Fear of being hit Fear of choking Fear of making an error
Handling frustration	Being retired on a well-hit line drive Making a good pitch and having it hit "9 miles" Teammate committing an error
Handling embarrassment	Striking out with the bases loaded Getting picked off Allowing the winning run to score on an error
Handling loneliness	Infielder with only 2 ground balls in the game Outfielder with no chances during the game Long intervals between appearances or innings
Handling slumps	Hitting slump with falling batting average Fielding slump Consecutive losses or high ERA Not playing several games in a row
Adjusting to change	Adjusting to strengths and weaknesses of opponent Adjust to the changing weather conditions Adjusting to a new relief pitcher or to a pinch hitter
Controlling emotions	Over excitement Challenging authority or the umpires Passiveness or indifference Allowing game situation to affect attitude Anger at bad call

All these situations occur many times during a baseball game or a season. The playing field is a laboratory for testing and refining the qualities that predict and make up a well-rounded life experience. By playing baseball you learn maturity, honesty, loyalty, adaptation, compassion, self-esteem, respect for authority, teamwork, sacrifice, humility, patience, striving for excellence, and more.

Significance of Home Plate

I see great relevance and meaning in how baseball's home plate relates to the eight life lessons learned in baseball. It seems to me that fear, failure, frustration, and embarrassment meet at home plate where the player must confront them squarely. In Little League, Pony League, Colt League, high school, college, minor leagues, and major leagues, home plate is always the same size—17 inches wide. This constancy parallels life. It tells us that whether you are a kid, a teenager, a young adult, an adult, or over the hill, certain rules, standards, and expected conduct remain the same.

As coaches, we must keep in mind the importance of the influence we exert. From my experience, I feel that what a person becomes is due to influence. We are influenced by what we see, what we hear, and what we read. It is critical that we conduct ourselves properly when leading young people. Remember, you and I are working to make them not only better ballplayers but also, and more important, better people. How many of our ballplayers will make it to the big leagues? Or even be drafted? The Bible says, "Many are called, but few are chosen." We must remember that we are preparing ballplayers for successful everyday living, not merely the next level of baseball.

Trust

Perhaps the most cherished quality coaches can provide their players is trust in one another. If we surround ourselves with ballplayers we can trust, it stands to reason they will trust the coach and trust one another. Long ago I broke down the word *trust* in the following way: T stands for *thankful.* Ballplayers should be thankful they are able to play and are on the team. The player who whines and complains would not measure up to the quality of trust. R stands for *reliable.* We rely on the ballplayer to make the ballclub look good on the field, on the campus, in the classroom, in the community. U stands for *understanding.* The player should understand how playing the game of baseball relates to everyday living.

The player should understand your philosophy and the fundamentals of baseball, and then relate those principles to everyday living. S stands for *sincere*. The player is sincere in applying what you are teaching on and off the field and making a sincere effort to be thankful and reliable. T stands for *truthful*. Players are true to the ballclub and true to themselves.

When your team has trust on your side you have a winner. A winner need not have the best natural ability to enter the select circle of other winners. The entrance to that circle is trust!

Types of Baseball Players

Although it's a generalization, through my career I found that baseball players fit into one of four categories:

- The *athlete* has outstanding natural ability, but you don't know when the player will perform. It might be today, tomorrow, or next week.

- The *competitor* competes only for himself and isn't concerned about the team.

- The *winner* will always be ready and will inspire his teammates to bear down and be ready to play on game day. The winner will urge the competitor to compete for the team, not only for himself. Furthermore, the winner does everything in his power to make the team look good on and off the field. Winners are mentally tough, motivate others, have intense desire, and are resilient and humble. If you have an athlete who is a winner, you have a blue-chip ballplayer. Be on the lookout for winners on your campus and put them in your lineup right away. They may not be the best runners, hitters, throwers, or fielders on your club, but I assure you that they will create more victories than the great athletes.

- The *donkey* is the ballplayer who just doesn't seem to fit. Many can be taught the principles of trust, faith, honesty, loyalty, teamwork, patience, and so on. In time, they will become valuable members of the team. But regretfully, a few will remain screwballs and wind up in Donkeyville—the point of no return. This is the player who doubts that marijuana and other recreational drugs will be detrimental and so becomes a user. The player soon descends to become a donkey (stubborn, stupid, slow, shady) and ends up in Donkeyville instead of the dugout. Let's do all we can to help our players avoid becoming donkeys!

Baseball Bulletin Board Material

Over 46 years of coaching, my love for the game has grown steadily deeper. Now that I'm no longer on the field every day, I can step back and measure what is truly great about baseball—the wonderful carryover to everyday living from learning, playing, and coaching the game. For example, the principles of faith and trust learned through teamwork, cooperation, and group support on the field represent the solid ground on which to build a husband, a father, a business associate, a community leader, a friend. The principles provide stability and a foundation for later life.

Over the years I've collected some slogans and lists that I call "bulletin board material." They summarize the principles we learn in baseball that we can apply to everyday life. The pinups in this chapter show a few of these.

Finally, I would like to leave you with words to live by and words to avoid.

- Five most important words: "Surround yourself with good people."
- Four most important words: "Take care of yourself."
- Three most important words: "Class, character, concern."
- Two most important words: "Thank you."
- Single most important word: "We."
- Single least important word: "I."
- Two worst words: "I quit."
- Three worst words: "I don't care."
- Four worst words: "Everybody is doing it."
- Five worst words: "Let somebody else do it."

Influence:

"As the family loses its influence in its children's upbringing, so does our nation lose control of its destiny."

The teacher and the coach are part of the family!

Let's spend a minute more with the five most important words—surround yourself with good people. Beginning with God Almighty is what I have found to be the best policy for life. "Trust in the Lord with all your heart, and do not lean on your own understanding. In all your ways acknowledge Him, and He will make your paths straight." (Proverbs 3:5–6) One of the main reasons some people excel is that they surround themselves with good people. Meanwhile, people who consistently get into trouble surround themselves with bad people (donkeys). If we apply the five most important words to our coaching, the rest will take care of itself. For example, we will take care of ourselves, we will treat people with courtesy and respect, we will show good character (character *does* count!), we will be concerned with others, we will not quit, and so on.

Signals of Negative Feedback:

Frustration, hopelessness, futility

Aggressiveness (misdirected)

Insecurity

Loneliness (lack of "oneness")

Uncertainty

Resentment

Emptiness

You will notice I did not say "I" is the worst word. Rather it is the *least important* word. We must take care of ourselves but let us not become an "I-tis" person—I, me, mine, what's in it for me.

And don't forget the two most important words—"Thank you." When Christ healed the 10 lepers (Luke 17:11–188) only one came back and said, "Thank you, Lord." Don't be one of the nine!

CHAPTER TWO

Making Baseball Fun

Bobo Brayton

Baseball is a fun, fun, fun game. We often give credit to Abner Doubleday or Alexander Cartwright for the origin of baseball, but actually it goes back much further than that. Through the research of Don Faye and Gene De Paul we find that baseball evolved through biblical times. They found that when you open the good book and take a look you can find the first baseball game because the first words in the Bible say, "In the beginning . . ." It continues from there.

> **"The journey on the way to winning is the fun of baseball."**
>
> Bobo Brayton, 1950
>
> **"It's fun to win."**
>
> Paul O'Neill, New York Yankees, 1998

Eve stole first, Adam stole second,
    Solomon umpired the game.
Rebecca went to the well with a pitcher, while Ruth in the field gained fame.
Goliath was struck out by David, Abel was hit by Cain. The Prodigal Son made
    a long home run, while Noah gave tickets for rain.
Jonah whaled and went down swinging only to pop up again.
A lion drive by old Nebuchadrezzar had Daniel warming up in the pen.
Delilah was pitching to Sampson, when he brought the house down with a clout.
The angels that day made a great double play, that's when Adam and Eve were
    thrown out.
St. Peter was checking for errors—he also had charge of the gate.
Salome sacrificed big John the Baptist, who wound up a head on the plate.
Now Satan was pitching that apple and looked like he might fan them all,
When Joshua let go with a mighty blow that went all the way to the wall.
The Lord himself took good aim and invented the very first baseball game,
And now we know why earth was made, to play His game so deftly laid.
Baseball is the American dream—its teachings carry us through life it seems.
Though it's not exactly life today, we learn these lessons when we practice and
    play.
Humble in victory, gracious in defeat are the lessons we learn whether we win
    or are beat.
The game itself will break your heart, those who win more than half or hit one-
    third are set apart.
The rest of us, in order to play, must develop strong minds and forgiving ways.
It isn't the outcome, through strife and rife, but how we tried that makes the
    diff.
Now we know why and how the game begun and to this very day it is still
    number one!

Now that we have discovered from whence the game came, we find that baseball is not exactly life itself, but the similarity keeps showing up. The game of baseball has been described by many people in many ways. Most argue it is an individual game played in a team concept. This allows for many individual philosophies and coaching approaches. In one philosophy baseball has been called a game of mistakes, so to be successful we attempt to eliminate the mistakes by greater preparation, greater dedication, better execution, better communal effort, and better discipline. Defensively we try to be in the proper position before the ball is even hit. We make the routine play all day, every day. We make the great play when needed. We play better longer. We play nine. Offensively, when we walk into the batter's box we are mentally right. We make contact and run hard. We adjust to the situation. We try not to expand the strike zone. Show me a team that expands the strike zone a half dozen times in a game, and I'll show you a team that will have trouble winning. Usually if good old WSU can avoid beating good old WSU, WSU has a chance to win. The old adage "It isn't whether you win or lose but how you play the game" has merit. Still, winning counts for a lot. Paul O'Neill, the right fielder of the 1998 New York Yankees, said it well. In an on-the-field interview immediately following the win over Cleveland for the American League Championship, he said with a wide smile on his face, "It's fun to win."

Baseball and Fun

Fun is a great feeling of playing well. Being impeccable in the defensive approach against the bunt, the steal, the hit-and-run, the double steal, and the squeeze play is a great feeling. Controlling the game through your improved play is a great feeling; playing better as the season progresses is a good feeling; building up to and winning a big game or series is a good feeling. Enjoying the journey through the season to a championship, enjoying being the best you can be—these are all good feelings. This is having fun. Fun is believing in your parents, believing in your coaches, believing in your teammates, believing in yourself. Fun is testing yourself. Fun is watching yourself progress to where you can compete to the best of your ability, where you can succeed, where you can win.

The Pony League movement has shown great foresight by developing the game for the success and fun of our youth. Their philosophy of "the playing field grows as the player grows" has been a boon to youth baseball from ages 5 to 18. This concept, more than any other, has allowed a greater number of boys and girls to succeed and have fun. Adjustments on the neighborhood team level, which include coach pitch, T-ball, and roll ball, take us right down to the cradle, making it easier for everyone to compete, succeed, and have fun.

In adult baseball and professional baseball we have made many changes to increase safety, equalize club financial resources, add fan interest, and just plain make the game more fun. Notable changes are the metal bat, the designated hitter, pitching rules, sliding rules, playing surfaces, adjustment of parks both indoor and outdoor, and night games. The playoff structures have been changed, and the use of the wild card has proven to be a major motivating factor in maintaining team and fan interest throughout the season. The 1998 wild-card races along with the Mark McGwire–Sammy Sosa home-run derby have baseball officials proclaiming 1998 as the greatest season since the Babe Ruth era. The world had fun!

Baseball Fundamentals

When taught in an atmosphere of dedication, confidence, and discipline, the fundamentals of throwing, catching, running, defense, and hitting are a whole lot of fun.

Throwing

The game of baseball can be reduced to a game of catch. There is an old saying "If you can't play catch, you can't play baseball." Show me a scatter-arm thrower, and I will show you a weak link in a baseball team. The fundamentals of baseball throwing and catching can be improved by playing catch. Known as the communication of baseball, playing catch is necessary to improve quality of play, to win, and to have fun.

A team that loves to play catch and consistently practices catching will win games. It is a great feeling to know people respect your arm. The anticipation that your good throw will make a difference in a ballgame is almost as much fun as making the throw.

Pitching and catching are the backbone of the game. Both positions are challenging and emphasize that throwing is fundamental to a fun baseball experience. A good thrower will probably have a chance to be a good pitcher. The catcher must also be a strong performer and can control the game with a good arm. You can win some games with poor pitching, but you can't even play the game with poor catching. A team with both poor pitching and poor catching is no fun!

Coach Buck Bailey, former long-time WSU coach, was conducting a throwing drill in the field house when an errant throw hit him on the side of his neck just below the ear. Many a normal person would have gone to the floor, and anyone else would have at least grabbed the spot in pain. But not Coach Bailey. In his gargantuan manner he strode right over to the player responsible for the wild throw, looked him right in the eye, and bellowed, "Sonny boy, how old are you?" The kid, shaking like a leaf in anticipation of being choked by those ham-sized hands or at the very least pounded into the ground, stammered out, "Seven—seven—seventeen," and waited for the worst. Buck hesitated a moment, growled, "How can you learn to be so wild in such a few years?" and stomped away, never touching the wound on his neck.

Running

Running is fun. If you can't run fast, the next best thing is to run hard. Add running smart, and we have a good player, one that all opponents fear. In fact, the mental pressure you put on the opposition when you get on base is as effective as the physical pressure. When a good runner gets on base, the whole game changes. Dr. John Olerud Sr. was a collegiate and professional catcher with average speed. Though his position usually dictates that he bat low in the order, even in pro ball he usually hit number two. He could handle the bat, he ran hard, and he ran smart. On one occasion in a crucial regional playoff game, he came from first to third on a ball hit short up the middle. After a great slide, he dusted himself off, looked at me in the third-base coaching box, and said with a grin, "I burned 'em with my speed." He was having fun.

Defensive Play

Defensive play is where running and throwing come together to create an integral part of the game. Infield play is challenging because every ground ball reacts differently. Thus the approach to each play is different. Practicing infield is enjoyable and culminates into great fun when making the plays in a game. You have a feeling of satisfaction, the confidence of knowing you can do it, and the knowledge that you are the best. The journey goes from practice to practice, game to game, year to year. The number one factor in winning is knowing you can, and it will happen if your team can communicate.

To be an outfielder you have to love to run because the essence of the position is running after fly balls and ground balls and retrieving them to the infield. To practice this position, you have to run and run and run. You learn this fundamental of outfield play, you take charge of your territory, you invite them to hit one out there, and you'll make the play. Dr. Bob Fry, as a center fielder for the 1965 WSU Cougar baseball team competing against Texas in the College World Series, made eight putouts and an assist, stole five bases including home, and managed to get three hits including a home run, all in one game. His performance fit the old cliche—he can hit 'em, go get 'em, and slide on both sides. He had fun playing the game!

Hitting

Hitting has many times been referred to as the fun part of baseball. Again, it is the confidence of knowing you can do it. You get a special feeling in your hands when you hit the ball right on the nose. Man, that feels good. This is where the game of baseball really is fun. A nationally recognized coach recently told me that he has eliminated the use of batting gloves so his players can get that good hitting feeling.

Building Fun Into Your Program

As part of your coaching philosophy, you can devise ways to pump fun into your program by adding fun to team meetings, the locker room, your practices, your games, your dugout, and your off-the-field baseball including road trips.

Team Meetings

Let the players know what the coaches expect. Teach them that being the best they can be is fun. Teach what all the great teachers in sport—Rockne, Leahy, Connie Mack, and Lombardi to name a few—have taught, that discipline and a dedicated work ethic are the basic building blocks in sport. Teach them that being a honed, disciplined athlete leads to better execution and higher confidence and thus to more wins and more fun. Confidence grows from a fun work ethic.

An example of a group who have excelled in baseball through a fun, dedicated work ethic are Japanese baseball players. Generally when you tell an American pitcher to run ten 50-yard sprints, the first 10 yards he will jog, the second 10 yards he will run, the next 20 yards will be a sprint, and the last 10 yards he will slow to a jog. There is a good possibility that he will run only 9 of the 10 sprints. The Japanese pitcher gets 10 yards behind the start line, runs to the start line and breaks into his sprint when he reaches it, continues to the finish line 50 yards away, and then jogs an additional 10 yards before stopping. He will likely run a couple extra sprints for good measure. Many people wonder why Japanese teams are so hard to beat. I believe this dedicated work ethic is the answer.

Tell your team how much the world needs leaders and that they can be leaders. How? Simply follow directions, be ready to learn, have an enthusiastic approach, maintain a positive attitude, and be a team player.

By adding a little fun to team meetings you will build camaraderie, fellowship, and leadership. Cocoa and cookies is a good beginning. The kids must have confidence in the coach. Once that is established everything comes easy. The coach must set goals, define stepping-stones, and give directions.

Locker Room

The locker room might include a sign pertinent to the moment, the orders of the day, a place to rest, some good music, occasional joking, and light horseplay. All these things develop camaraderie. At Washington State University we once had two of the greenest guys ever to leave home. If they had wanted to go home they couldn't have found their way. After about the first month of the school year, a Far Side cartoon was posted on the locker room bulletin board showing two college greenhorns, hand labeled (by the team's upperclassmen) Kevin and Ole. They were sitting at a table with a box of corn flakes, a quart of milk, two bowls, and an open cookbook. Kevin was saying, "It says right here in the cookbook, Ole, to put the corn flakes in first." Ten years have passed, and that dog-eared cartoon remains in the locker room—Kevin and Ole live on.

On the Field

On the practice field you must provide organization and immediate goals for the day. Everyone needs to know what he is doing and where he is going on that specific day or week or before the next game. Here—out on the practice field—is where the players must have some fun. Your approach, your methods of teaching and directing, show up here. This is their workyard, their ballyard, where life begins and ends every day. Make sure that they are successful, that they work hard and make progress, that they hear a lot of "'atta boys."

Games from the good old days can be a lot of fun. You can use them when the number of players you have is limited or when you want to work in a less formal setting. Some of the old favorites are One Old Cat, Over the Line, Work Up, Five Hundred, Fungo Baseball, Long Ball or Home Run, Pepper, Long Pepper, and Flip. The guys will come out early and compete like heck if you get them started. The drills of baseball and the game itself can be made fun by oral embellishment from the coaches and players. Much of the chatter doesn't even sound like the original words. For instance, the phrase "come on now" is always a slurred "hon now." Remember other old favorites—"hon you babe," "hon horse," "work your fee," "way to go," "turn it loose," "atta babe," and again a lot of "atta boys." The old vaudeville saw about leaving 'em laughing, or at least feeling fuzzy, is a good philosophy.

At the end of an early fall practice during the second year that John Olerud Jr. attended Washington State, I called the team together in what we called a Coug Up. As I was about to speak regarding the practice, running, and so on, I noticed an undertone among the players, with even some laughing. I asked, "Hey, what's going on? Cut me in on the joke." It seemed that some of the guys had seen Ole at a movie with a real cute girl. As far as anyone knew this was Ole's first date ever, and it was making big news among the troops. Ole the Monk had turned into a lady's man. As it worked out the girl was his sister who had just come to college as a freshman. Ole left them laughing—at themselves.

Game day is what we practice for. Pregame, the game itself, and postgame should all be organized and scheduled to the second. The game must start on time—you never know when it will end. The presentation of the game itself is so important. Part of this presentation is the fun atmosphere that you create around your park for the good of the game and the good of the fans. The pride you create in your players about their appearance and performance is a fun thing. A well-groomed park, excellent fan amenities, the competition, qualified officials, the music, the announcers, and even the scoreboard add up to an enjoyable baseball experience for everyone. Play ball! Have fun!

Dugout and Bullpen

The dugout is the player's home, his cocoon. It should be kept clean, comfortable, orderly, and active. Baseball is a game in which everyone is not physically involved all the time. The coach must invent things to do in the dugout to keep everyone in the game and have fun as well. Many of the nonstarters will enjoy doing different chores. Some will insist on doing their chores. Some chores fit specific people better than others. For example, substitute catchers can work between innings warming up pitchers. They can also work the bullpen. Next-game pitchers can chart the pitchers or hitters. To maintain efficiency and keep interest high, assign chores in short stints. Keep that dugout hopping and fun.

The bullpen, or "bully," an extension of the dugout, is a special spot in the lives of at least one-third of your team. Players can enjoy bullpen duty by doing other activities besides throwing and keeping the place neat. They can learn to swing the bat and bunt, learn to juggle, learn to handle the ball, learn how to pitch by watching, learn to roll the ball up one arm, around the neck, down the other arm, under the leg, around the back and so on, learn to throw two balls at once for strikes or to the bases. You'll be a hero. Hey, the bullpen isn't boring—it's fun. Just remember, when it's time to pitch, "Keep your head down, throw hard, and mix in a strike now and again."

Off the Field

As a coach you spend more of your time in off-the-field coaching than on-the-field coaching. This has been referred to as incidental coaching or coaching around the edges. It occurs on the travel bus, in the locker room, around the cage, before or after practice, anywhere a coach talks to a player. It is amazing how much improvement can be accomplished with some conversation and some extra work. It can be fun.

Know your players—the good things and the amusing things, what they do, who they run around with, their problems, their strengths and weaknesses, their parents, where they are from. Give your players support and help. If your players are collegiate or high school age, know their academic program, counsel them, show them you care about them now and in the future. A couple of good questions to ask are, "How is that tough history class treating you?" or "How are the folks doing?" Give them a phone call occasionally. It's an ego booster to answer a roomie's question of, "Who was that?" with a casual, "Oh, just the coach." Why he called doesn't really matter; it's that he called. A team activity unrelated to baseball is a good way to have fun and to cement relations. Promote a basketball, volleyball, or flag football team in the off-season, or attend a game together. Invite the girls to a sock hop in the locker room to get them thinking the old coach is human. Have a racquetball, horseshoe, or tennis tournament. Have picnics and parties. The memories of white-elephant Christmas gifts hang on for years. Remember, the way to a ballplayer's heart is through his stomach, so put on a good feed every once in a while. Memories of a good steak or a three-layer chocolate cake go a long ways in building trust and friendship.

An important aspect of off-the-field relations is the road trips. A vital part of these trips is knowing what is expected. A written itinerary for all personnel plus interested parents, fans, and office people at home will help cut down on faux pas and put everyone at least knowing where they are to be and at what time. A travel absolute is to leave on time.

The Cougars left on a southern swing to California at a designated time, 6:00 A.M. Our number one pitcher, Stacy Morgan, missed the bus. He borrowed a car, drove eight hours to Klamath Falls, Oregon, where it broke down. He called his father in Chico, California, who drove to Klamath Falls, picked Stacy up, and drove to Redding, California, in time for Stacy to join the Cougars for breakfast the next morning. His experience was the fun topic for the remainder of the trip. Stacy is now a successful coach in Grants Pass, Oregon, and I'll bet his teams always leave on time.

You as coach must be their guide, their daddy, their poppa. These trips give you many opportunities to know your players in informal, fun situations. During the playing days of Oregon coach Don Kirsch, bus trips were really fun. They were a time of great camaraderie and fellowship, a time to harmonize, tell jokes, play road games, play cards, study together, or just visit and get to know one another better. The Ducks were having a rare bad year, and it happened to coincide with the advent of the Walkman and other self-entertainment media. During a deathly quiet trip to Idaho, Coach started thinking about the team's record and the effect of noncommunication. In the middle of the desert he told the driver to pull over and declared a moratorium on all headsets and portable radios. Much grumbling ensued, so he gave them a choice—either put away the self-entertaining media or get out and walk. The sagebrush country looked windy, cold, and lonely, so everyone conformed. They found out that person-to-person communication was fun, especially when they won 12 of their last 14 games.

Sometimes discipline can be fun when handed out in a way that the disciplined are hardly aware of but the point is made. On a long bus ride from Pullman to Reno, some of the boys were getting a bit restless, much to the chagrin of Coach Brayton. He decided he'd had enough and remembered the old one about tired boys being good boys. He stopped the bus and ordered everyone out but the coaches, the team manager, and the trainer. They had not passed a building of any description or even a car for the past 50 miles, and from that spot you could look ahead for 50 miles and see the same thing. He said, "A little exercise will do you guys good. We, the chosen few, and the bus driver will drive down the road two miles and wait 15 minutes. Those of you who are there will go on with us the rest of the way, those who aren't can hitchhike." They were all there in 13 minutes, and after some laughing and grousing about the jog, almost all were asleep in minutes.

Here's another get-the-point discipline that has never been forgotten and always brings a laugh when the boys get together. After losing a tough doubleheader to Oregon, Coach Brayton got on the bus and instructed the team manager to give everyone two dollars for meal money. He justified this skimpy allotment by explaining, "You guys play like hamburgers, you can eat hamburgers." So the next day they won a doubleheader. It was fun and they all ate steak.

Giving Back

Players have fun giving back. This is a wonderful opportunity to see them as people away from the baseball field. We learn a lot about the true person when working with them. You will see them as workers, organizers, and communicators and observe their attitude toward people. You can accomplish this in many ways, such as team autograph-signing sessions; clinics for Little Leaguers; clinics for area elementary and secondary schools; visits to area schools, shut-ins, hospitals, and senior centers; and participation in antidrug and alcohol programs. The list goes on and on. When you are doing good things for people you feel good, and that's when the fun begins.

The Baseball Family

The baseball family might be the largest family in the world. If you have ever played or coached a game, or if you are a baseball fan, you are a member of the baseball family. This gives you the right to enter any baseball park in the world after paying the admission fee. This gives you the right to be an expert on baseball playing and management. This gives you the right to cheer for any team you wish. It also gives you the right to second-guess any coach, manager, player, or management personnel. You can choose to associate yourself with any subfamily, whether you've been invited or not. If you're a Red Sox family member, you can declare war on any Yankees family member. If you're a Trojans family member, you're automatically at odds with any Bruins family member. You can wear a Cubs shirt and be a Cubs family member even though you've never been near Chicago, much less Wrigley Field.

With these rights go the privilege of responsibility. None of us are bigger than the game. We owe the game; it doesn't owe us. The fan in the Bob Uecker seat in the stadium or the one home listening or watching probably doesn't owe the game to the extent of the guy playing second base in the All-Star Game. For instance, one player, not the team, was wearing a rag around his head in place of a cap during batting and fielding practice before a major-league game. As a family member I felt this was ludicrous and a degradation of the game. I wrote this individual, explaining to him as a father might, that we all, especially high-profile players, owe the game its identity, its integrity, its perpetuity, and its tradition.

These seem to be tenuous times in baseball, so we need everyone's help. Because the season of 1998 may have taken baseball off the endangered list, perhaps individual acts are not as crucial as they once seemed to be. But in my opinion they are. Yes, we hate and we love in the baseball family. The attitude of the family during the McGwire-Sosa run for the home-run record was an impeccable example of love and respect for family members. Hey, we still love Babe Ruth, we still love Roger Maris, and we still love the guy who spit on the umpire. To be a member of the baseball family is the ultimate in family fun.

CHAPTER THREE

Competing With Class

Hal Smeltzly

We all know true baseball fans—those traditionalists who can give you statistics back to the 1920s and, in the same breath, quote Roger Angell or George Will. They will debate with you about which was the greatest team of all time and what records will or will not be broken. But when all is said and done, what you will always get is a smug smile and the assurance that, whatever else you say about baseball, it is most assuredly a game with class.

During the early weeks of September 1998, the word class came up repeatedly. Our new American hero, St. Louis Cardinal Mark McGwire, showed class in almost every move he made. The Roger Maris family was described as a class act. As Chicago Cub Sammy Sosa ran from his position in the outfield to hug and congratulate McGwire on his record-breaking home run, announcers spoke in awe of his inherent class. Class is a widely used term and can apply correctly in a number of situations. For the purpose of this discussion, I will use one of the dictionary's definitions: excellence, excellence as it applies to behavior, performance, appearance, and sportsmanship.

The Coach Sets the Standard

Let's begin by taking a hard look at yourself as you prepare to adapt to the personalities of the young athletes you will be working with as you mold and develop your team. In today's society in which a two-parent home is often the exception rather than the rule, you will find young people desperately searching for role models, people they can admire and emulate.

It has been my experience that young people are looking for quality leadership from the person in charge. First impressions are a critical factor in the success or failure of coaches as they recruit, make personal contact with players, and interact at the first team meeting. Therefore, it is important to review and evaluate your leadership attitude so that you are prepared to work with parents, players, and administrators whom you may be meeting for the first time.

Leadership Style

To be a successful coach, you must work at keeping your people skills appropriate and effective. Review your thought processes. What assumptions or convictions about certain things, ideas, or individuals do you hold as true? For example, coaches have preconceived attitudes about human nature and what makes players respond. Some coaches believe that reward and discipline should be used only in exceptional cases.

Most of the time they will choose to go with the flow when working with players. This leadership style works better with older, more experienced players.

Joe Torre, manager of the New York Yankees 1998 World Series Champions, is a classic example of an outstanding manager who is able to adjust to pressure from both management and outside sources and adapt his go-with-the-flow leadership style to the experience and skill level of an exceptional group of professional players. Remarks from the Yankees' clubhouse describing Torre's leadership style include, "Joe doesn't get rattled, no matter how tough things may be," and, "Joe makes it seem like it's not that bad." Joe Torre hates team meetings; he favors casual one-on-one sessions by the players' lockers. Probably the key to the go-with-the-flow style is best summed up by another player's comments: "He's a player's manager. We had two rules: play hard and be on time. Although Joe doesn't say much, when he does speak, everyone listens."

You must make a decision about what leadership style best suits you and your team. Selecting the correct style of leadership requires you to evaluate the situation. Consider how skillful, motivated, and committed your players are to having a successful season. These are critical factors as they will definitely influence your efforts to communicate. Your players must understand your intent, so that they will want to help you and the team accomplish a successful season. Inexperienced players will need your direction. You will have to tell them what they should do and how they should do it. For a team with returning players, you will need to assess the level of direction required. As the team gains some competence and experience, the players will become even more motivated. As players develop, you will find that you can gradually take a more flexible style. This can apply to the individuals or to the team as a whole. Times will come, however, when you may need to return temporarily to the direct style of leadership.

The important point to recognize is that the players generally behave in accord with the coaches' attitude. This applies to Little League as well as the major leagues. The attitudes of the head coach impact directly on the leadership a coach is able to exhibit. This will determine the effectiveness of individual players and the team as a group.

Values

Values are an important self-evaluation checkpoint. Your values will influence your priorities. You place value on such things as honesty, integrity, and sportsmanship. Strong values are what you put first, defend most, and want least to give up. You will find that individual values will at times be in conflict. For example, you, as the head coach, submit a travel voucher incorrectly summarizing expenses. You know it is incorrect and likely will not be looked at closely. What you value most will likely guide your actions. In this situation your values on truth and self-interest will be in conflict. I hope your choice would be to correct the report and reinforce the value of being honest. What you value most will likely reflect your actions and will greatly influence players and direction they take.

Another important element of self-evaluation, I would suggest, is a review of the elements of developing respect. Gaining the respect of players is important. A respected coach influences players by teaching, coaching, disciplining, and setting a good example. A coach must bring out the best in every player. He has to eliminate counterproductive attitudes, values, and behavior. For example, if after you and your assistant coaches have done your best with a player he still does not meet the standards you have set, you may have to drop him from the team. You cannot allow him to disrupt the cohesion you are trying to develop on the team.

Respected, successful coaches create a leadership climate that causes most players to develop the right values. Successful leadership is the quality of bringing people into the coach's way of thinking about values and procedure, having them agree that this is the course to follow to be successful. This mutual agreement on how to go forward is not built on fear or intimidation but on respect for the head coach. A respected coach can often change a player's motivation from self-interest to becoming a selfless player who makes a positive contribution to the team.

Remember that a coach, whether you like it or not, is always on display. A coach's actions say much more than his words. Players will watch you closely and imitate your behavior. Accept the obligation to be a good role model and do not ignore the effect your behavior has on others.

Being a positive and respected role model centers on a person's integrity. Integrity means being honest and straightforward and avoiding deception. It is important that you be sincere, honest, and candid. Integrity is the basis for trust and confidence that must exist if a team is to be successful. If you compromise your personal integrity, you break the bonds of trust between yourself and your players. You must demonstrate integrity in your personal and professional life in an ongoing way.

Leadership in Action

Directed democracy best describes my first choice of leadership styles. I discovered early in my career that this style allowed me to communicate best with my players and be persuasive with their parents, my employer, my boosters, and the media. One of the elements of the directed democracy style of leadership is having every team member know that he is important, that he should feel free to discuss with the head coach what is on his mind. His input is important. The players are aware that there is one person in charge—the head coach. The head coach makes the final decision after considering what he has heard from others and what his experience tells him is the right move on a particular occasion.

At Florida Southern, we have an opportunity to recruit players who will fit our baseball program and school environment. My view has been that you recruit or select your problems. Therefore, you should take special care to choose the type of individual you want to work with in your program.

My experience has been that players who come from winning programs and have a solid relationship of respect and caring with family members are likely to be successful team members. These individuals are more secure and stable, more approachable about adopting important values and goals.

The success that Florida Southern has had includes 15 conference championships, 18 NCAA regional championships, 8 national championships, and combined winning record of 1,358 wins and 416 loses for a .766 winning percentage. This has been made possible because over a 30-year period, administered by three head coaches, attention has been paid to specific details. This includes team-member selection, individual and team teaching of fundamentals, and appearance and behavior. Whenever a Florida Southern team is together as a unit, whether on the field or traveling, they are going to present a sharp, classy appearance. This standard has been in place for 30 years, passed on from veterans to incoming freshmen. The sense of pride that dictates appearance also carries over to the way players respond to the people they meet, whether it is a waitress who serves them or the bat boy for the opposing team. Confidence, courtesy, and composure are all part of the makeup of the Florida Southern athlete.

The most significant of these details deals with the teaching of fundamentals and team preparation. Every team member has been exposed to the fundamentals of every phase of the game, from the first day of practice to the preparation for the last game of the season. In a two-hour practice we will spend a significant amount of time on teaching everything from bunt defenses to rundown plays.

The rationale behind this heavy emphasis on fundamental instruction is simply that teams that can flawlessly perform the fundamentals will be successful. When players become convinced that converting routine defensive plays into outs is possible, they begin to realize that they can play with any opponent. A fundamentally sound team will begin to believe in themselves and sense that even if they have fallen behind, if they can keep it close they will find a way to win most of the time. Winning teams view themselves as well-conditioned, well-coached, and prepared to take advantage of any mistake an opponent makes.

Teams at Florida Southern over the years have developed these attitudes and skills. Florida Southern's baseball program has high expectations every season. When that is matched with the program's winning tradition, you have the elements that make national champions.

Handling Adversity

Successful coaches have a presence about them, a certain excitement that makes players want to listen. Good leadership skills include patience and determination, having the strength not to be impulsive. Instead, a successful coach is deliberate and decisive, even when the heat is on and in the face of criticism. The successful coach will have players who want to play for him, players who are ready to give their all for him.

When a team is not playing well, the public may expect the head coach to become upset with the team, jump up and down, yell and scream, throw the water cooler, do whatever it takes to get the players' attention. But if the coach has projected himself to the team as always being under control in stressful situations, the team will know that such an outburst would be out of character, mainly for show. The coach would run the risk of losing their respect.

Coaches who can stay under control, who can keep a cool head and steady hand as their teams travel through rough times, will be able to maintain a positive relationship with their players. When you are upset, keep it simple. Tell your team that you are disappointed and frustrated by the team's play. Young people will understand this low-key statement. Players don't want to disappoint their coach. The coach must try to find solutions and things to be positive about.

Team meetings following poorly played games are not usually in the best interest of the team or the coach. The coach is not at his best emotionally and has not had an opportunity to absorb all that may have gone wrong during the game. Take time to prepare your remarks so that you can present meaningful suggestions and corrections in a composed fashion. Some coaches often choose to chastise, challenge, and sometimes even publicly humiliate their teams. This approach may serve as an emotional outlet for the coach, but it will be counterproductive when it comes to the relationship and respect between players and head coach.

When the coach meets with his team, he should look for ways to improve the situation, not show anger and frustration. As far as the public is concerned, how you handle a team that is not playing well is a matter of perception. If you are emotional and yell a lot and you win, you are a great motivator! If you yell a lot and you lose, you are too tough on the team and just don't understand young people. If you are under control, even laid back, you are considered to be a players' coach, provided you win. If you lose, you are not enough of a disciplinarian! The bottom line is that you are expected to win. When you win, what you are doing is perceived as the right way to get it done. The public is unpredictable. Don't be tempted to make changes just for the sake of change or public relations. Trust your experience, your preparation, and a self-controlled approach. Trusting yourself and acting in a timely fashion will serve you well.

Players don't want to see their coach discouraged in bad times. There must always be a sense of hope. It is never over until the last out! The successful coach can convey that feeling and in the end will find that teams will pull together and be successful most of the time.

Standards for the Players

Excellent behavior involves many elements. When you coach a youth team, excellent behavior is basic, and you can easily describe expectations. Teaching older players about excellent behavior can be more complicated and demanding. Perhaps the best approach to explaining and developing the idea, at any level, is to look for one or two common threads that are part of the fabric of the idea of excellent behavior.

In recent years it has become acceptable for a head coach or school authorities to develop a code of conduct for players. This code or policy statement gives players an idea of what is expected of them athletically and academically. These general rules usually apply at any level. They cover the how players should act on or off the playing field. It is beneficial to all concerned if the code of conduct is general in nature. This allows enough built-in flexibility so that it is adjustable to the variety of situations that arise. Having everyone understand what is expected is a vital element in team development and success.

Coaches are usually the ones to enforce the code; thus the relationship between the coach and players is important. Team members' respect for the head coach and how the team members view themselves as team members are what make a code successful.

What happens when rules are broken? Most of the time the player who breaks the rule pays a penalty. To be effective, the penalty should be handed out soon after the infraction. Make sure the penalty fits the infraction and share what is happening with the rest of the team. The team will learn something from the experience, and the purpose of the code will be reinforced.

> "The player who loses his head and can't keep his cool is worse than no ballplayer at all."

Excellence in performance is an area that requires focus and discipline from players and coaches. It is a given that a team must be physically, mentally, and emotionally prepared to play well. Being physically prepared includes two important areas: strength and endurance. If the individual and team are to be successful, they must be willing to work at conditioning over an extended period. The ongoing challenge for the head coach is to motivate players to work hard at conditioning. Remind players that hard work will improve their luck.

Mental preparedness is important, and players must understand what playing smart means. Learning the physical skills and techniques is one thing, but winning teams are the teams that have all players tuned into game plans and strategies. This includes everything from cutoff and relay assignments to what to do with a scouting report on your opponent's hitting tendencies. The ability to focus on the task at hand is what separates successful players and teams from the losers.

Emotions are important. Players need to be taught, and at times directed, to control their emotions. Coaches also have to learn to motivate the team without losing emotional control. Players and teams that balance their emotions are less likely to have the pitcher overthrow the ball or have a hitter overswing at a pitch. Several other skills require self-control to achieve optimum performance. An old but often-quoted baseball adage sums it up: "The player who loses his head and can't keep his cool is worse than no ballplayer at all."

One of the most difficult challenges for a coach and team on and off the field is to project an image that is positive. It is a fine line between being perceived as confident and self-assured or, on the negative side, being considered arrogant and cocky. Coaches need to remind themselves and the team that everyone involved is in the public eye. The more success a team and coach enjoy, the more attention they will receive. This attention often includes criticism. Responsibilities go with representing a team, a school, and a conference. A positive public image requires that all players follow social customs in the community.

Coaches must accept the responsibility for how a team looks on the field and in public. Appearance is one of the few factors you can control. If you pay attention to appearance and how you want your team to behave, the impression you want to make on others will result in positive reinforcement. In time, your team will be the team you want it to be. It's your call. If you want your team to be successful, then look and act successful. Having a team dress in a specific way for an event or for travel goes a long way in projecting a good image. Players must learn that public and fan approval is a necessary part of the athletic scene and that each player represents every other player.

Do not assume that your players know how to put on a game uniform correctly. How a team looks sends an important message to the opposing team. A professional appearance and attitude, combined with a well-organized pregame practice, can make the point to the opponent that they are about to engage in a tough battle. In some cases, you will find that you can take the opponent right out of their game plan. When a team begins to doubt themselves because they are impressed with what they see before a game, chances are they will not do well. More than one game has been lost before it ever started.

Sportsmanship Makes the Difference

Most people involved with sports can easily judge fairness and sportsmanship. Probably the most important single factor in developing a class athlete and a class team is to develop a healthy attitude about competition. This includes respect for the opponent and oneself and being under control in difficult situations. When your players internalize these attitudes, the result is that they will be reliable and successful.

Parents, coaches, and administrators should all share the understanding that self-reliance, honesty, and composure under stress are valuable in situations much wider than the sport in which they were learned. Players who learn about fairness and sportsmanship have learned self-respect, respect for their opponents, and the ability to identify with the feelings of others. Perhaps the most important responsibility of the head coach is to encourage in players a sense of pride, self-discipline, and excellent behavior. In the short term, this will bring credit to them and the team they represent, and in the long term will ensure a lasting commitment to sportsmanship. The result is that they will in turn earn the respect of the people around them and the assurance that they are, indeed, a team with class.

CHAPTER FOUR

Hustling Should Be a Habit

Bobby Winkles

I played baseball for six years in the Chicago White Sox organization. Unfortunately I did not have much ability. I played shortstop, and my biggest asset was hustle: I was first on the field, first in the dugout after an inning, ran hard on every ball hit, and talked it up in the infield. I believe that two invitations to spring training with the White Sox came as a result of the way I went about my job. I didn't have much ability, but my motor was in high gear all the time.

In 1958, while playing AAA in Indianapolis, I knew the time had come to retire. My manager, Walker Cooper, called me over one July day and told me there was only one thing keeping me from the major leagues. I became extremely enthusiastic and blurted out, "Tell me what it is, Coop, and I'll go to work on my weakness." He answered, "It's your ability."

After the 1956 season, I had started study toward an advanced degree at the University of Colorado, and in 1957 had received a master's degree in physical education. So in 1958, after my talk with Walker Cooper in July, I called my advisor, Dr. David Bartelma, to ask about coaching positions that might be open. He told me that Arizona State was starting a program, and that they were looking for a young coach with a master's degree. After one phone call, the job was mine. How lucky can you get! I was allowed to finish the season at Indianapolis, which ended on Labor Day, and then reported to Arizona State. I had a month and a half to prepare. For those six weeks, I mapped out my plans on how to coach a college baseball team. Some of my notes were as follows:

- We will play hard for the entire game.
- No player will be bigger than the team, no matter how good he may be.
- We will play fast games.
- We will be a team with character.
- I will be friends with all high school coaches and major league scouts.
- Any high school player can try out for the freshman team.
- We will be a disciplined team. Discipline will be the same for all players, and it will be fairly applied.
- We will be in great physical condition.

I also drew up a list of rules. They encompassed much more than behavior on the baseball field and during the game. They covered being a student, being a good citizen, keeping in touch with parents, developing character, adhering to a dress code and hair-grooming code, being responsible, being polite, and developing self-discipline.

Running Was to Be Our Discipline, Hustle Our Trademark

This chapter is not about hustle or lack of hustle by other teams. This chapter deals only with the Arizona State University baseball program from 1959 through 1971. Coaching is not throwing out the bats and balls and saying, "Let's play ball." Coaching is time consuming and hard work. Coaching is much more than determining a game plan. The coach has to be patient and consistent in repeating his desires. He must be compassionate and tough. He must be a counselor, a father figure, and a friend.

Preparing the Players and Their Families

In high school or college, proper preparation should take place before the season starts. The good coach doesn't wait until the first practice to drop the bomb of rules on his team.

In high school, the coach should have an early meeting (preferably during the second or third week of classes). Because some high school athletes play several sports, the coach should schedule the meeting at a time when all those planning to play baseball can attend. Written rules and regulations are better than oral ones. The players can keep a copy in their rooms at home and refer to it from time to time. When practice starts, the candidates will be familiar with what is expected of them if they plan to play baseball.

Parents play a large part in the success of a high school coach. They go to games and pay attention to what happens on the field. The parents know if every player is treated the same. A good friend of mine, Charlie Webb, followed the Arizona State University philosophy. Camelback High School was his first coaching job. Charlie not only let the players know the philosophy but also let the parents know. He notified parents, in writing, what he expected of their sons. Charlie has informed me that there were few complaints or problems with parents. He coached at Camelback his entire career and was very successful. Most coaches know that parents can be helpful to the program or, at times, a hindrance. Do what you can to make them helpful.

College is somewhat different from high school. The college student is away from home for the first time. At Arizona State, we allowed any freshman or junior college student to try out for the baseball team. There was a sign-up sheet outside the baseball office. In my day, freshmen were not allowed to play varsity sports, and we were not limited to a maximum number of practice days. We would have approximately five freshmen on scholarship. That gave 16 players a chance to play freshmen baseball, and there would be between 50 and 75 signatures on the sign-up sheet. During the second week of school they all came to our home for dinner. Ellie, my dear wife of 45 years, would make sloppy Joes and potato salad and served that, along with chips and sodas, to all the candidates. They would sit on the floor, and then each one would stand and introduce themselves, tell where they were from, and name the high school they attended. Each candidate filled out a form that gave his parent's or parents' name, address, and phone number. We gave each candidate a list of rules. Some were surprised to learn that the rules included more than the activities on the baseball field. Included in these rules were how we expected them to conduct themselves off the field and in the classroom.

Once practice started, we made cuts daily. In approximately 10 days we had the squad picked. We then let the parents know what we had told their sons and that we would notify the parents if there was a problem. It's amazing how few problems you have if the student-athlete knows that their parents are going to be part of the program by being kept informed. In my opinion, coaching is not a democracy. To me, the best coaches in college and high school are benevolent dictators. They make and enforce the rules but at the same time have compassion and love for their players.

Discipline

Discipline was strict at ASU. I never let a player stretch the rules. As a coach, you know when a player is leaning toward abusing the rules. That's when you have a talk. You do the talking, and the player does the listening.

I kept a class schedule of each player. I could check his grades with the professor, and I knew where to find him. It's never easy to tell a student-athlete that he must change his behavior or the next time he might be only a student. The day following such an encounter, I made sure to make contact before practice. Here the class schedule was my guide about when I might run into him before or after a class. Or perhaps I might find him in the cafeteria. I greeted the player with a smile. I would say something like, "How's it going?" I might put my arm around him and ask if he was OK. It might have been corny, but I never wanted a player to start practice with his head down. In my opinion, the coach who can administer discipline and show, through compassion, that everything is OK the next day gets respect from his players. As a coach, I wanted every player to look me in the eye when he came through the gate to the ballfield. A player cannot give his best if he is afraid of making a mistake. My players always knew that whatever happened the day before was forgotten by the next day.

We ran a minimum of 20 minutes after nearly every game. It was a matter of conditioning, not because we won or lost. The players knew this was our routine, and they knew it was not punishment. Discipline was in addition to our routine. If I needed to make a point, the player or players stayed after the routine running and ran until I felt I made the point. A coach should not, in my opinion, discipline a player for physical errors. They happen. Mental mistakes, however, were subject to discipline. Self-discipline is defined as an activity, exercise, or regimen that develops character and improves a skill. At Arizona State, we used the word encouragement a lot. Discipline was not meant to be punishment. Rather it was meant to encourage the player to avoid making the same mistake when the next opportunity arose. We know that fundamental drills are not always a lot of fun. We also know that the proper execution of these drills is essential to winning, especially in a close ball game. We had an encouragement highway that we called Route 440, representing the number of yards around the outer limits of the baseball field. During drills, if a player didn't execute properly, he took a trip around Route 440. The trip was not a leisurely stroll. We required that the players complete it in less than two minutes.

For example, the bunt with a runner on first is to be put down the first-base line. The first baseman has to hold the runner while the third baseman can charge and possibly force the runner out at second. With runners at first and second, the bunt goes down the third-base line. The third baseman stays at third to protect against the steal, and the first baseman charges home plate to make a possible play at third base. During practice we gave the bunter two chances. If the player didn't execute the bunt correctly, we directed him to Route 440. When he finished the trip, we awarded the bunter another opportunity to execute the bunt correctly. Failure resulted in another run around this famous highway. We did not use base runners for this drill, as they take up time. Fast pace in fundamental drills makes for more work in less time.

In the hit-and-run drill, we did not have to hit behind the runner. The focus was on hitting ground balls. Route 440 was waiting for those who hit the ball in the air.

The double cutoff is an important play. The defensive team that executes the play correctly has a chance to throw out runners at either third base or home plate. The throw from the outfielder is critical. If the outfielder missed both infielders, he was on his way around the perimeter of the ballfield. Because we considered this a mental error, not a physical one, it merited a trip on Route 440.

I would like to reiterate that running at Arizona State was not considered punishment! Running was considered encouragement. The players understood, and running was never a problem. I have always argued that the best conditioned baseball team will win a lot of games in the last three innings. One NCAA championship year we played 25 one-run games and won 22 of them. I attribute many of those wins to being in excellent physical condition.

Hustle and Attitude

Most who saw us play during my tenure at Arizona State University assumed that we were the fastest-playing team in the college ranks. We were known as a hustling team that wasted little time during any game. We played hard, regardless of the score.

Definitions of the word hustle include the following: (1) to proceed or work rapidly or energetically, (2) to be aggressive, (3) to urge, prod, or speed up, (4) a competitive struggle. A hustler could be defined as (1) an enthusiastic person determined to succeed or (2) a go-getter.

When speaking of hustle in baseball, some people bring up false hustle. They question why players run when it's not necessary. Some examples of false hustle given by those critics are running to the plate to hit, running from home plate to the dugout after a strikeout, sprinting back to the dugout after making an out, entering the practice field by running instead of walking, running to and from the mound, sprinting from the bullpen to the mound.

My answer to the idea of false hustle is that it doesn't exist. When a team excites fans, major-league scouts, broadcasters, and high school coaches by running everywhere and playing a fast game, it is a plus for the game of baseball. These critics forgot to look up the definition.

Hustle is an attitude. Attitude is a tendency or orientation, especially of the mind. Hustle as an attitude is not inherent in human beings. Attitude is developed. In baseball there are those who hustle and those who don't. There are those who have great attitudes and those who don't. Because I believe that hustle is an attitude, let us discuss attitude. Where does an attitude originate, and how does it develop? An attitude can be flexible, which means it can go from good to bad or bad to good. It can change in one hour, one day, one month, one year, or never. An attitude can be changed for better or worse by a parent or parents, friends, teachers, coaches, employers, spouses, or sweethearts. As a baseball coach, whatever your philosophy may be, you will need attitude changes in some of your players to be successful. You need all team members to think as you do. Baseball is a team sport, and everyone on your team must recognize the importance of doing what is best for the team. They must have the same attitude as you do during practices and games. You cannot give up on a needed attitude change until you have exhausted all your methods for changing it. There are many cases when a good player has a bad attitude. You don't understand why he refuses to conform. You can only go so far with such a player, but it is best for you and your team to go on without a dissident member of your squad.

In 13 years at Arizona State, we had just three players who couldn't get the idea of team attitude. We asked each of them, all regulars, to leave the team. We allowed them to keep their scholarships, but they could not play on the baseball team. They were all juniors, and each one signed a pro contract.

Rick Monday played for our 1965 NCAA championship team. Later he would spend 15 years in the majors with Oakland, the Chicago Cubs, and the Los Angeles Dodgers. One day, while playing for the Cubs, he hit a ball toward the stands down the left-field line. He thought it was foul by several feet, but if you have watched games at Wrigley Field you know about the wind. This day it was blowing a gale toward right field. Rick didn't run until he realized the ball was going to be fair. He ended up on first base instead of second or third. The broadcaster, who had been with the Cubs for years, made this statement: "That's the only ball Rick hasn't run 100 percent on during his career with the Cubs, and that includes one hoppers back to the pitcher." I was proud that Rick played at ASU and that he was still running out balls 10 years later. That one time was an exception, and the broadcaster was quick to come to Rick's defense. Had that happened at ASU, however, I would have removed him for a pinch runner no matter how important that game may have been.

Self-Discipline

It was always a wish of mine that every player who played at Arizona State would be able to cope with the ups and downs of life after he left the program. Theory is a big part of the academic process. What happens in life, after sports, is not theory. Being successful is a grind; it does not just happen. In my opinion, 98 percent of success is hard work, doing what one enjoys, and self-discipline. Luck and inheritance are part of the other 2 percent. My saying to players was, "the harder you work, the luckier you get."

> **"The harder you work, the luckier you get."**

As you read this portion of my chapter, you will notice that many of the rules and regulations were closely associated with self-discipline. When a player left the program and hadn't progressed from being a boy to being a man, I would be dissatisfied with myself. One of our rules was that players would wear no facial hair and no long hair, with the back of the hair trimmed so it would not touch the collar. Alan Bannister played 12 years in the major leagues. Out of high school, he was the number one draft pick of the California Angels. He opted to attend Arizona State instead of accepting a $53,000 signing bonus. He was also a surfer from California. At our prepractice meeting, we gave the candidates our hair policy. Alan was a great young man, a good student, and a fine baseball player. He dropped by my office a few days before practice to visit. I reminded him about the hair policy. He said, "Coach, I just had my hair cut the other day." My answer was, "The barber didn't finish the job. You had better go see him again before Monday." He looked real neat on Monday.

Speeding Up the Game—How and Why

In my opinion, it is embarrassing for a team to be outhustled. It is even more embarrassing for the coach. Psychologically, we felt that the way we played gave us an edge when the ability of both teams was even. This is not to say that other teams did not hustle; we just did it a different way. One of our on-field rules was for the batter to run to home plate to hit and run back to the dugout after a strikeout. We felt that running to home plate showed we were ready to hit. Our hitters never stepped out of the batter's box. Even when taking a sign from the third-base coach, our batter's back foot stayed in place. Another rule was that players never argued a call by the umpire. To strike out is an embarrassment. We ran back to the dugout to get out of the eyes of the fans. I suggested that as a reason, and the players accepted it. They didn't have a choice. We ran to first base on a walk and ran back to the dugout, at full speed, after an out at any base. Running was our game—to us running was hustle. All the player had to remember was run, don't walk.

Our pitchers were required to run to and from the mound. I believe we were the first team to do this. This was a definite time saver in the length of a baseball game. Psychologically, you have an edge over a pitcher who walks to and from his position. The batter, in the back of his mind, could be thinking that the pitcher can't wait to pitch.

In 1973 when I managed the California Angels, our team ran to and from the mound. We were the first major-league team to do so. The pitching coach and I talked to Nolan Ryan and Clyde Wright about the idea. Our talking points were that the Angels had not drawn well and it would shorten the game. They agreed to try it. We had a meeting of the pitchers and catchers, and it was a success. We had the shortest average game time in the American League in 1973.

At Arizona State, we believed that our pitchers needed only 5 pitches to get loose when the weather was warm. It always bothered me to see pitchers take 10 to 12 warm-up pitches between innings. When our catcher made the last out of an inning, we had a system. We let the catcher put on his chest protector and mask, and we had two extra men putting on his shin guards. Our pitcher, in many instances, was throwing his 5 warm-up pitches before the other team had entered their dugout. Another thing—we did not allow our pitchers to leave the dirt area of the mound between pitches. This procedure saved time and energy. I'm five feet, nine inches tall, and many of our pitchers were over six feet. I seldom went to the mound, but when it was necessary for a visit, the pitcher would walk to the lower level of the mound, and I would stand on the rubber. When asked by a Phoenix reporter why this happened, I replied that I was five feet nine, that the pitcher was taller, and that I liked to look the pitcher in the eye when we talked. He printed the explanation, and after that the fans knew why the visits always looked a little goofy!

We had all of our College World Series games televised or radioed back to Phoenix and the surrounding communities. The broadcasters asked me if the team could take a little more time between our last out and the first pitch. They had no problem getting in two minutes of commercials with the other team, but they were having trouble with us. My answer was, "You had better sell 30-second time spots." In the 1969 College World Series finals, Larry Gura beat Tulsa 10-1, in 1 hour and 39 minutes. Fortunately, we did not have to contend with aluminum bats. Today those types of games are improbable. Table 4.1 shows the running times of our six 1969 NCAA championship games.

— TABLE 4.1 —

Running Times of ASU 1969 NCAA Championship Games

Game	Running time	Game	Running time
Texas 4, ASU 0	1:46	ASU 11, Tulsa 3	2:16
ASU 2, UCLA 1 (11 innings)	2:19	ASU 4, NYU 1	1:58
ASU 4, Mass 2	1:57	ASU 10, Tulsa 1	1:39

Character Building

Definitions of character include the following: (1) moral or ethical quality, (2) good repute, (3) the aggregate of features and traits that form the individual nature of a person, and (4) qualities of courage and honesty.

You have heard it said that a person or a team has character. Win or lose, in my opinion that's the best compliment a coach or team can receive.

I never cared what a player thought of me while he played at Arizona State. I did care what he thought of me 10 years later. I believe a coach can be a large influence in character building. When a coach takes time to make a definite contribution to the life of his players off the field, he has every right to feel good about himself.

The rules discussed earlier in this chapter were mostly about hustle and attitude. The prepractice meeting at our home was about more than just baseball. Several rules were about character. We did not set down rules that were impossible to abide by. Anyone who sets down rules that players can't follow is unfair. We established the following additional rules for on- and off-field behavior:

- You are here first as a student, second to be a person of character, and third to be the best baseball player you can be.

- You will say yes sir, no sir, yes ma'am, or no ma'am to all professors and coaches. Huh, uh huh, yeah, and naw are not in your vocabulary. (We pointed out that if you said all these words fast, it sounded more like a hog grunting than a person talking—huh-uh-huh-yeah-naw. Try it!)

- Go to class and do your homework. There will be no study hall for members of the Arizona State University baseball team. When attending class you will sit in the first two rows and look the professor in the eye when he or she talks to you. You will wear shoes and socks; thongs are not permitted.

- Anyone caught drinking will be suspended for one month. (Our first-string catcher got tipsy one night, and I received a call from the police. I went to pick him up to keep him out of jail. There was not much communication on the way back to his dorm. We suspended him for 30 days, and he coached first base every game because I wanted him in view of the fans.)

- Anyone caught smoking in public will be suspended for one month. (That never happened.)

- We go by Lombardi time. If you aren't five minutes early, you are late.
- There will be no swearing on the baseball field. Hell and damn are considered swear words.
- We have an obligation to your parents. If you get into trouble, they will get a phone call from us. It would be wise if you called them first. It would make them proud that you had already called.
- No throwing bats or helmets. If you want to get the person responsible for your strikeout or pop up, drop your bat and helmet, get up some speed, and dive head first into the dugout. (Our dugouts were concrete.)
- No fighting or arguing with a teammate. If you have a problem let me know. We will be glad to vacate the baseball dressing room, put you inside, and lock the door.
- If you have a problem, call me anytime—day or night. I will help in any way possible.

A Closing Note

Being a successful coach takes time, patience, and knowledge of the game. I disagree with those who judge the success of a coach on winning alone. Few coaches have the luxury of several good players every year. To me, the successful coach is the one who gets the most out of his players.

I never coached third base. I feel that a coach can do a lot more coaching by being in the dugout. When I see a team play hard, hustle, and execute the fundamentals, a tip of the hat goes to their coach. He did the best that he could with what he had.

You may have surmised by reading this chapter that baseball at Arizona State University was all work and no fun. Nothing could be further from the truth. The team knew what to expect from me. They knew what was acceptable and what was unacceptable. They knew they could joke with me and they knew I was not an uptight person. The players were never embarrassed in front of others and any serious discussion was in the privacy of my office and away from the field.

I spent 43 years in baseball. The thirteen years at ASU were the most enjoyable. There was never a day that I wished to be in another profession!

CHAPTER FIVE

Coaching With Integrity

Robert E. Smith

The primary focus of this chapter is not on how to coach baseball but on *why* one coaches baseball. A person should not become a baseball coach unless he loves to compete, wants to win, and has a strong commitment to excellence. At the same time, one should not become a baseball coach unless he is willing to lose in order to win the ultimate game. That is what integrity is all about.

> *"Whoever wants to know the heart and mind of America had better learn baseball."*
>
> Jacques Barzun

As a baseball coach one needs to decide this: Am I going to be part of the problem or the solution? The problem to which I refer is the moral decline occurring in our world, affecting virtually every area of society. Baseball is not exempt.

The good news is that the sport of baseball can be a part of the solution if we as baseball coaches are willing to take the high road and be coaches of integrity. This is undoubtedly the most difficult, but also the most rewarding, road to travel.

A sector of our society wants us to believe that there are no absolutes, no final bases for right and wrong. Thus we need not be concerned about being persons of integrity or helping our athletes become people of integrity. As one who loves the game of baseball, I know the instant gratification that comes from winning a game, getting a hit, scoring a run, or striking out a batter. All are important but not at the expense of compromising values.

Following the defeat of Napoleon in the 1800s, the Duke of Wellington was quoted as saying, "The Battle of Waterloo was won on the playing fields of Eton." If that was true in England and Europe in the 19th century, the athletic fields of today certainly should offer us the opportunity to develop leaders for our day, our country, and our world. But it won't just happen! We as baseball coaches must be proponents of a countercultural movement to put morality and integrity back among our nation's priorities by having such traits characterize our baseball coaching activities.

President Herbert Hoover stated, "Next to religion, baseball has furnished a greater impact on American life than any other institution." If President Hoover were alive today, could he still be expected to give such a respectful salute to our game?

In writing on the topic of coaching with integrity, I would like to rephrase President Hoover's comment: "Next to ministers, priests, and rabbis [and I would add caring parents], baseball coaches have the potential of making a greater impact on the youth of America than any other group or profession."

Jacques Barzun was correct when he indicated that "whoever wants to know the heart and mind of America had better learn baseball." With this acknowledgment of the high place of baseball, our American national pastime, comes a deep sense of responsibility for those of us who choose to claim the title *baseball coach*.

In society today, we are faced with growing disrespect for leaders, a lessening acceptance of the existence of lasting values, and a desire to win at all cost. Baseball does not escape these societal influences. Baseball coaches at all levels are regularly tempted to take other than the high road—to cut a corner, stretch a rule, or shade the truth—to accomplish the short-term goal of recruiting a player, preparing a team, or winning a baseball game.

But it does not have to be that way! Many coaches have maintained an example of integrity over a lifetime of coaching the great game of baseball, simultaneously realizing lasting joy and accomplishing great good.

Integrity is defined as a state or quality of being complete, undivided, or unbroken. It includes moral soundness, honesty, and uprightness. In this chapter, I would like to unwrap the meaning of integrity in the life of a baseball coach by analyzing the complete role of the baseball coach and reminding the reader of some incomplete, shortsighted actions that lack full integrity.

Integrity is a relational word. A baseball coach's integrity shows up in his relationship with those affected or influenced by his coaching. To place the concept of integrity in its proper context, a baseball coach must reflect on his relationship with his players, their parents, his colleagues (assistant coaches), his family, the umpires, opposing coaches and their players, his institution or organization, and most important his God. For integrity to have an aspect of completeness, a coach must consider each of these relationships. It is difficult to consider the integrity of a baseball coach without giving thought to what he believes to be important, the emphasis he places on true values, how he prioritizes his time, and the effect of his actions on others.

Dr. W. Richard Stephens, my predecessor at Greenville College, both as baseball coach and later as college president, likes to describe our graduates as "those who can be trusted when no one is looking." Because a baseball coach finds that he often makes his decisions in full view of his players and fans, I would expand Dr. Stephens's definition to describe a good baseball coach as "someone you can trust, both when no one is looking and also when many are looking—perhaps second-guessing."

Before discussing some of the temptations that a baseball coach faces, let me present a fundamental principle that I believe will go a long way toward coaching with integrity. As a baseball coach, think of your responsibilities to your players and all those you influence as opportunities for building lifetime relationships. Never recruit a player for a season, two, or four years. Rather, recruit him to begin a lifetime coach-player relationship. Never talk to the parents of your players, or an opposing coach or umpire, with the view of it being a one-time meeting or short-term friendship. From the beginning of any relationship, take the big picture approach. Let your relationships be built on the expectation that your actions will produce friendships that will last for life.

I love to be called "Coach." Next to the terms of endearment within my immediate family (Dad, Paw Paw, Honey), Coach beats them all. It is better than Prof, Dr., or President. One of my great joys is to have a player from my early days of coaching return to campus and still call me Coach. Over the years I have tried to send my ex-players birthday cards every year and regularly stay in touch with them. I admit this is easier to do on a college campus where an alumni department has names and addresses, but I have found great joy in these continuing relationships. As I travel, I enjoy stopping to visit with a former player. To have one of these young men get in touch with me when he needs advice or counsel, or when he wants to share something of happiness in his life, is a greater joy than even winning a baseball game—and I love to win baseball games.

Coaching at various levels brings different challenges, though many are the same. Let me list some of the slippery slopes that can lead a baseball coach downward in ways that are not marked by integrity.

Failing to Walk the Talk

During the decade of the 1990s, seemingly more than ever before, coaches and athletes have openly defied their responsibilities as role models. Sports pages almost daily carry stories of baseball players and coaches whose lives have become entangled with the law, whose wives have been betrayed, and whose commitments to integrity are no longer deemed important.

As coaches practicing integrity, we dare not give up or let up. The darker the night, the brighter the light that will shine. In a time when there are certainly fallen baseball stars, it is all the more important that as coaches we provide our players and fans a lifestyle that walks the talk, that consistently practices those actions we know to be just and right.

Baseball coaches are role models. We cannot get around that responsibility and privilege. As articulated earlier, the question is whether we will be a part of the problem or the solution.

In preparing to write this chapter, I talked to over a dozen coaches for whom I have great admiration and respect. When I asked what they believed to be important for a coach who desires to show integrity, their responses most often centered on the necessity that the coach have the priorities of his life in order.

For me, this means that my first commitment is to God, my second to my family, and my third to my job. Without question, the most tempting slippery slope of my life has been that of getting those three priorities out of line. It is easy to give lip service to these priorities and quite another to practice them regularly.

As a baseball coach, I urge you to take time to meet the spiritual needs of your life. Dr. Bob Briner, my closest friend from childhood days until his recent death, has written a book titled *Squeeze Play.* In this book he gives numerous practical insights for men who are caught between the pressures of work, home, and spiritual faith.

Finding the proper balance makes life much more rewarding and it enables you as a coach to be the role model who consistently walks his talk. Coaches, remember that both the quality and quantity of time you spend with your family are important. Do not let the pressures of your work crowd out the things that are far more important than baseball wins and losses.

Bending the Rules

Baseball is a game of intricate rules. Just the basic rule book of baseball contains enough rules to last a lifetime. But baseball coaches face many other rules and regulations of the organizations with which their teams are affiliated. This is not improving; it is becoming worse. From youth organizations to collegiate organizations, we find ourselves feeling a continuous squeeze. To conform to so many rules often seems to take away our freedom to coach the team or help our players.

Coach Keith Madison of the University of Kentucky shared with me the constant temptation he has felt to bend the rules and compromise his integrity and standards. It is easy to say that a rule is ridiculous or that a certain rule was put in place because of football or basketball violations. We might well reason that baseball really does not need such a rule.

The rule that has been most tempting for Coach Madison to compromise is related to practice time during the off-season. He noted, "Since the NCAA allows coaches only two hours per week in the off-season with any one player to work on skills, it is very tempting to go overtime, especially when you have good rapport with a player and he is eager to learn."

To maintain the high road, Madison keeps his players well informed of the rules and regulations. In turn, they help keep him accountable, for he does not want his players ever to view him as one who cheats or takes shortcuts.

Ron Polk, head coach at the University of Georgia, recommends that coaches have guiding principles but refrain from providing too many detailed rules for players. This certainly squares with what I found to be true, particularly as I matured as a baseball coach. In my early days, I was more insecure and tended to have many rules for my players. I felt it gave me more structure and a higher degree of control. But with time I learned what Coach Polk discovered, and both my players and I were better for it.

Coach Bobby Knight of Indiana basketball fame preaches that the more rules an organization possesses, the greater the opportunity for an unscrupulous coach to find ways of taking advantage of a situation and using the systems that are in place.

The late Coach Bob Starcher from Malone College indicated that one of his biggest temptations came in the area of teaching borderline plays; for example, pickoff moves that are difficult for umpires and opponents to detect. Another is the maneuver of a third-base coach who asks to see the ball when a runner is on third base. The young, inexperienced pitcher is tricked into stepping off the mound and tossing the ball to the third-base coach, who steps aside. As the ball rolls to the fence, the runner scores. Is that good baseball? No, that is not what coaching with integrity is all about.

Overselling Your Baseball Program

By his very nature, a successful coach is a sales representative. We all like to make a good first impression when discussing our institutions and programs. But a coach can easily step over the line in his recruitment by failing to be truthful in describing his program and what it will give to the potential player. This slippery slope of overselling can include both what a coach promises and what he fails to mention or reveal. Complete honesty in advertising your baseball program is always the best policy. Your reputation as an honest coach will spread quickly. Know your program's strengths and weaknesses, work hard to improve your baseball program, sell your program enthusiastically, and do not promise more than you can deliver to each player.

Integrity begins at the mouth. Your word must be trustworthy. There is no place in baseball for a coach who talks out of two sides of his mouth. Do not promise a player or his parents some lofty hope that goes beyond what you can deliver.

Your players will compare stories, so make sure that only one story comes out of your mouth.

Hal Smeltzly, athletic director and former baseball coach at Florida Southern College, reflected on his belief that coaches are often tempted to tell players and parents what they want to hear rather than what they need to hear. This is particularly true in recruiting. "If you want to take the high road," Smeltzly writes, "be honest with parents and players about where the player will fit into your program and what they will find on your campus when they get involved in college life."

No surprises—particularly, no unkept promises! They will certainly come back to haunt a baseball coach and rob him of joy and effectiveness. Truth, plainly stated upfront, will prevent many future problems.

Using Intimidation as a Strategy to Win

Some notoriously inappropriate role models in baseball today would try to make it seem that a baseball coach can bully and intimidate his way to success. This approach to coaching can be seen in the coach's relationships with umpires, his players, and his opposition. By his actions, this type of coaching incites others to act in unfair ways that take away from the glory and good of our great game.

Collegiate baseball statesman Elmer Kosub writes that one of the toughest challenges facing today's baseball coaches is helping to control the tidal wave of violence that has swept across our country. Recognizing the baseball field as a potentially powerful classroom, Kosub challenges coaches to become role models by controlling their own violence and tendency to incite those around them and by setting and maintaining acceptable standards for their teams and fans.

By any measure of comparison, Coach Gordie Gillespie, formerly at Lewis University and St. Francis College, is a highly successful baseball coach. He admits that he too has been tempted to take the low road. He writes: "As a young coach, I emulated a Billy Martin-type manager and tried to get a competitive edge in baseball games. I wanted the play to favor Gordie Gillespie and his team, even though it might be the wrong call. One day when I was going through a tirade, a great umpire said to me, 'Gordie, will you shut up!' Then he asked me in no uncertain terms, 'Do you want the play called right?' I meekly answered, 'Yes.' He told me to go back to the dugout and he and his partner would call the play right. I never forgot that lesson." If it is good enough for Gordie Gillespie, it is good enough for me.

Kentucky coach Keith Madison believes that some coaches feel they can intimidate their opponent or even their own players, but he stressed that in baseball you win with execution not intimidation. He favors "proper intimidation through better preparation, execution, and playing with aggressiveness and confidence." Good advice, Coach Madison!

Jeopardizing the Player's Health

A coach's drive to win can, if not checked, result in rationalizing actions that could jeopardize the future health and well-being of a ballplayer.

In youth baseball there is a temptation to stress specialization early and, with that specialization, to expect a level of concentration and practice that is too strenuous and demanding. Mr. David Osinski, one of the game's finest instructors, points to the coaches and parents who insist on early specialization for the child. This often happens irrespective of whether the child has the attributes to play the position successfully at higher levels. Such preselection, Osinski notes, hinders the development of the player. The youngster masters only one position and does not learn other facets of the game that can be enjoyable and improve self-confidence.

At all levels of baseball, there is the tendency to rush the injured athlete back into play or practice before the player completes an entire rehabilitation program. Subtly, or sometimes not so subtly, the coach makes the player feel that if he doesn't return to the lineup he is letting his teammates down. A coach of integrity will be guided in these matters not by the short-term needs of the team but by the long-term needs of the player. The lifetime coach-player relationship calls for wisdom to overrule emotions. Install a team trainer or doctor with unquestionable veto power over you and leave medically related judgments to the doc.

Failing to Support the Mission of Your Institution or Organization

Almost all baseball coaches lead teams associated with institutions and organizations that define for the coach and players the goals for the baseball team. These often include such worthy objectives as the development of leadership, learning, integrity, health, and a commitment to excellence. From the early years of youth baseball to college and adult programs, baseball is played with the expectation of contributing to the growth and development of each player.

Eager and enthusiastic coaches have a strong tendency to forget varied institutional goals and act as if the only allegiance players have is to the baseball program. The baseball player must know the expectations of the school, college, or program and be held accountable for those expectations just as he is for the way he performs on the field.

In reflecting back on many years of successful coaching, Hal Smeltzly said, "I think the times I felt challenged and pressured by boosters and parents the most were when I insisted that all players had to have a 2.5 grade point average in their studies if they were to go on road trips with the team. I spent a career trying to prove that athletes and teams could be successful without compromising the academic side of the college experience. I found that players responded to my 'no travel' rule. I have had a number of former players thank me for taking a tough stand on academic matters. They felt it made a difference in their college life. They became convinced that it was possible to be a winner on the baseball field *and* in the classroom."

Coaches, do not become myopic and fail to see that your institutional or organizational commitment makes baseball a contributing part of the total program of which your team is a part.

Flaunting Victory and Excusing Defeat

One of my former players, Coach Larry Winterholder, presently a baseball coach at Taylor University, recently reminded me of the inappropriateness and lack of integrity that shows itself when the last out has been recorded. How do we coach with integrity following the conclusion of the game?

Let's start with the winning coach. Today's society often exhibits an in-your-face approach to success. Inflated egos and warped understanding of the importance of winning a baseball game can easily result in unethical conduct. Excessively exuberant postgame demonstrations, aimed at putting down the opposition or the umpires, have no place in baseball. Celebrate victory graciously. Congratulate excellence enthusiastically but do not enjoy victory at the expense of the losing team. The fundamental principle I mentioned earlier is still the goal—to treat all with whom you are involved, including opposing coaches and players, in a way that develops lifetime relationships. The golden rule of doing unto others as you would have them do to you is sound advice for the winning coach.

For the coach of integrity who loses, I also have a word of advice. In your postgame actions, do not seek to find and display on the field something that would attempt to rationalize or justify your loss. There are certainly lessons to be learned from losing. One of the most important is how to lose with a sense of respect for your opponent and a willingness to accept and learn from your mistakes and defeat. That learning best occurs in future team meetings and practice sessions, not through postgame tantrums.

A Closing Note

A baseball coach who stays in the game for any time will face the seven temptations I have discussed. If we recast the seven stages of the slippery slope into a set of positive guidelines, a coach can counteract the temptations.

- Lead by example
- Play by the rules
- Practice honest salesmanship regarding your program
- Win with sportsmanship
- Look out for your players' health
- Support your instititution or organization
- Be humble in victory, gracious in defeat

It is important that the training and preparation of coaches include assistance in correctly overcoming these slippery slopes. My reference to the television program *To Tell the Truth* dates me, but that early television quiz show used an appropriate command. The emcee would request, "Will the real [name of celebrity] please stand up!" As a baseball coach, you can be sure that the real you will be the one who stands up when you face the inevitable pressure situations. Do not wait until those times come before you wrestle with some of the issues of morality and integrity. They will determine what kind of coach you really are and what the lasting results of your life as a baseball coach will be.

As baseball coaches, we can face the 21st century with optimism, for we hold in our hands the potential for helping to shape the future of our nation. We are preparing youth for future leadership.

In my role as a college president I have come to believe that one of the greatest needs today is the development of *servant leaders*—not just leaders. People will always be willing and eager to step forward and lead, for a self-seeking ego often causes individuals to desire positions of leadership. A paradigm of leadership that we desperately need is one that is unselfish and puts others ahead of ourselves. Baseball coaches can be excellent role models of servant leadership if their greatest concerns are not just the win-loss column, or looking good, or being politically correct. Rather, let the major goal be the maximum development of those whom the coach has the privilege of influencing for good. That is where integrity shows and where it pays great dividends.

Let us work to ensure that in 2028 the president of the United States, like President Herbert Hoover a century before, can again say, "Next to religion, baseball has furnished a greater impact on American life than any other institution."

PART II

Program Building and Management

CHAPTER SIX

Organizing and Orchestrating a Winning Program

Ron Polk

Webster's New World Dictionary defines the word *winning* as gaining a victory, being victorious, achieving a triumph. Thus, in baseball when one team scores more runs than the other, that team has gained a victory, has been victorious, has triumphed over the opponent.

Coaches who have picked up this book are for the most part hoping that its contents will help them win more games. Thus, those readers may turn first to the chapters that detail strategy and on-the-field preparation to achieve wins. They are interested first in learning the X's and O's from successful coaches who have gained numerous victories. No one can blame a coach for picking up a baseball book written by successful coaches to learn the secrets of success, for every coach wants to be successful.

But is the scoreboard the only method of measuring success by a coach, player, or baseball team? If success is measured only by wins and losses, does this negate the fact that one who loses the game as a coach, player, or team might still be a winner?

This chapter will provide coaches with information that will help them win baseball games, allow the young men they coach the opportunity to achieve success on a daily basis, and establish a winning baseball program—even if, at times, the scoreboard indicates that the opponent has won the game. Success as a coach should never be defined solely by the scoreboard! Coaching success can also be defined by the means and methods employed by the coach to produce winners in young men. After all, baseball is just a game, and the game can produce positive results for all who play it, whether they win or lose.

Follow with me as I describe what I feel a coach must do to organize and orchestrate a winning program, besides merely coaching the team in practice sessions and on game days.

Coaching Staff and Support Personnel

Probably no task is more important in organizing and orchestrating a winning program than surrounding oneself with quality assistant coaches, managers, trainers, secretaries, a sports information coordinator, and even bat girls. It is vital that all support personnel work toward goals each day to produce positive results both on and off the baseball field.

Each year I produced for coaches and support personnel detailed job descriptions and administrative responsibility sheets. Everyone fully understood what I expected of them and how their jobs would enable us to meet the daily obligations of the baseball program. We held daily meetings with the entire coaching staff and scheduled periodic meetings with the other personnel to ensure that everyone had a way to share information within the baseball program.

The head coach must ensure that everyone is working in the same direction for the best interest of all concerned. For instance, it is important that all personnel within the program have direct input in the selection process when vacancies occur on the staff (either on the paid or volunteer staff).

Securing dedicated, first-class individuals to work with student-athletes and the public is crucial to the success of any program. I believe that to have a successful coaching career you must surround yourself with quality people. You must encourage both positive and negative comments from these associates to ensure that you meet all the needs of the baseball program. Look for people who will cross their t's and dot their i's if you want to maintain a high sense of purpose and organization. Show me a highly structured and organized baseball program with a staff dedicated to doing everything in a first-class manner, and I will show you a program that will be successful both on and off the baseball field.

Those working within a quality baseball program will quickly understand that a major investment of time is required from all involved. To do even the little things right takes a time commitment. This investment of time in doing a first-class job will reap major benefits in the results achieved by the program, not only in wins on the field but also in public relations. Further, the student-athletes will respect the program and learn that careful preparation will be useful in later life.

It's the Little Things That Count

A person walking in the countryside has a much greater chance of tripping over a small rock than a large boulder. Seeing a large rock and carefully moving around it, we avoid tripping over it. But the small rock often trips us up because we do not pay careful attention. I have always stressed to my coaches that we must take care of the little things, because if we do the bigger things will take care of themselves. The same holds true for players on the baseball field. If they do not take care of the little things that happen each game, then they will never come close to taking care of the larger things, among which is who won the game that day. The extra inch a player might gain in his secondary lead at second base will be one less inch he will have to travel when he tries to score on a hit to the outfield. The college coach who writes a personal letter to a high school coach who just won a big game does a small thing. But it is a huge thing to the coach who receives the letter.

To have a truly successful program, a baseball coach and his staff must make a great commitment to doing the little things each day. What follows are some of the details, some of the little things, that we did throughout the baseball season to organize and orchestrate a winning program.

Recruiting

I have always followed the practice of answering all letters and returning all phone calls before I left the office each day, no matter how late at night it might be. I asked my assistant coaches and staff to do the same. Coaches are often so busy during the day that they push their mail and phone messages across their desks. I felt that answering mail promptly and returning all calls was one of the top priority items on my daily schedule. You must handle the recruiting aspect of your position in a professional and classy manner because the recruitment of student-athletes is the lifeblood of any competitive baseball program. It was always our intention to do this in such a manner that each recruited young man, and his parents, felt that we had their best interest at heart. Even if a boy opted to attend another college or university, we sent him a letter congratulating him on his decision and thanking him for his interest in our university.

It was important for us that all discussions with the boy and his parents were up front, and never would we use negative recruiting about another school. Instead, we represented our school and baseball program in a manner that reflected a classy approach to the recruiting process. We also made every effort to involve the young man's high school or junior college coach in the recruiting process. That way the coach was fully aware of our interest in his player. If a potential recruit decided to attend another school, we sent his coach of a copy of the letter we sent the boy thanking him for his interest in our school. By keeping coaches informed on what we were doing in our recruiting, they felt comfortable with our staff when we called on them again to help us evaluate and recruit their players.

Further, we sent our yearly and press media guide to all high school and junior college coaches whom we have dealt with in the past. We would also often send personal letters to these coaches wishing them the best for their spring season. We even made it a practice to send congratulatory letters to boys who decided to sign professional baseball contracts instead of attending Mississippi State. Additionally, we sent letters to all our former players in pro baseball and to all the players who competed against us in the Southeastern Conference.

When we brought recruits on campus for their official visits, we wanted them to have a tremendous experience and get a feel for what college is all about, both on and off the baseball field. We made every effort to have our current players interact with the recruits so that the recruits could ask them about their experiences as student-athletes at our university. When the recruit arrived on campus, one of our staff members would call his parents to be sure they knew their son had safely arrived on our campus. The little things that one does in the recruiting process go a long way in building strong relationships between a coaching staff, the young man, and his family.

Publications

One of the ways that we kept everyone informed about our baseball program was by producing and distributing attractive and informative media guides, game programs, and poster and pocket schedules. We maintained a massive name and address list of people to whom we sent these materials before the opening game of our season. Poster and pocket schedules were distributed by our sports information and ticket departments to businesses throughout Mississippi and the surrounding states. We sent pocket schedules (50,000 each year) to all our season-ticket holders. The coaching staff monitored the quality of these publications to ensure that they were free of errors. The sports information department and our baseball office worked together to approve each of these publications before they were sent to the printer.

At the beginning of fall practice, our players each received a 520-page baseball playbook, their textbook for the baseball season. It contained all the information, including signals, that they had to learn before the first pitch of the regular season. The book was also available to the public, serving as a tremendous vehicle for promoting our baseball program. Understandably, the books we sold did not include signals!

Contact With Former Players, Managers, and Coaches

We always wanted to be sure that our former players, managers, and coaches remained a part of our baseball program. Before each season, I would type a personal letter to each one to send along with our media guide. Further, each would receive a birthday card and Christmas card each year, and, if they were married, I would send them an anniversary card. We also sent each of our baseball alumni a season pass to all our home games, hoping to keep them involved as much as possible.

Every two years we hosted an alumni baseball weekend for all our former baseball players, managers, and coaches. By having this weekend every two years rather than each year, we made it a weekend they all looked forward to with great interest and anticipation. We would have a golf tournament for them on Saturday morning followed by a dinner on campus for them and their families. On Sunday afternoon we would play the alumni baseball game. All players dressed out in game uniforms with special alumni baseball caps. We played a nine-inning game matching various teams (by years) against each other. We generally had well over 100 alumni back on campus for the weekend.

Communicating With Parents and Scouts

In our efforts to make the parents of our players an integral part of the baseball program, we sent them a letter after our fall practice ended and again after the spring season ended. These letters provided information about what their son's involvement with the baseball program was all about, both on and off the field. We encouraged them to stop by the coaches' offices when they were on campus to discuss their son's academic and athletic performance. We provided complimentary chairback seats for all the parents and assisted them in making hotel reservations for road trips.

We fully recognized that the professional baseball scouts who attended our games had a difficult job as they traveled around the country evaluating talent for the professional baseball draft. We wanted to make their scouting of our kids easy. Thus, in the fall we sent them our spring schedule of games, a roster with all the information they would need on each boy, and a VIP pass that they could use to get into all our home games, including a chairback seat behind home plate. We also sent all the scouts in our files a media guide in the spring. We wanted to establish a professional relationship with these scouts, for many of them help us throughout the year in evaluating players whom we might be recruiting.

Camps and Clinics

One of the best tools a coaching staff can use for improving public relations, evaluating prospective student-athletes, and providing additional income to assistant coaches is conducting summer and winter baseball camps on campus. We have averaged over 1,200 kids in our camps and, if the camp staff does its job, these kids leave with a great feeling about our university and baseball program. Our camps have always been work and instruction, with the camp sessions starting at 9:00 A.M. and continuing through the day until 10:00 P.M., with breaks for lunch and dinner. The camp staff is carefully selected for coaches who have great knowledge of the game and enjoy working with kids of different ages.

Besides baseball instruction, we have always had various lectures for the boys on the importance of academics and how to handle themselves in a first-class manner in everything they do off the baseball field. We encourage their parents to attend all the sessions. At the end of the camp, we have a closing ceremony when we honor all the campers in front of their parents and friends. Many of these boys and their family members buy Bulldog clothing items at these camps, which provides outstanding program awareness throughout the state.

We inform the camper and their parents that our baseball camps are strictly for those interested in improving their baseball skills. We do not have any free-time activities planned. It is all baseball!

Each year we conduct a clinic for all the coaches in our area to get them on our campus and provide them with information they can use at their respective baseball programs. Our coaching staff conducts most of these clinic sessions, but we often have some of the outstanding coaches in our area give a clinic session as well. It is important to have all the coaches in your area familiar with your program and coaching staff. If you can be of assistance to them and their program, you should always make yourselves available to them.

To promote our baseball program and pass along information about the team and our student-athletes, we as a coaching staff made ourselves available for all baseball clinics, civic clubs, alumni meetings, high school and junior college banquets, and any other group that invited us to speak. This is time consuming for the coaches, but we feel it is a crucial aspect of our public relations. It ensures that our baseball program remains highly visible throughout our area and surrounding states. It is vital that the assistant coaches have as many speaking opportunities as the head coach, so that they can refine their public-speaking abilities for the time they become a head coach.

Building a Fan Base

Organizing and orchestrating a winning baseball program must also center on the fans who support your program. The more fans you can draw, the more attractive your program becomes to the high school and junior college players you would like to have involved in your program.

When I arrived at Mississippi State in 1976, the program was selling few baseball season tickets. We all felt it was important to our program to start making an effort to sell season tickets and get our fan base involved. We sold our first season tickets at minimal cost to build up the fan base. As our on-field performance improved, we could raise the price of our season tickets. We now sell over 4,100 season tickets each year and have a waiting list for those who wish to buy season tickets in our chairback section.

We also allowed vehicles to park on the elevated banks beyond the outfield fence. This area was tailor-made for vehicles, and the fans could sit in their vehicles and watch the baseball games. We charged the vehicles' occupants just as we did those who bought a general admission ticket. As our on-field success grew, more fans started bringing their cars, trucks, and campers to the games. At first, we forced them to remove their vehicles after each game, but with demand so high for priority parking spots in the outfield, we finally had to allow them to park their vehicles in the outfield for the entire season. Later, we had to deed plots of parking spots in the outfield as the demand grew even more. Now we have cars, trucks, and campers three rows deep from foul pole to foul pole with permanent spots in the outfield. Fans drive their vehicles into what they call the outfield lounge a week before the first home game. The vehicles are "locked" into their deeded plots for the entire season, and their owners must remove the vehicles a week after the last home game. I'm not sure how many other amateur baseball programs can pull off an outfield lounge as we have at Mississippi State, but it has been an enormous success for us.

In 1986, due to the large crowds we were drawing to a relatively small stadium, we passed a bond issue and sold the rights to the chairback seats for a lifetime. That allowed us to build a 7,000-seat stadium, with half of those seats being chairbacks. This was a major plus for our program, for now the fans had seats with their names inscribed and did not have to arrive at the stadium early to scramble for a premium seat.

Once we got the fans to attend the games, we wanted to provide them with great entertainment by putting on the field all-American kids who played hard. The players always respond to large, enthusiastic crowds, and these fans made the boys play even harder. For that reason, we won most of our home games. We played quality music before the games and between innings and had a first-class public-address announcer working our games. We built plenty of concession stands and rest rooms for the public and tried to have someone sing the national anthem before all games. We even bought the largest American flag we could find and erected a flag pole right over our center-field fence. We attempted to do everything first class, for we wanted our fans to know that we had a great product and wanted them to be a part of the program.

Playing Environment

We made sure that our playing field was well maintained. Our players and the visiting players enjoyed competing on a top-quality field. We dressed our field staff in colorful shirts. Our diamond girls proved extremely helpful to the program, serving as the first all-girl groundskeeping crew in college baseball history. They also served as ushers for our fans, staffed our novelty booth in the stadium concourse, and picked up the bats during the game. We also used the diamond girls to assist in hosting recruits on game days.

We always tried to put together a quality schedule for our players and fans. Each year we tried to plan at least one regular-season tournament. When we had the opportunity to host an NCAA regional on our campus, we went all out making sure that the competing teams' players, coaches, and staff left our campus with a favorable impression. Our outfield lounge fans invited the visiting teams to eat in the outfield after each game they played or when they came back to the stadium to watch other games. We hosted a pretournament catfish dinner for all the teams and provided courtesy cars to the head coaches.

We have always had a pregame routine for our players to get them mentally and physically ready for each contest. Our pregame outfield-infield was a multiple-ball routine that made our players look first class. We always played "Sweet Georgia Brown" on the public-address system while we were executing this drill. We followed a pregame running program in the outfield to ensure that our kids were physically prepared to take the field.

We took great pride in our uniforms, which included the names of the boys on the back of each set. We asked our players to wear their uniforms properly, be clean shaven, and always have their hair trimmed. We also asked our players to sign autographs for the fans before and after the game. These little things are crucial to building a strong relationship between players and fans.

We worked out a contract with a scoreboard company, allowing them to sell advertising on the board. In this way we could afford to erect a very large scoreboard with a message center and animation capabilities.

We staffed our press box with two people who were responsible for the scoreboard on game day, so we always had quality information for the players and fans. It is important that the person taking care of balls, strikes, outs, and score by inning be able to produce this information on the scoreboard in a timely fashion. A great scoreboard means a lot to the players, the media, and most important, the fans.

Mass Media

We developed, with the assistance of our local radio station, a radio network for all our baseball games, both home and away. In time, it turned into the largest college baseball radio network in the country with 26 stations. Some of the stations would carry only our conference games, and others would carry all the games. Nothing we did as a baseball program was more significant in creating fan interest and enthusiasm than putting in place this extensive radio network. We were able to secure the services of a first-class play-by-play announcer who has remained with Mississippi State for many years and provides stability and continuity to the broadcasts.

We deemed it vital to the success of our baseball program to provide the print and electronic media every opportunity to associate and identify with our players and coaches. A week before our first game each year, we held a press conference, sending out invitations to all the media outlets in the state. We held this press conference before a men's basketball game, so the media would be able to cover two events. I would bring our cocaptains to this conference to respond to questions from the press after I made my general comments concerning the upcoming season. During the season, all our coaches and players were available to the press before batting practice and immediately after the game.

Another avenue we used to promote our program throughout Mississippi was a weekly television show produced and directed by our campus television station. This 30-minute show was broadcast by 14 television stations throughout the state, making it the largest television network in college baseball. We had interviews with the coaches and players on each show besides a weekly feature on some aspect of the baseball program. We also showed highlights of game action during the preceding week, and occasionally we had a coaching clinic segment providing basic baseball skill information. Our television station on campus would also prepare a highlight video whenever the team made the College World Series. We sold this highlight tape to the general public.

Team Activities

College baseball teams spend a lot of time on the road, so we made every effort to provide the team with a first-class travel experience. We would stay in first-class hotels and serve the players quality meals. We were fortunate to have our own athletic department bus, which contained card tables and several television monitors so the team could watch movies on road trips. We worked out an advertising tradeoff with a local video store so our managers, before each road trip, could select current movies for the team.

Because it is difficult for the baseball team to attend church services on Sunday mornings, especially when playing on the road, we would always have an optional chapel service for our team. Often we would have someone come in from outside the team to conduct these services. Otherwise, a member of the coaching staff or one of the players conducted the service. When at home, we would have the chapel service after our pregame meal. On the road, the service would be conducted in a meeting room at the hotel after our pregame meal.

We always thought it important to eat all our meals on road trips as a team rather than passing out meal money. This ensured that the players ate quality meals and provided us with an opportunity to meet with the team afterward. At all our pregame meals we gave the team a detailed scouting report on the opponent we would be playing that day. For SEC games, we put these scouting reports in writing so the players could study and analyze them throughout the series.

At the completion of our fall practice each year, we would have all the players, coaches, managers, trainers, and diamond girls gather for a banana-split party. The last week of practice we would have the banana-split world series (best three out of five), with the losers having to buy a deluxe banana split for the winners. The diamond girls squad would also divide up before the series opener to determine their winners and losers. This was always an enjoyable occasion. This was the time for the diamond girls to name their bat buddies for the season. Throughout the year the diamond girls would take care of their player, manager, trainer, and coach bat buddies by baking them goodies.

Also at the end of fall practice, we would pass out a player evaluation form that the players would use to rank all the position players and pitchers and pick their starting lineup versus a right-handed and left-handed pitcher. Then before the first game in the spring, we would do this again with the team captains and coaches filling out the forms. At the banana-split party in the fall, we would pass out the results to all team members to use in our ~~player-coach meetings~~ that we conducted following fall practice. I have always felt that it is helpful to have comments from everyone concerning the makeup of the team, and we wanted the players to play an important role in the total evaluation of the baseball team.

Communicating With Coaches, Visiting Teams, and Umpires

About four times during the spring baseball season we would send a card to each of the high school and junior college coaches who had previously coached our team members. On this card we would provide each coach with information on how his boy was doing during our season. I deemed it important to keep the boys' coaches informed about how their young men were doing during the baseball season because often they would have no other way to know, especially if they were not in Mississippi.

In the fall, we assigned a member of our coaching staff to send information to the head coach of each team that would be playing games at our stadium. Our goal was to provide information helpful to the visitors in planning their trips to Mississippi State. Included in this information would be a listing of hotels in our towns with phone numbers and room rates, names and phone numbers of restaurants in town, a pregame schedule of events listing batting practice and infield-outfield practice times, and starting times of the games. We would also offer free laundry service for their teams and list the names and phone numbers of our managers to work out the arrangements for the pickup and delivery of these laundry items.

We feel that public relations from our baseball office to the umpires working our home games is an important responsibility. We assigned one of our managers to the umpires from the time they arrived at our stadium to the time they left for home. This manager would be sure to escort them to their dressing room and provide them with food and soft drinks. The umpires would be sent detailed information about the games they would be working, including starting time for each game, ground rules, hotel and restaurant information, and phone numbers they can call in case of an emergency in their travels to and from our stadium. At the end of the season we would send each umpire who worked our home games a thank-you note signed by all members of our coaching staff.

Foster-Parent Program

Most of the boys who were members of our baseball team, including the managers, lived outside our university location. We thought it important to have a local family serve as foster parents to each boy during the time they attended our university. At one time, any family in town could become foster parents to our baseball players. Later, the NCAA banned this type of program. Now the NCAA allows foster-parent programs as long as one of the family members is employed by the school. We had two meetings each year with these families when I spoke to them about the foster-family program and the baseball program. They "chose" their foster son for the year by drawing a boy's name out of a baseball cap. (Each had to have a new boy each year.) The foster parents could have the player over to their home for an occasional home-cooked meal, and we encouraged the foster parents to let the player's parents know that they were available for them and their son any time as long as they followed NCAA rules and regulations. We had a meet-the-players dinner before our first game each spring when the players and managers would sit with their foster parents during dinner.

Honoring Our Players

Any time one of our players achieved a high honor for his skills on the baseball field or in the classroom, we made sure to present him with a plaque or certificate at an athletic event. Often this would occur before our football or basketball games on campus when we expected a great crowd. Also, any former player who appeared in a major-league game was brought back to the campus in his off-season and honored at one of our athletic events. We thought it important to recognize our current and former players when they accomplished something significant.

During our last home series of the spring, we would honor our senior baseball players and managers before one of the games. If their parents could appear on the field with them, it made for an even more special occasion. Our public-address announcer would prepare and read a brief script on each boy while he walked out to the home-plate area to be recognized by our fans for his involvement in the baseball program.

Each year in late spring, we would take a team picture for our sports information office to use in case we played in postseason tournaments. We would also use this team picture to order picture plaques for the boys to buy for themselves and their families. Because we ordered so many of these plaques each year, the price per plaque was very reasonable. Each player would now have a beautiful picture plaque to hang on his wall to remember the experience of playing college baseball at Mississippi State. We would also make these plaques available for sale to the foster parents and other fans of the baseball program.

We presented attractive awards each year to players and managers who lettered. For the first year, they would receive a letter jacket. For year two, lettering and a blanket. For the third year, a travel bag, and for the fourth year, a watch.

At the conclusion of fall practice, when the players completed their player-coach evaluation forms, we asked them to name their cocaptains for the spring season. The two players receiving the most votes from the players would be our cocaptains. I would meet with them a few times each year in my office concerning anything the club wished to tell me about the direction we were taking with their baseball program. When I went to home plate to exchange lineup cards with the umpires and the opposing coach, I would always have one of the cocaptains come with me to meet the umpires and the coach. At the end of the year, I would present the two cocaptains attractive plaques for their service to the baseball team.

After fall practice ended we would display for the team several items they could buy for themselves or their families for Christmas gifts. These items all contained the Mississippi State baseball logo with the name of the person wearing the item. We had available team jackets, sport shirts, sweat pants and sweat tops, pullovers, and sweaters. A local sporting goods store made up the items for the team, and the team would pay the regular commercial rate for these items just before the players went home for the Christmas holiday season.

A Closing Note

A coach who wishes to organize and orchestrate a winning baseball program must do a lot of behind-the-scenes work. To maximize success on the field, it certainly helps if he is a great on-field coach, but often what the coach does off the field is just as important in building a polished, first-class baseball program. I hope the information I have provided on how we organized our baseball program will help you do the same for your program.

CHAPTER SEVEN

Establishing a Successful High School Program

Ken Schreiber

Baseball programs at the high school level function in varied ways. Some programs operate at the minimum, and others may parallel college and professional programs. The attitudes of the coach and the community will probably determine the level at which the program will function.

Before setting out to develop a program, a coach should ask himself the following questions:

- What type of a coach do I want to be and what kind of coach am I capable of being?
- How much time am I willing to put forth in developing a program?
- How much latitude will my school administration and community allow me in building up a program?

Developing a program can be difficult but fun. In the development stages, results can usually be seen on a regular basis, thereby motivating the coaching staff and team members to continue their progress. When a program has reached a certain plateau of accomplishment, results may become less visible and past results may become expectations. Such expectations are not always realistic or fair and could possibly take some of the fun out of being successful.

If maintaining a program becomes a hardship, or some of the fun escapes, the coach may have to develop strategies to recapture some of the zeal previously experienced in conducting the program. These strategies may have to cope with meeting expectations, fair or not, maintaining what has been developed, or continuing to progress.

Establishing a successful program can be accomplished by several different methods, using different philosophies. As I mentioned previously, the coach's personality and the school system's attitude affect the decision about which method the coach will pursue, but most successful programs will incorporate certain common principles. This chapter will highlight some of the principles, as well as some of the policies, that we employed in establishing our program at La Porte High School.

Three-Stage Program

At La Porte we have divided our total program into three stages. We conduct the first stage during summer. It begins immediately after the conclusion of regular-season and tournament play and runs through July. This part of the program is equivalent to college fall practice. We drop the seniors from the regular season and use the players with future eligibility who we expect will contribute the following season.

We put together a summer schedule that runs through July. Although we emphasize winning, this part of the program is mostly for observation, instruction, and experimentation. The coaching staff can work toward detecting strong and weak areas and attempt to put the pieces together for the following year. The players get an opportunity to gain additional game experience and, in some cases, adjust to a new position.

At the end of the summer season, each player will meet with the coach to discuss his strengths and weaknesses and his projected role in the program for the following season. At this meeting we give the player a written critique outlining what he can do to improve himself between this time and the beginning of stage two.

The second part of the program is conducted during winter, in January and February. This eight-week program is important because we pick up where we left off last summer. Because we live in a cold-weather state, we conduct this phase of the program indoors. Regardless of how big our indoor facilities are in Indiana, a sport like baseball will be restricted. We find these limitations to be pluses as it forces us to break down the game. It gives us the opportunity to work on a lot of one-on-one, individual-position instruction. We also stress conditioning during this period so that when we move outdoors the players are less likely to become injured.

Stage three is the beginning of the regular season, what we had been preparing for in the two previous stages. As we are making the move outdoors and determining the team members for the regular season, we begin to focus on the team concept. We emphasize team drills, fundamentals, and strategies. Two weeks before the season opener, we devote additional attention to the pitching staff. We put them into a schedule that we expect them to follow during the regular season.

The three parts of the program complement each other and help develop continuity in preparing players for this year's team.

Program First, Individual Second

We subscribe strongly to the principle that the total program should be stressed more than the individuals who make up the program. Does this attitude seem to come across as authoritarian or antisocial? In society today we hear so much about individual rights that we tend to lose sight of the responsibilities of the individual.

The principle of program first and individual second is based on the premise that the individual, though important to the program, will move on in a short time. The program will remain for other individuals to benefit from. Therefore the overall program receives top priority when establishing policies and making decisions.

We run a no-nonsense program. When we establish rules and regulations, we maintain that attitude. We give each player a copy of the policies before he tries out. After reading these policies, the player and his parents must sign a statement indicating that they have read the rules and agree that the player will uphold them while a member of the program. The responsibility belongs to the athlete and his parents.

Our athletic department has established a code of conduct that all athletes in our school must follow. This code explains policies and penalties concerning alcohol, drugs, tobacco, misdemeanors, and felonies. Each individual sports program has the option of adding to this code with policies of their own. These addenda must be in print and approved by the administration.

It is in this addendum that our program addresses such items as academics, absences, tardiness, appearance, attitude, promptness, locker room behavior, care of equipment, and respect toward opponents and umpires.

Any player who we cut when trying out is welcome to try out again in future years. A player who makes the program and then quits is not welcome to try out in future years.

Coaches, as well as players, have responsibilities. Job descriptions that detail the responsibilities of each coach are made up for every coach in the system. Job performance of each assistant coach is evaluated annually by the head coach, and the head coach is evaluated by the athletic director.

We deal with violation of rules immediately and without concern about the value of the player or the success of the team. We enforce the rules on a consistent, fair, and firm basis.

Setting Realistic Goals

The ability to recognize the facts and then establish goals based on those facts is invaluable in directing a successful program. The coach of a successful program should have the aptitude to evaluate players' abilities accurately. The more exact he is in defining those abilities, the more precise he can be in establishing individual and team goals.

It is fine to be optimistic and show hope for the best when dealing with team members, but the coach must be realistic when setting goals. If the coach sets goals so high that they are unreachable, the players will have difficulty developing confidence in themselves and the program. On the other hand, if the coach sets goals that are too easily accomplished, the players and the program could be functioning under false pretenses. The progress of the players and the program will be impeded.

A coach must be honest with himself, as well as with the players, when it comes to evaluating personnel and the challenges that lie ahead.

Do It Your Way

Thousands of books have been written, an equal number of films have been made, and ten times that number of clinicians have spoken on the topic of how to play baseball. Most of the methods and theories presented have valid approaches to the game. The successful coach will decide what methods and theories best fit his personality and then incorporate them into his program.

High school baseball has different problems than college and professional programs. At the high school level we have to use the material that is available to us on a year-to-year basis. Colleges can recruit talent, and the pros can sign talent to meet their needs.

How many high school baseball games have been won by a "swinging bunt" hit in front of deeply positioned third basemen or an "opposite-side" ground ball that sneaked through an overshifted infield? In many such cases, the coach of the defensive team positioned the players because he was remembering what he read in a book, saw in a film, or heard at a clinic. He might have been unaware of what level of baseball he was coaching or the abilities of his pitcher or the abilities of the opposing batters.

You must understand the level of play you are coaching. If a team has a healthy kid on the mound who throws with a lot of velocity, his coach might play most of the opposing batters opposite what the book suggests, that is, he might rotate fielders for right-handed batters as if they were left-handed and vice versa. Most high school batters are not going to pull hard-throwing pitchers with regularity.

The same is true for other facets of the game. Do what is best for your situation. Let the type of personnel you are using and your mental approach to the game be the deciding factors. Don't let other people dictate the way your team should play!

Throw away the book but be ready to take the heat if it backfires! The experts who read "the book" will let you know in many different ways just how misinformed you are about how the game should be played.

Put the brakes in storage! Aggressiveness should be part of any program that wants success on a long-term basis. You can incorporate aggressiveness into most activities that take place on the baseball field. Regardless of the talent available, aggressiveness can put pressure on the opposing team, offensively and defensively. You might have to replace the steal with the hit-and-run, but you can still achieve movement on the bases.

Do not allow fear to enter your program's makeup because it will inhibit the players' aggressiveness. If players are fearful of making mistakes, they will tend to play cautiously, waiting for things to happen instead of making things happen!

It is encouraging to see the opposition enter the stadium with the veins in their necks ready to pop. This type of tension can tighten the joints, reduce quickness, and lessen mental alertness. These conditions could lead to defeat. A player might exhibit the same physical characteristics if he becomes obsessed about losing. Although losing should not, of course, be a goal of any program, fear of losing might be just as detrimental to a player's performance as fear of making mistakes.

In order for the players to play without fear, the coach must be willing to coach without fear!

Basic Before Cute

Short-term success can be achieved by having super talent. All the coach has to do is fill out the lineup card properly and then stay out of the way. If a program is blessed with super talent every year, then this success can possibly be maintained long term. The possibility of this talented team losing occurs when they face a team of similar talent that is sound in the fundamentals of the game.

Many programs, with or without good talent, look for shortcuts to success. While looking for alternatives to teaching sound, fundamental baseball, they work overtime incorporating pickoffs, hidden-ball tricks, and gimmick plays. When one of these plays works, it draws delight from the home crowd, justifying to the coach all the work put into this type of play.

Usually a coaching staff that goes into depth in teaching gimmick baseball needs to be concerned with base runners, because they are bound to see their fair share!

We are aware of programs that teach numerous pickoffs to first, second, and third bases. You can bet that when an opposing runner reaches one of these bases, the fans are in for a clinic on how to hold runners on, and the game is going to be lengthened by several minutes. The one base that these programs seem to ignore is home plate. While their pitcher is throwing a game to the bases, attempting to hold runners on, he loses concentration toward home plate and the batter.

This example is true for any aspect on the game. If coaches emphasize the cute stuff at the expense of the basics of the game, they should not be surprised at their lack of success.

Time to Coach, Time to Not

We have already discussed realistic goals, but probably just as important to establishing a successful program is realistic coaching. Coaches have varied degrees of knowledge that they can impart to their players. Some coaches are extremely knowledgeable about the game. Other coaches have knowledge that can be described as anywhere from adequate to nearly nonexistent.

Regardless of how much knowledge a coach has, of equal importance is his ability to transfer it to his players constructively. Some coaches feel they must convey all their knowledge to all the players all the time! Other coaches feel that it is only necessary to pass on knowledge to certain players, at certain times, and in certain situations.

Overcoaching can be just as detrimental as not coaching enough. The successful coach can identify the need for work on a skill and then be able to fulfill this need with the knowledge to correct or enhance the skill.

How many times have you observed the following situation? While a batter is in the cage working on his timing and skills, a coach is standing by relating every flaw that he can detect in the batter's technique. The young man ends up so confused that instead of swinging aggressively with a quick bat, he starts thinking about all the flaws that are being pointed out to him. He thus loses his aggressiveness and exhibits a slow bat.

When teaching or working on mechanics, a coach should stress only one at a time. No other factors should be addressed while the player works on this one mechanic. The player should concentrate on a single thought. We've all heard stories of coaches who take .350 hitters and coach them into .250 hitters! That is a good example of overcoaching.

A coach should not concern himself with impressing players about how smart he is, but how smart he can be when knowledge is needed!

Positive but Constructive

Coaches of successful programs have certain philosophical principles that apply positive reinforcement. Seldom do the coaches in these programs use terminology that allows their players to develop excuses for failure.

Regardless of how many players a program has to replace from the previous year, positive coaches do not use the term *rebuilding*. Reality is that at the high school level players move on every year. Therefore rebuilding could be an annual declaration.

Another practice that successful coaches stay away from is defending players who fail by constantly referring to their youth and inexperience. When a young man is a member of a team, he should be expected to execute at the level of play at which the team is competing. Focus should be on performance, not on the youth or inexperience of the players. It's fine for the coach to have these factors in *his* mind, but he should not use them as an excuse for failure. Eventually the players seize upon these excuses and develop an attitude geared toward failure.

The positive coach does not use the theory of kicking fannies in defeat and patting backs in victory. It has been proven that the best time to administer constructive criticism to an individual or team is after a success. Players are more susceptible to accepting criticism when they are in a positive mood. Some of the best teaching and learning can be done after success.

On the other hand, when a player or a team has just failed, the coach should allow some time to elapse before applying constructive criticism. When postfailure discussion does begin, it could be more effective if some positive reinforcement is interjected.

When conferring with his players, the successful coach knows when to turn it on and when to turn it off. This communication skill gains the respect of the players, and they will know that his coaching is about more than just winning and losing!

Coach to Your Strengths

Work first toward the strengths of your program and the individuals who make up your program instead of trying to combat your opponent's weaknesses. The coach who attempts to expose the possible weaknesses of the opposition by making his players adjust to the opponent's style of play could be falling into a trap.

Joe Brock, a coach in Stayton, Oregon, wrote an article several years ago for a coaching journal. He emphasized the bunting game; his team might execute as many as 15 bunts a game. After reading the article, we decided no team that put down 15 bunts in one game would beat us! We would set up our defense to take away the effectiveness of the bunt. We're not stupid, right?

Shortly after reading this article, we had an opportunity to meet Coach Brock. During our conversation we discussed his article. We told him how we would defense his team if we ever played him. We would play our team up. Coach Brock asked if we normally play up. When we answered no, he taught us a lesson by stating, "Then we have you doing something unnatural in your system of play." He said that his article didn't imply that they have to bunt the ball, but because they work on the bunt so much and do it so effectively, they make the opposition do things they usually don't do. When teams play up on his hitters, they have just that much more field in which to hit safely.

Since this lesson from Coach Brock, we subscribe to the philosophy of emphasizing first what we do best and then worrying about the opponent's quality of play. We don't put our kids into situations that are strange to them or that could affect their performance.

Organized Practices

Most established programs in any sport conduct well-organized, meaningful practices. Regardless of whether a program is well-staffed or understaffed, practices can and must be organized and consequential. The goal of practice is to do what needs to be accomplished, in quality fashion and in the least amount of time.

Baseball can be a boring sport if a coaching staff allows it. Most of the boredom shows up at long, unorganized practices. Programs conducted in certain areas of the country must contend with another detracting factor, the weather. There is nothing romantic about standing around for two and a half hours in freezing weather, watching inactivity in an unorganized practice. Bring on basketball and soccer!

At La Porte we have a basic philosophy about conducting baseball practice. We believe that success results from pitchers being able to throw strikes (and early in the count), defensive people being able to play catch properly and thus able to make the routine plays, and hitters being able to make contact. Sounds easy! Some coaches show their players an abundance of videos on how to play the game. Some coaches develop a reading list of books for their players to learn the fundamentals. The successful coach conducts well-organized practices. His players witness ground balls, fly balls, pitched balls, and thrown balls by the hundreds and thousands. You learn the game by doing the game.

> *We believe in the Sesame Street approach to teaching fundamentals. We tell, we show, we do, do, do, again and again!*

When indoors, we break the game down into a lot of individual and position work. Once we move outdoors we devote a lot of time toward team concept work.

We believe in the Sesame Street approach to teaching fundamentals. We tell, we show, we do, do, do, again and again! When working on team concept drills, we work extensively to establish these drills into our team's thinking caps. Throughout the season, we review these concepts on the theory of doing a little frequently rather than a lot seldom.

Equipment and how you use it can strongly affect how organized your practices are. Programs that have facilities where equipment can be used in practice have a tremendous opportunity, but the coach must take advantage of the opportunity. The ambitious program will find ways to accumulate and use the needed equipment.

When you are considering equipment, baseballs are a must—lots and lots of baseballs, baseballs of any description. Programs that attempt to conduct practices with a handful of balls are kidding themselves. When working on a skill or a mechanic, a player should not have to be constantly interrupted by having to round up baseballs. The only skill this improves is how to pick up baseballs.

Equally high on the priority list should be cages and protection screens. These pieces of equipment permit multiple drills to take place at the same time, allowing you to conduct practices in less time. The players are more active and are protected from potential injury. There are no substitutes for baseballs, cages, and screens when it comes to conducting well-organized, meaningful practices.

Make every effort to use drills that simulate game situations, even in your conditioning drills. The players and the teams that practice the little things and emphasize details have the best opportunity to excel. Players learn from practice—well-organized, meaningful practice.

Administration and Financial Support

In the opening statement of the chapter, I mentioned that the community could be one of the determining factors in developing a successful a high school baseball program. A coach of a developing program could appeal to several groups within the community when attempting to attract support, but probably none is as important as the administration of the school system. That is the body of people responsible for the total system, including the baseball program. They determine policies that all programs must observe. It would be wise to ascertain the attitude of this group before setting out to develop the baseball program.

Perhaps the administration initially displays a conservative attitude toward the baseball coach eager to develop a successful program. In this situation the coach should not be discouraged. Most administrators at the high school level give more attention to the so-called revenue sports, the self-supporting programs that may pay for some of the other sports, including baseball.

The best thing a coach can do to impress the school administration is to do what he was hired to do—coach baseball. The better job he does coaching, the more attention his program will likely receive in the future.

Although the administration might not want to open their checkbook to fund the development of the baseball program, they might allow the program to raise financial support on its own. If this is a possibility, the coach must decide if he wants to do it, and if so, what avenues he wants to pursue.

The ideal method would be to charge admission to games. To do this successfully, a program must first field a quality product that appeals to fans. Second, they must have a facility conducive to charging admission. Charging admission might be the most difficult option for a high school baseball program, but it could be the most satisfying. It would give the program a feeling that it had arrived and no longer had the label as one of the "other" sports.

Fund-Raising

Fund-raising is the method most often used by sport teams that do not have the power of developing a fan base. If the school administration allows fund-raising, the coach should construct a well thought-out plan about how the program will conduct the fund-raiser or fund-raisers.

Three important factors have to be considered before initiating a fund-raiser. First, the coach should decide how much money the program needs. A program should not become caught up in seeing how much money it can raise; it should raise only as much as it needs. Coaches of some programs become so obsessed with fund-raising that they subconsciously put the importance of the program on a back burner. Keep in mind that fund-raising is a part of the program, not the program itself.

Second, it should be determined what type of fund-raiser would be most beneficial to the program. Fund-raising that can both generate funds and promote the program is usually easier to market.

A third factor to consider is when to conduct the fund-raiser. Strongly consider the off-season when making this decision. When the playing season rolls around, the fewer distractions you place on the players, the more attention they can devote to baseball.

Regardless of what route you take to raise revenue, the successful program should strive to become self-supporting. It might take time, but it can be done. What a great feeling it is to no longer be considered one of the "other" sports.

A Closing Note

The success of a high school baseball program starts with the coach. He should be the architect of the total program. The coach who can master the X's and O's of the game and impart them effectively to his players can be a good coach. The coach who possesses those skills and is also capable of carrying out the duties of psychologist, groundskeeper, equipment manager, promoter, and administrator can establish a baseball program that will be successful for the long term.

CHAPTER EIGHT

Building a Recruiting Network

Mark Marquess

In fielding a competitive Division I college baseball team, you must have two ingredients: good players and solid coaching. Early in my coaching career, I thought that coaching was the more critical of these two components. But the longer I have coached, the more convinced I am that recruiting is the lifeblood of a successful college baseball program. You must have talented players if you want to succeed. You cannot hope to outcoach an opponent who has better talent. If I have to hire an assistant baseball coach, the first and most critical factor I consider when making my decision is that coach's ability to recruit. If a head coach at the college level cannot recruit or does not have an excellent recruiter on his coaching staff, he is unlikely to have a successful baseball program.

In evaluating the overall value of recruiting and the success of a baseball program, I have concluded that the higher you advance in baseball (Little League, Babe Ruth, high school, college, minor leagues, major leagues), the less the importance or impact of coaching on the success of a team. Obviously, good coaching can and does make a difference, but rarely does superior coaching beat better talent. Recruiting talented players is at least as important to the success of a team as the ability to teach the fundamentals of baseball or manage a baseball game.

One of my former coaches at the college level, John Ralston (who coached football at Stanford University where I played defensive back), gave me some sound advice when I became a college head coach. He told me that a college coach had two important seasons—the competitive season, when his team played their games, and the recruiting season, when the coaching staff recruits their future players. If he hopes to have a winning program, a college coach must approach the recruiting season with the same desire and dedication as he does the competitive season.

Recruiting Philosophy

When establishing a recruiting program at the college level, a coach must first develop a recruiting philosophy or approach. What type of student-athlete will he recruit? Will he recruit high school players? Junior college players? A combination of both? From which areas of the country will he recruit? Local? State? Regional? National? International? In addition, what are the financial limits of his recruiting budget?

In deciding whether to recruit high school players or junior college players, most college coaches prefer to recruit high school players. They feel that by recruiting high school players they will have a player for at least three years and thus be able to build team morale and team chemistry. If a college coach recruits strictly junior college players, he will have a more difficult time creating stability in his program because most junior college players will stay for only one or two seasons. I feel the ideal recruiting approach focuses on the high school talent pool, with only a couple of recruits being junior college transfers. Those junior college players can fill specific needs of your baseball program. If you recruit the majority of your players from high school and get a couple of junior college transfers, you can build a good, solid foundation for your team, composed primarily of high school players and supplemented by a few transfer players who will fill specific needs.

To determine in which areas to recruit, a coach must first look at his recruiting budget. If the resources are limited, it might be impossible to recruit nationally, or even regionally. Each college will have its limitations, but that should not keep you from being successful. In the West, I can give you two examples of college baseball programs that take totally opposite approaches in their recruiting philosophies. At Stanford University, we recruit nationally because of the makeup of our overall student body and the academic qualifications required of our student-athletes. Thus, each year over half of the members of our baseball team are from outside California. Our recruiting approach requires a large recruiting budget, but it is an approach that has worked for us. On the other hand, Cal State Fullerton, which has an outstanding baseball program, recruits primarily local players. The majority of the Cal State Fullerton players live within a 100-mile radius of the university. Cal State Fullerton's recruiting budget is significantly lower than Stanford's, yet their recruiting approach is just as successful. In other words, a college coach must find a recruiting approach or philosophy that works for his school.

In choosing a recruiting philosophy, each college coach must work within a financial budget. I strongly recommend that a coach cut other parts of his budget, whether it be equipment, travel, or other items, to put extra money in his recruiting budget. If sacrifices must be made financially, they should not come at the expense of recruiting. Remember, recruiting is the lifeblood of any successful college athletic program.

Who and How Many to Recruit

After a coach has determined his recruiting philosophy, he must then decide what positions he needs to recruit for the upcoming year (pitchers, catchers, outfielders, infielders). It has been my experience that you always recruit pitching. I have never heard a college coach say he had too much pitching. The other position I recruit each year is the catching position. A good college baseball program will have at least two, or maybe three, catchers. It is difficult to teach a college player to be a catcher if he has never caught before, so you must always have at least two or three catchers in your program. A catcher is probably also able to play at least one other defensive position when not catching, usually first base or third base.

I also recommend that you recruit shortstops and center fielders. The best athletes on most high school teams play those positions. You can move a good high school shortstop to another defensive position in college if he is a good athlete. Most high school shortstops can also play outfield in college. At Stanford, most of my better players and athletes played shortstop in high school. Even Jack McDowell and Mike Mussina, who became great major-league pitchers, played shortstop in high school when they weren't pitching. Of course, there are always exceptions. Sometimes a player will play third base or first base in high school and be quite successful at the same position in college and in the major leagues. A couple examples are Robin Ventura and Will Clark. Finally, the most important high school or junior college player to recruit is the rare athlete who you feel can both pitch and play another defensive position on your team. That recruit is critical to your program because you get two players for the price of one.

Sometimes, at the collegiate level, we make a big mistake in not letting the tremendous athlete who is our number one pitcher also play another position. We might make the opposite blunder by not giving our starting shortstop a shot at pitching. Recruit and play the best athletes.

A coach must also determine the number of players he will recruit in a given year. Obviously, that will depend on the needs of each program, but I strongly suggest that you recruit at least three times the number of players you need in a given year. For example, if you feel you need to bring in 5 recruits this year, you should probably recruit 15 players to get 5. Again, the number of players you decide to recruit will fluctuate depending on your program and your success in recruiting. It is always better, however, to recruit too many players rather than too few.

How to Find Recruits

The next step in the recruiting process for the college coach is to build a recruiting network—a system that he sets up to find the baseball talent in the recruiting area that he has defined. That area might be local, within a 100-mile radius, regional, or national. Whatever his recruiting area, a coach must have a system or plan to find the best players in that area. One recommendation I would make is that whatever your recruiting area—local, regional, national, even international—you must never miss a local player who has the talent to play in your program. There is a natural inclination to look beyond your area, to buy into the idea that the grass is always greener elsewhere, but you must not fall into that trap. Most local players would prefer to stay near home and play locally in college, so don't miss recruiting the local player who can play in your program.

In establishing your recruiting network, you should first establish a mailing program to all the high school and junior college baseball coaches in the areas you are recruiting. In that mailing you will ask the high school or junior college coach to recommend players from his team or opposing teams who he feels can play baseball at your level. Be sure the coach gives you his home and school phone numbers and the address and phone number of the recruits he is recommending.

Second, you and your staff should phone at least two coaches in every high school and junior college league in the areas you are recruiting. By calling the coaches, you minimize the chance of missing any players. In addition, by spending time on the phone you build up a relationship with the high school or junior college coach, which will grow over the years and help build a solid foundation for your recruiting network.

Another source for finding high school and junior college players is a scouting service. These scouting services are fairly new for baseball but are becoming more prevalent each year. They provide a tremendous service for college baseball. For a minimal fee, they will provide the names and addresses of the better players in the areas you are recruiting. The advantage of a recruiting service is that it can save you a lot of time and leg work in identifying the better high school and junior college players.

Two other sources are available to a college program in identifying talented high school and junior college players. One is the baseball alumni of their particular institution, who should be encouraged to call the coaches when they hear of talented baseball players in their area. Second, pro baseball scouts may sometimes help college coaches in identifying talented players.

By setting up a mailing program and spending a lot of time on the phone, a college coach will eventually develop a solid recruiting network for identifying talented high school and junior college players.

There are no secrets to identifying talented players. It just takes time and effort. The more years you recruit, the better contacts you make, and thus the more successful you will be in identifying talent.

Evaluating Recruits

Once you have a list of talented high school and junior college players, you then must evaluate their ability. The evaluation process will eventually determine which baseball player you are going to recruit. The first step is for the recruit to fill out a baseball prospect information sheet (see sample on pages 90-91). This information sheet will provide valuable information on the recruit as an athlete and student. Besides the information sheet, you should request a copy of the recruit's high school or junior college transcript. You should evaluate the recruit's transcript to see if he is qualified to attend your university.

If the recruit is qualified academically, the next step is for your coaching staff to make some phone calls. You should call the recruit's high school or junior college coach if you have not already spoken with him. In addition, you should call one or two other coaches in the recruit's league and ask their opinions on his ability. If possible, you should also try to call a professional baseball scout who may have seen the player. After these phone calls, you will have a good idea of whether the player is worth further evaluation. In some cases, it is obvious after these phone calls that the recruit is a great player whom you must recruit. On the other hand, you may determine that the player does not have the ability to play at the college level.

The next step is for someone on your coaching staff to see the recruit play. There are many showcases, tryouts, and games that allow college coaches the opportunity to evaluate high school players. I strongly recommend that one person from your coaching staff be the main person to evaluate all your recruits. By having just one coach evaluate the players, you will make fewer mistakes in the evaluation process. Obviously, the coach who evaluates the recruits must be qualified to identify talent.

At the conclusion of the evaluation process, your coaching staff will determine which players you plan to recruit for your program. Your staff should phone those players to see if they have an interest in your school. A recruit will indicate his interest in your school and baseball program if he agrees to visit your institution as one of his five official visits. If a recruit is unwilling to commit to making an official visit to your university, it is unlikely you have a chance of successfully recruiting him. Go on to the next recruit and don't worry about the ones that got away.

Summer Camps

Another way that college baseball programs can evaluate talent is by running summer camps for high school players. These camps must follow strict NCAA rules, but they offer another opportunity for college coaches to observe some outstanding baseball players.

For five days, college coaches can work on their campuses with players from high school, providing them with instruction and the opportunity to compete against other outstanding players. The high school players have an opportunity to live on a college campus and get to know the coaches first hand. In most cases, high school players who attend these camps already have some interest in that particular college program. It is a great opportunity for both the college coaches and the high school players to get to know each other. To run such a camp effectively, however, requires a lot of planning and preparation. Each program must decide if such a camp is worth the time and energy. When a summer camp is run poorly, it will have a negative impact on a player's perception of that college baseball program.

Recruiting Phone Calls and Correspondence

Once you have chosen the high school or junior college players you wish to recruit, you must implement a plan of communicating with these players. There are two basic ways of communicating with a recruit—by mail or by telephone. Nowadays, another important way of communicating with the recruit is e-mail. Some of us old-time coaches are taking computer classes so that we can take advantage of this newer method of communication!

For mailings, you should develop a program of sending at least one piece of mail each week to a recruit. In those mailings, you should emphasize the strengths of your baseball program and your university. If you know the academic interest of the recruit, it is always useful to send him information on that particular major. Some of the better recruiters in college baseball do a fantastic job with their mailings, sending two or three pieces of correspondence each week. The recruits and their parents enjoy the literature and learn a great deal about the baseball program and university.

As far as phone calls are concerned, NCAA rules allow you to make one phone call per week to a recruit. It is critical that you take advantage of that opportunity and call your recruits each week. I suggest that you try to call a recruit on the same day each week and at the same time

STANFORD UNIVERSITY
BASEBALL PROSPECT INFORMATION SHEET

Date: _____

SS#: _____ - ____ - _____

Name _____ Nickname _____ Phone (____) _____

   Last First Middle

Street Address _____ City _____ State _____ Zip _____

High School/JC _____ Yr. of Graduation _____

Father's Name _____ Alma Mater _____

Father's Occupation _____ Work Phone (____) _____

Mother's Name _____ Alma Mater _____

Mother's Occupation _____ Work Phone (____) _____

Brothers and Sisters? (name and age) _____

Any in College? _____ Where? _____

Will you need financial assistance to attend Stanford? _____ Religious Preference _____

Ethnic Background: African American ____ Caucasian ____ Hispanic ____ Native American Indian ____ Other ____

Hobbies _____

High School GPA (4.0=A) in College Prep Courses _____ Counselor's Name _____

PSAT Score: Date taken (month/year) _____ Verbal _____ Math _____

SAT Score: Date taken (month/year) _____ Verbal _____ Math _____ Re-take SAT date _____

ACT Score: Date taken (month/year) _____ Verbal _____ Math _____ Soc.Sci. _____ Nat.Sci. _____ Comp. _____

What do you plan to major in at Stanford? _____

List all honors you have won and/or positions obtained outside of athletics _____

_____

_____

BASEBALL BACKGROUND

Baseball Coach's Name _____ Home Phone (____) _____ Alma Mater _____

School League _____ Honors received in Baseball _____

_____

List other Varsity Sports in which you are participating _____

Height _____ Weight _____ Bats _____ Throws _____ Birthdate _____

Batting Average (soph. year) _____ (junior year) _____ (summer team) _____

Playing Position: 1st choice _____ 2nd choice _____ Speed (distance and time, if available) _____

If Pitcher: Record _____ ERA _____ Strikeouts _____ Innings Pitched _____

Summer Team: Coach _____ League _____ Coach's Phone (____) _____

The top two players you played against who will be graduating the same year as yourself:

_____ _____

Name

each day. That way the recruit will expect your call and will look forward to your conversations. It is also imperative that you know exactly what points you want to make with the recruit during that phone call. Do not miss an opportunity to sell your program and university. Remember, you have only one call per week, so don't waste it!

One of the keys to the entire recruiting process is your ability to communicate the positives of your baseball program and school. Your ability to sell yourself, your baseball program, and your university will be the deciding factor in recruiting. Be sure to do the most efficient job possible with your mailings and phone calls. And learn how to use e-mail!

Home Visit

Sometime during the recruiting process, I strongly recommend that one of the coaches on your staff make a home visit to each of your top recruits. You may have to make a home visit early in the recruiting process to get your recruit to agree to make an official visit to your university. If the recruit has already agreed to make an official visit to your institution, you can make your home visit either before or following his official visit. But in either case, you must make a home visit if you hope to persuade the recruit to attend your university.

The home visit is a great opportunity for you to sell your program and school to the player and his parents face to face. I believe the home visit is extremely important to parents. They have an opportunity to ask the coach questions about the baseball program and the university. The home visit usually forms the parents' first impression, which is important in any relationship, especially in the recruiting process.

After the home visit, you will have a much better idea of your chances of persuading the recruit to attend your school. You will learn what is important to the recruit and his parents in making their final decision. The home visit is one of the key elements in the entire recruiting process and will test your ability to sell your program.

Official Visit

The NCAA allows a high school or junior college baseball recruit to make official visits to five colleges or universities. An official visit allows a college to pay the recruit's expenses to visit their campus for a 48-hour period. If a recruit selects your university as one of his five visits, then you definitely have a chance of persuading him to attend your institution. Conversely, if a recruit does not select your university as one of his five official visits, then in all likelihood your recruitment of that player is finished.

The 48-hour period when a recruit visits your campus is the key to the entire recruiting process. It is the culmination of months of hard work during which you and your coaching staff have identified your recruits, evaluated their baseball talent, and spent endless hours on the phone trying to persuade them to attend your school. In 28 years of recruiting at the college level, it has been my experience that in 9 out of 10 cases, a recruit makes his final decision based on his experience during his official visit.

At this point, I will point out that the official visit is not only a time when a recruit can judge whether he feels comfortable with a particular college and its players and coaches but also an opportunity for a coaching staff to evaluate whether that recruit will fit into their baseball program. Occasionally, after an official visit, the coaching staff may decide that a recruit will not fit into the program. It doesn't happen often, but the official visit can persuade a coaching staff that they no longer wish to recruit a player.

Because of the importance of the official visit, the entire visit must be highly organized. The coaching staff must sit down and make up an itinerary for each prospect's visit. The entire 48-hour period should be accounted for during a recruit's stay on campus. A visit that is unorganized and haphazard will result in failure. The coaching staff should approach the official visit as they would a practice, and a good coach would never think of conducting practice without a practice plan.

In setting up the official visit, the coach must decide when to schedule it. First, an official visit should occur only when your students are attending classes in regular session. It does no good for a recruit to visit your university when no students are on campus. Second, I strongly recommend that you have your recruits visit when your team is practicing. Recruits enjoy seeing how the baseball team works out and getting a first-hand look at their future teammates. Finally, I would try to set up recruiting visits on a weekend when there is a home football game. In most cases, the atmosphere of a college football game on campus adds to the overall excitement of a recruit's visit. But if I had to choose whether to have a recruit visit when we were practicing baseball or when there was a home football game, I would select a weekend when we had baseball practice.

In making the itinerary for a campus visit, you should try to achieve four goals. First, you need to make the recruit familiar with your baseball program and your style of coaching. That is why you should have a team practice during the visit. Second, you must have the recruit obtain information on the academics of your university. Most coaches will set up an academic meeting with a recruit during his visit. The recruit might meet with a professor from an academic department in which he has expressed interest. Third, during the visit the recruit should see the academic and athletic facilities of the university. Many coaches make the mistake of showing their recruits only the athletic facilities. You must show the recruit the academic facilities as well. Finally, you must ensure that the recruit spends time socially with your players, alone with them, without the coaches present. It is during that time that a recruit can ask questions about the program and university that they are afraid to ask in front of the coaching staff. What is it like to play for Coach Smith? How tough is it academically? What is the social life like?

One of the more important decisions the coaching staff will make about a recruit's official visit is determining which player on his team will be the recruit's host. The host is responsible for the recruit during his entire visit. The host should be an upperclassman (sophomore, junior, or senior) who has experience in the baseball program and in the school academically. I feel it is unwise for a freshman to be a host because a freshman hasn't been there long enough to know a lot about the baseball program or the university. The host should be outgoing, friendly, and, most important, a good salesman for your baseball program and university. In some cases, the host may be from the same geographical area as a recruit, maybe even from his high school. I also recommend that you have one host for each recruit. I do not feel it works out as well if a host is responsible for two or three recruits. A host can give more individual attention to one person. It is important to make the recruit feel special. During a recruit's 48-hour visit to your campus, he will spend the bulk of his time with his host. The host is a key player in the official visit, so be sure to select the best host possible.

Follow-Up to Official Visit

After a recruit has made his official visit, the coach has a golden opportunity to close the deal. The recruit should have his most favorable impression of your school immediately after his visit, and a coach might be able to get the recruit to commit to his university right then. Even if the recruit is unwilling to commit after his official visit, the coach has an opportunity to see where his school stands in the recruiting process. If after the official visit the recruit is not excited about your school and baseball program, then you are in trouble. At the conclusion of the official visit, it is imperative that you, as a coach, get some indication from the recruit about where you stand in the recruiting game. If it doesn't look good for your school, then you need to know that and focus on those recruits who you still have an opportunity of recruiting. At the conclusion of all your official visits, you hope to have convinced enough outstanding high school and junior college players to attend your university and play for your baseball program.

Evaluating Your Recruiting Efforts

After all your recruits have made their decisions and you know how many new players will be joining your team for next year, you need to sit down as a coaching staff and evaluate your recruiting efforts. You may decide to make changes in your process to be more effective next year. Recruiting is no different or less important than coaching your baseball team. After each season, you evaluate your team's win-loss record and make changes to become more successful. Recruiting is no different. You must always try to improve how you recruit. Remember, good players make good coaches, and an outstanding recruiting effort will provide you and your school with an excellent baseball program for many years.

CHAPTER NINE

Marketing and Promoting Your Program

Ron Fraser

College baseball must take the gloves off and compete for survival.

Good coaches emphasize fundamentals, so before discussing the marketing and promoting of college baseball, you should go back to square one and make sure you have a program to market and promote.

At Miami, the reality that on-field success doesn't necessarily translate into program or job security touched home in the late 1970s. Being nationally ranked and going to the NCAA regional every year and the College World Series most years wasn't enough. Because of an inflationary economy and because it was part of an athletic department that at the time had a weak football team, on the field and at the box office, baseball consistently found its budget being reduced.

It didn't take a rocket scientist, or even a baseball coach, long to figure out that with repeated budget cuts, pretty soon what would be left wouldn't be worth much. The original fundamentals, that survival comes first, dictated that the first drive was to stay alive.

Today, with the alarming trend of eliminating entire programs, it is more important than ever for the coach to take control of his destiny. By building a revenue-generating operation, the coach implements the first steps to ensure program, and job security. All things being equal, the program that generates income and has increasing revenue potential will be saved from extinction ahead of programs having no revenue potential.

Building respect for your product is at the core of any business-building strategy. I fought my entire career to gain respect for college baseball, and I wanted tangible results like increases in salaries, attendance, and television coverage. College baseball coaches must recognize that their game is one with great tradition and accomplishment. It can compete as a viable entertainment option for the student, campus, and community populations as well as being attractive to the corporate sector.

The key word is entertainment, for entertainment is what sports has evolved into and how it must now be marketed, promoted, and publicized. The competition is no longer simply other sports. These days, sports must be treated as a business, positioned to compete as an entertainment alternative to television, movies, surfing the net, reading, bicycling, or whatever activity people and families choose to do with their discretionary time and dollars.

College baseball must take the gloves off and compete for survival. Prosperity can follow, but as any emergency-room doctor will attest you must forget everything else until the patient is out of danger. And so it evolved at Miami, where the early success formula—marketing baseball first as entertainment and principally to families—has withstood the test of time and is effective to this day.

The inspiration needed to take control of my destiny hit me one day as I was parking at the office and noticed the shiny, new Lincoln pulling in next to me. For a kid like me from Jersey, Lincoln was the guy on the penny and someone who we heard was on the $5 bill. I remember thinking that the guy with the Lincoln must really be successful, and then I saw who he was—my concessions guy. So I got out of my car and helped him out . . . out of our business. The next season we took over our food and souvenir operation and saw the program's net income increase considerably.

The moral to that and most stories is that many things others can do, you can do better yourself. Even if you can't, at least you'll sleep better knowing you are in control of your fate. After my budget kept getting cut, I made up my mind that if I was going to lose the program, I might as well lose it because of things I did, not because football couldn't cut it. I would leave myself no excuses.

I believe in hard work and hanging in there until you get it right. Abraham Lincoln failed to become elected many times before first winning office. Thomas Edison failed in thousands of experiments before inventing the electric light. Sir Winston Churchill delivered the shortest commencement address in Oxford history when he admonished the graduates and guests, "Never give up!" Several seconds later he repeated, "Never give up!" And then the great man sat down. Nothing else needed to be said.

With the Hurricanes, the people of South Florida noticed that we were trying something different, and they came out to see for themselves. More than a few liked what they saw, enough that when Florida State came to town so many people showed up that we had to seat fans on the field in the bullpens.

As long as you are sincere, people generally will give the one thing every program needs, a chance. What the program does with that chance is up to you.

Principles of Marketing

These principles were the cornerstones of our success, and we hope they can be of some help to you.

Get the House in Order

Society has adopted the family structure as its dominant order. Coaches will do well to adopt this time-tested framework. Start with players and coaches and continue through the extended family of administrative staff and stadium staff. Then transfer this family atmosphere to your stadium. Remember, people support and give to other people, not to inanimate stadiums and not to nameless, faceless teams.

Once you develop a family atmosphere throughout your organization, the benefits will follow. Remember, people begin forming impressions about you and your program long before they set foot inside your ballpark. These impressions arise from a variety of sources, so by creating a family culture the message will remain consistent, no matter the messenger or vehicle.

After you have instilled family culture, ask these questions to determine if your program has the groundwork in place to be successful:

- Do you have clear and concise directions to the stadium, a current schedule, a roster, and a list of promotions posted at every telephone? Have you trained everyone who may come into contact with the public?

- Is stadium access clearly marked? Do you have a traffic plan for typical games, for big games?

- Are parking areas clearly marked? If you charge for parking, is the tab reasonable and competitive? Are the parking attendants well groomed, dressed appropriately, and trained to answer the frequently asked (and easily anticipated) questions?

- Is the ticket operation adequate to handle the expected crowd? Are prices reasonable and competitive? Do you offer a variety of ticket options, both season and single game?

- Is the stadium staff well groomed, appropriately attired (which helps people recognize your staff), and trained in customer service, venue knowledge, and program knowledge?

- Are the concession and novelty stands clean, convenient, and numerous enough? Is the food selection varied and the products top quality? Are the attendants scrupulously clean and helpful? Are prices fair and competitive? Is this food that you'd regularly feed your family?

- The staff in the parking lots, at the ticket booths, gates, concession and novelty stands, and the ushers—do they smile? Do they say, "Thank you. Yes, ma'am. No, sir."? These people are the front-line ambassadors for your program and its contact with the customers.

- Are the rest rooms plentiful and immaculate? The typical number one complaint among fans is rest rooms. Make sure yours pass the white-glove test.

- Are your promotions organized? Do you have giveaways for all age ranges, kids through adults? Do you give fans a promotion schedule to encourage repeat visits? Is your announcer scripted and an asset to the in-game operation? Is your mascot similarly scripted and integrated?

- Finally, do you have a plan for dealing with customer complaints and problems? Have you developed fair policies for dealing with your customers? Do you have efficient channels for resolving problems? Do you have a tested emergency plan in place? Make certain that everyone in the operation understands and is prepared to act on these plans. Lives, and jobs, may depend on it.

In resolving the issues posed by these questions, you will have established a solid foundation on which to build a revenue-generating engine that can serve, or perhaps save, the program.

Market to the Family

Having established the proper atmosphere, it is time to invite others to join the family—but whom? Would you rather direct your marketing efforts at someone who buys tickets and concessions one at a time? Or would you rather court the entire family and double, triple, or quadruple the payoff? Even to a coach, the answer is obvious.

To be successful, we had to differentiate our product as an entertainment option. Just as the *Fortune* 500 companies do, we needed to establish an identity, a brand. The brand we chose was this: good, clean, G-rated family entertainment. In Miami, a town not known for such pleasures, this brand distinguished us.

Already knowing that traditional baseball fans would likely be satisfied with our excellent schedule and high caliber of play, we needed identify other potential customers and learn what they expected. Our market research included standard demographic questions and a section on what Miami baseball had to do to win the public's business.

The results really opened my eyes, showing that mothers represented almost 40 percent of the primary baseball fans. The survey spoke even louder with a want list that included reasonably priced family entertainment that one could feel safe bringing children to and recommending to friends and associates.

Now confident a significant market segment was accessible, we drew our target on the moms. Doing so required a two-prong approach—price and promotion.

> **Our credo was this: It's Showtime!**

Because the Archie Bunker show was popular in the 1970s, we offered an All in the Family season ticket that admitted two adults and three children for $20. That broke down to about seven cents per person per game and removed price as an obstacle for just about everyone. For the others, we always had enough promotions with free tickets available so that anyone who wanted to see Hurricanes baseball could. We were building an aircraft carrier, not a canoe.

We developed an integrated marketing, promotions, and public-relations strategy that featured top-quality baseball and name opponents for the purist; we created a family-friendly atmosphere before, during, and after games, with plenty of promotions and prize giveaways for the family and nonbaseball fan; and we introduced an endless array of attractions for the kids, including special giveaways, youth-oriented promotions, and a mascot.

Every game became family day or family night. We'd play baseball bingo, with fans holding the chosen lucky number vicariously standing in the batter's box with a Hurricanes player and winning a prize ranging from a free soda for anything except a hit to a new bicycle or a vacation trip when the player got a hit.

We'd have pizza-eating contests on the field, face painting on the concourse, and special promotions and offers at the concession and souvenir stands. All were designed to ensure that each game at the park was a unique experience.

Our credo was this: It's Showtime! It didn't matter if we'd done a money scramble or some other promotion a hundred times, there would always be people in the stadium who had never seen one. Therefore, our responsibility was to put on a show as if it were the very first time, to do all we could to deliver something they'd never seen before—a total entertainment package.

Each game was a different opportunity, and we played it out to the fullest. Fans got free seat cushions on Monday, the chance to win a color TV and VCR on Tuesday, and an exhibition game against a major-league team on Wednesday. Ringmaster of the circus was announcer Jay Rokeach, and for more than 30 years he helped draw and keep the crowds in the game.

Early on I said that I'd retire if we got our box scores printed in the morning paper, but once we did, we set our sights higher and invented a new challenge—becoming part of the local culture. We did this by designing a program that offered plenty of surprises over and above the promotion schedule. That way people would never know what was going to happen next, and we hoped that the fans thought enough of us to talk to others. We knew the program had really been accepted when Hurricanes baseball became a topic of conversation around the copier or water cooler.

We developed our Miami Maniac character and held auditions to choose someone to bring to life 15 pounds and $3,200 worth of fur and foam. A half season and a series of well-meaning but uncharismatic candidates passed before we struck gold by recruiting an outstanding young man from South Carolina, John Routh.

In 1982, John first donned the Miami Maniac costume, the same one that fans had either ignored or derided. For the next 10 years he was Miami baseball's single greatest attraction. The young man was a ballpark magnet. Kids followed him as if he were the pied piper, and adults couldn't take their eyes off him. People said they watched the Maniac more than the baseball because they knew Miami would win almost every game at home, but no one had any idea what the genius inside the Maniac costume was going to do. A quality mascot, properly integrated into the overall marketing and promotion plan, can be a home run for any program emphasizing families first.

Fun, Fun, and More Fun

Promotional ideas are like interns. Some turn out better than others, but there is no such thing as a bad one. Keep the good ones, work with those that have potential, and move on.

Something for everyone, we called it. There was little that we didn't attempt. We gave away dozens of used cars (most of 'em looked really good at night) and even a brand new two-seat Mercedes. You name it, we gave it away—hats, bats, balls, food coupons, seat cushions.

We had pizza-eating contests. We invited the fans onto the field following Sunday afternoon games to run the bases and get autographs. Our rule was that all players and coaches had to stay until the last autograph was signed and the final kid was happy. And we always thanked the autograph seeker because we knew the day would come when people would stop asking.

We invited fans on the field after a game to help the teams eat a 90-foot banana split or a 60-foot submarine sandwich, always sponsored by a local company. We had some high-powered friends give us use of an ocean liner for a night (you read it right, this does say ocean liner) to take a four-hour boat ride. We cohosted this "Cruise to Nowhere" three years in a row, and our program received half the proceeds, sharing with the favorite charity of the maritime sponsors.

Hundreds of first-timers showed up for the chance to win a diamond at the diamond. The winner of our Coach for a Day promotion was a great lady, an every-night fan who in her day job was a judge.

One thing we learned—be dead serious about the baseball in your program, but when it comes to marketing and promotion, don't take yourself too seriously. Have a sense of humor. Remember, your fans expect the team to be an active, willing part of *their* family.

Above all else, our goal was for people to come out and have fun, whatever it took. When fans have a good time, they do two other important things—they come back and they tell others. When word of mouth can make or break you, this was by far the most effective advertising we could have ever done, and we could not have bought it at any cost.

We weren't afraid to try something if it meant having fun and getting fans involved. Do something. Do anything. There's an old advertising saying: If you don't market and promote, a funny thing will happen. Nothing.

One of our first promotions was getting sponsors to pay for the baseballs. The sponsor got an announcement, a picture of the ceremony, and an autographed ball. As small as that sounds, for years we never had to pay for a game ball.

Do something. Do anything. Do it now.

Get Others Involved

Few programs and fewer coaches succeed on their own. We certainly didn't. Don't be too proud to ask for help. The first rule in personnel is to surround yourself with the best people possible, preferably people who are smarter than you are.

Soon after I made the commitment to do everything possible to save my program, I met a young man who was already working at the university. I thought Rick Remmert had great potential, and I was impressed with his work ethic. So I asked him to join my staff as college baseball's first full-time marketing and promotions director to help me do something that had never been done before. We made a great combination. Although marketing may have been a success had I hired someone else, we would not have been *the* success we were without Rick, and we certainly wouldn't have had as much fun. Thanks, Rick.

If you don't have knowledge about how to market or promote, ask those who do. Read a book or attend a seminar. Learn what you don't know. For years we were fixtures on the seminar circuit, and we borrowed most of our promotional ideas from those think tanks. Little is new in promotions; almost everything is a variation on something from another market or another sport. Find out what successful programs are doing and adapt these techniques to your market. There's no need to reinvent the wheel.

Miami baseball was blessed with many friends. Do not underestimate the generosity of others or the contributions they can make. One of the best things we did was organize our Coaches Committee, consisting of some of the area's top business and civic leaders. At first, frankly, we were just hoping that if we associated with achievers from the real world, maybe some of their knowledge would rub off. At the least, these executives could certainly give objective, free advice about the true potential of the program and how to go about reaching it.

Although the money and sponsorship deals these Coaches Committee members brought the program from their corporations were helpful, perhaps their most important contribution was providing entry to their powerful network of colleagues and associates. It was always awesome when a Coaches Committee member, with one phone call, got me in front of a mover, a shaker, and a decision maker who, on my own, I had been trying unsuccessfully to see for months.

The final lesson taught by the Coaches Committee was that if you are going to ask someone's opinion and ask for help, then you have an obligation to listen to and to work with that person. Nothing is more frustrating for volunteers than to have their time and input ignored or devalued. Remember, while some can give money, others can give time. Volunteers are crucial to the success of athletic programs.

Whether you have a booster club, student group, or alumni association, ask for their help, give them direction in the areas in which you need assistance, and then join with your coaches in becoming active participants in helping these people help you. Many long-term relationships and sponsorships grow from these collaborations. One person can only do so much, but there is no limit to what people working together can do.

Do not take for granted the help others give the program. You have a responsibility to recognize, reward, and share the credit. This can take many forms, from ceremonies and announcements at the stadium, to throwing out the first pitch at a game, or just taking the time to say thank you or write a note of appreciation. Regrettably, "thank you" is one of the most underused expressions in our language.

Corporations play a key role in any success. What you offer them combined with the way you treat them will ultimately determine if they become repeat supporters. Give something of value in exchange for a sponsor's investment and be willing to work with them in structuring an arrangement that will benefit you both.

In diversifying the elements of your package, a sponsor can tap into a number of corporate accounts, such as advertising, marketing, employee relations, customer relations, and charitable donations. This gives a program a fighting chance at getting that $7,500 package sold—$1,500 from each of five budgets rather than trying to hit one budget for the whole $7,500. Smaller sponsors have different needs and circumstances. Develop programs to help them help you. A small business may have cash-flow problems but often turns out to be among your most effective and loyal backers. Work with them. If a company can't pay $2,500 at one time for a sponsorship, take $500 a month for five months.

Don't forget your supporters. If the first time you see a sponsor is when the contract is signed and the next time is when you are pitching the renewal, you'll likely be removed from the game. We made it our business to learn about our sponsors' operations and called each of them at least once a month year round. Remember, although your season may be February through June, theirs runs all year.

One or two days a month we'd hop in the car and visit as many sponsors as we could. We'd just drop by and stick our heads in the door. Sometimes we'd leave a couple of promo items, but always we'd let them know that we appreciated their business.

We'd finish by asking them if there was anything we could do for them. One of the great lessons is that no matter your cause or product, you're not really selling anything. You are trying to help people get what they want—in our case some family entertainment, a break from the 9-to-5 grind, a place to advertise a product or entertain clients. When you help people get what they want or need, they in turn will give you what you want—in our case by buying tickets, a yearbook ad, or a sponsorship. Don't sell. Help people and watch them help you.

Get the Word Out

To be successful, your program needs to be heard. Although the coach is the lead dog, everyone associated with the program, from the players and coaches to the office and stadium staffs, is a critical member of the public-relations team. Remember, every conversation is an opportunity; use it to your benefit. And never forget the program's responsibility to give back to the community. Again, the head coach is the point person, but when a coach, player, or staff member is out participating in community activities, the program is out there too.

Hurricanes baseball was fortunate to receive extensive media coverage, but we took none of it for granted. As it is with autograph requests, a day will come when people stop thinking enough of your opinion to ask for it.

By maintaining open, honest relationships with the media, programs should be able to incorporate proactive public relations into an overall marketing and promotions strategy. Even the best news is of little value if the target audience does not hear about it.

Ultimately, the time a coach spends marketing, promoting, and publicizing a program will be just as valuable as time spent on pickoff plays. For if there are no dollars coming in, the day may come when the lights are turned off and the doors are locked. This has happened too often in college sports, and the unfortunate lament is that much of it was preventable.

Be your own insurance policy by being the pro in promotion. Remember that two-thirds of promotion is motion, so get off your seat, get on your feet, get out in the street, and compete. You may just save your program and job, and more than likely you will enjoy a life-enriching experience.

My Top 10 Most Memorable Promotions

We staged literally thousands of promotions, some of which you may be able to adapt to your program. Here are some of the most memorable:

1. **Attendance Record Night.** After our promotions kicked in, crowds grew so large that the fire department put a cap on attendance. Once we reached the maximum, we couldn't let anyone in until someone else left. We all know the drill—two out, two in. When I asked the fire chief, who was also a friend, what would happen if I ignored the warning, he only half jokingly told me that he'd have to arrest me.

    Imagine the headline in the paper the next day: "Coach Arrested for Putting Too Many Fans at a College Baseball Game." I'd have retired right then because that would have been the greatest thing I could ever do for college baseball.

2. **Five-Thousand Dollar Dinner.** To retire the debt on Mark Light Stadium, we invited a few of our friends to dinner, but this was no

ordinary feast. Tickets cost $5,000 per person, and we held dinner on the baseball field, featuring some of the world's finest delicacies, including truffles flown in from the Black Forest. Until that night, I didn't even know where the Black Forest was.

At the end of the night, one of the guests came up to me and said it was the most fun he'd had in his life and he'd like to pay for the whole evening. Can you imagine that guy waking up the next morning and finding out that he'd paid $29,000 for dinner, which didn't even include the tip?

3. **Ten-Thousand Dollar Money Scramble.** A local bank supplied the $1 bills that we crumpled and scattered on the field. We chose two fans at random to retrieve as much as they could within 30 seconds.

We got lucky the very first time. One of the contestants was an older woman. She had bad hands and didn't go to her left very well.

4. **Trip to Somewhere.** Participating fans arrived at the stadium with their bags packed in hopes of winning a trip. No one except our marketing and promotions staff knew the destination until we stopped the game and selected the winners, who left on their trips directly from the stadium.

The first time we did this I thought was going to be our last. One of the prizes was a weekend at the famous Fontainbleau Hotel on Miami Beach. A student won, and it turns out her boyfriend was the quarterback on the football team. Unfortunately, the girl's mother didn't know her daughter was even dating anyone until the next morning when she picked up the newspaper and saw the front-page photo of her daughter and the quarterback getting in a limo for a weekend at the Fontainbleau.

5. **Open-Heart Surgery.** First prize was a free open-heart operation, but there was a catch—the prize was not transferable and had to be used within a year.

We had good attendance that night from Miami Beach, and all the retirement homes brought groups.

6. **Lucky Numbers.** We sold advertising on paper scorecards that also had a number stamped on them. At various times during the game, the announcer would select and call a number. The fan holding that number won 1 of 15 prizes that we gave away on average every game. The prizes ranged from a free soda to a television set to a used car to a vacation trip.

One of the media came up to me and said that I had no shame, that we were selling nothing more than pieces of paper. And I said, "Yeah, but there's printing on both sides."

7. **Bathing Suit Day.** A local manufacturer wanted publicity for his new line of bathing suits. University of Miami bat girls (and a few ringers) were the models.

It was a good gate. We charged everyone with binoculars and cameras double.

8. **Lobster Bake.** We arranged for the Maine Black Bears to bring down a little extra baggage—a thousand live lobsters. The teams joined paying fans after one of the games for dinner on the field.

The next night my third baseman threw the ball into the stands. When I asked him what happened, he tells me, "Coach, it wasn't my fault, the ball had drawn butter all over it." What could I say?

9. **VIP Suite.** By the early 1980s, we had dozens of corporations wanting to become involved but didn't have a suitable place for them to entertain. We decided to build college baseball's first VIP suite and cajoled a local contractor into doing the job for free. One problem with commando construction, though, was that no permit was pulled and the job was shut down halfway through before being permitted, revised, and completed.

Now I'm not advocating anyone breaking the rules, but sometimes with our program we found it easier to ask forgiveness than permission.

10. ***10* Night.** Following release of the Bo Derek movie *10,* I had one of my versatile players, Sam Sorce, play all nine positions and DH in the same game, hence *10* Night.

For a month, we announced that we had invited Bo Derek to throw out the first pitch. But most of our fans didn't hear the key word "invited." Bo Derek no-showed us, but a lot of desperate guys did show up.

PART III

Creative and Effective Practice Sessions

CHAPTER TEN

Conducting Innovative Practices

Ed Cheff

A coach's ability to establish a philosophy of teaching baseball that is effective and respected by the players is critical to success on any level, from Little League to the big leagues. Once a coach has defined this philosophy, he must consistently incorporate it into every aspect of his teaching laboratory—the practice session. Although age groups, facilities, size of staff, institutional restrictions, the environment, and so forth will differ, some aspects of teaching baseball are generic to nearly any situation. Creativity and innovation are also part of a baseball coach's responsibility to his program. By borrowing concepts and ideas from successful teams in all sports (football, basketball, wrestling, and so on) and linking them with personal knowledge, the coach can enhance the development of a quality baseball program.

Developing a Philosophy of Teaching Baseball

To be successful, a coach must establish a consistent philosophy and teaching strategy for his program. He must first earn the respect of his players. He will then be able to define expectations for his players and motivate them. The coach should develop a season-long practice plan and decide how to schedule individual practice sessions, varying them in length, purpose, and pressure. By adhering to a consistent set of principles, a coach can make the most of precious practice time.

Earning the Respect of Your Players

Coaches must display an intellectual knowledge of baseball strategies appropriate to the playing ability of their players and their opponents. A creative approach to teaching is also extremely beneficial. There is no "baseball by the book" appropriate for every team and every level. Using appropriate technical and psychological aspects to teach skill performance is a prerequisite for earning the respect of your players.

A coach also earns respect by demonstrating a work ethic. Coaches constantly challenge their players to make a total commitment to reaching their full potential. Coaches who do not make the same commitment they ask from their players create a hypocrisy that can damage beyond repair the coach-player (teacher-pupil) relationship. Players will tolerate some weaknesses in a coach, but hypocrisy is not one of them.

Defining Expectations

Define for your players the foundation of a good practice and be explicit about what you expect of them. Teams earn the opportunity to win based on the quality of their practices.

Practice is more than just a series of drills and a repetition of biomechanical exercise. The coach should try to integrate emotional balance, intellectual appreciation for what is being performed, and total physical effort combined with a tough mentality (the ability to make a positive reaction to a negative situation). To achieve integration of these elements, you must structure and monitor your practices so effort is explicitly defined and recognized.

Establishing the Master Plan

Before the first practice you should develop a checklist indicating the time you will give before the first game to teaching every conceivable aspect of the game—team offensive and defensive execution, defensive plays by position, base running, the bunting game, hitting and pitching biomechanics, situational hitting and pitching, and communication systems (players to players, coach to player, and so on). Prioritize the components you see as vital to your team's success and emphasize those in early practices. It is not important to run more than one bunt defense versus a first-and-second bunt situation or to have more than two or three options against the first-and-third steal. Review the checklist weekly to determine what you need to teach before you lose a game because you had not practiced something as simple as defending a squeeze play.

Organizing and Scheduling Practice

We all know that pressure can negatively affect skill performance and cause sound offensive and defensive strategy to break down. Therefore, the goal is to develop players who have faced specific game situations in practice, complete with pressure to perform, so they can say, "I've been here before, many times," when they confront challenging situations in a big game. Fear of failure and playing not to lose are trademarks of teams that do not simulate game pressure in their practices. A coach cannot hand out confidence to players. They must earn it in practice.

In any form of instruction an optimum teacher-to-pupil ratio is important, especially in youth and high school baseball. Practicing the execution of offensive and defensive strategies is obviously a large-group activity. Because the offensive aspects of the game—hitting, bunting, base running, and so on—relate to every player at every position, it is possible to teach with larger groups. But baseball demands many different defensive skills from nine guys playing nine positions. It is often best to teach individual defensive skills in pre- and postpractice sessions because it is easy to create a small teacher-to-pupil ratio that facilitates skill development.

The duration of the practice is not nearly as important as the quality of the practice. Many factors are involved in determining the length of time a team will practice on a given day. In many cases a 60-minute workout may be the best length for practice. On the other hand, a specific Saturday might see players putting in two hours of small-group time between 9 A.M. and 1 P.M. and returning at 2 P.M. for four hours of team offensive and defensive execution work. Often the coach needs to devote far more time to practice than the players. Preschool 6:30 A.M. conditioning workouts have value and are appropriate for the high school or collegiate player. It is not appropriate for student-athletes to allow athletic pursuits to come ahead of academic commitments. If a coach truly cares about his players, he will monitor their academic progress just as he monitors their athletic development. He will make sure that players establish and follow proper priorities.

Motivating Players

Practices afford a daily opportunity for players to make positive statements about themselves on the field and to demonstrate the quality of player they aspire to become. I want our players to be aware of the personal practice legacy they will be remembered for at Lewis-Clark State College. We realize that some players, due to greater levels of experience, skill development, and maturity, will be better game performers than others. But every player on the team can be a great practice player while striving to become a gamer. Players who will not perform in practice should never see the field on game day, regardless of their talent. Earning peer respect in practice is vital to the team's success. The staff and players need to understand and agree that practices are characterized by a high level of intensity and game-level enthusiasm.

Regardless of the structure of practice—full-team offensive and defensive situations, a live batting practice setup with skill drills incorporated, or group drills—we're in a fire-up mode, challenging players to maximize their physical, mental, intellectual, and emotional performance. We often conduct teaching with a great deal of pressure that calls for game-situation performance. Specific individual or small-group skill drills, however, will be rather low key.

Spoken communication to players is often emphatic and loud so that everyone on the field is aware of a coach's response to the effort given by a player. Some comments are negative, matching a negative effort by the player, and positive comments are voiced for positive responses. An analytical response from the coach defining the player's effort is called *reality evaluation*. We use reality evaluation so that players are never confused by how we define acceptable effort. If the coach does not like individual actions in a team setting, he should conduct a small-group workout after practice or schedule a prepractice group for the next day. Once the coach develops the proper practice tempo, it is important to keep it going.

When the coach challenges players to demonstrate maximum effort in every practice, the "I did my best" mentality will surface, especially in players new to the program. For many players, the statement that they did their best is often inaccurate because developing players do not always know what their best is. Players must trust that the coach is the best judge of a player's potential level of play. A coach should never demand more than a player is capable of giving and should never accept less than the player's best.

Components of Practice

To conduct practices efficiently, a coach must organize work on all aspects of baseball—hitting, pitching, playing defense, base running. Of course, work in these areas usually occurs simultaneously. Batting practice, for example, offers the opportunity to do defensive and base-running work. We have developed in our program a structure for starting practice, teaching hitting, teaching defense, and scrimmaging.

Starting Practice

In our program, players begin practice 10 minutes before the posted starting time with a quarter-mile warm-up run. The stretching routines, form running, plyometric work, and so on never include social conversation. Once practice begins all focus is on the activity at hand. By changing stretching and form-running routines we foster renewed attention to that important component of practice.

We follow these routines with throw-and-catch drills. Besides warming up the muscle groups involved in the throwing action, we want to incorporate sound throwing mechanics, correct catching technique, and appropriate ball-glove exchange. We feel these drills are an important part of our practice, so they are structured and monitored.

We start by having our players line up in two straight lines, equally spaced, facing one another about 20 feet apart. One line parallels an outfield foul line, and the other is in the outfield. In the first 20 throws we establish a rhythm so that every throw and catch is in unison. It is our way to get the players to focus immediately on the first skill-development part of practice. To increase the length of our throws, the line in the outfield will back up approximately 20 more feet (lined up with the pitching mound). We will throw for a prescribed amount of time depending on how much throwing we will be doing in practice drills. The line in the outfield then moves to 90 feet (lined up with second base), and after a prescribed time at this distance we make throws specific to positions.

Outfielders play catch with outfielders and work on throwing off a simulated catch of a fly ball, throwing after charging a simulated ground ball, and so on.

A good catch-throw warm-up for the catchers is to have them work on the infield. Because we carry four catchers, each base is occupied. The catchers at first base and third base simulate proper footwork and throwing fundamentals while throwing to each other, just as the catchers do at home plate and second base. The catcher receiving the throw simulates a block and tag play he would make at home plate.

The catchers then practice the footwork and action they use in pickoff plays at first. The catcher at home simulates a catch and throws to the catcher at first base. The catcher at first base then simulates a catch and throws to the catcher at second base and so on around the diamond. After a set number of throws, they practice throwing to third on steal attempts. The catcher at home simulates a catch and throws to the catcher at third. The catcher at third simulates a catch and throws to the catcher at second and so on around the diamond. It is important to incorporate specifics of ball handling and footwork as well as throwing.

Middle infielders should work every day on simulated catch and throw from a double-relay position. Corner infielders should simulate catch and throw from a cut position, employing either a relay throw or a cut and throw to second base. Two or three times a week infielders should play four-corner, quick-hand catch and throw.

Catch drills properly executed can set the mood and tempo of a great practice. We change drills daily to maintain the challenge of executing for the players.

Structure for Teaching Hitting

As I mentioned earlier in this chapter, several principles are involved in teaching a complex skill like hitting a well-pitched baseball. When teaching hitting, you should adhere to these principles. Recognize also the four related, yet distinct, components of hitting:

1. Performing the biomechanics of the basic swing properly and making the subtle adjustments necessary to hit the entire zone
2. Acquiring accurate information about the speed and trajectory of the pitch
3. Achieving rhythm and timing with the pitcher
4. Understanding the pitcher's arsenal of pitches and how he uses them

A hitting practice that takes into account these four components is far more valuable than one that deals almost exclusively with the biomechanical component. Too often coaches seem to attribute hitting failure to mechanical problems and then make mechanical adjustments to solve what might be visual, rhythm, or timing problems, or the hitter's lack of appreciation for the pitcher's strategy to get him out.

Five-Station Hitting

We believe it is beneficial to focus the entire hitting practice toward a particular type of pitcher. For example, a typical collegiate left-hander throws an 82- to 84-mile-per-hour fastball, prefers to throw with some armside run and sink, doesn't like to pitch in much to right-handers but will miss in, and changes up off the fastball with armside sink. His breaking ball is between 70 and 72 miles per hour and is his preferred pitch to left-handed hitters. He relies on right-handers hitting 6-3 ground-ball outs off the deuce and is usually effective with his change-up against right-handed hitters because of their lack of patience.

Before the hitting drill, we remind players of our hitting philosophy versus left-handed pitching. This might be something as simple as the following:

- Right-handed hitters look away for the fastball and react to the deuce. Keep the breaking ball off the ground by staying balanced with weight slightly back. Focus on cutting off the bottom third of the ball. If the pitch is acutely changing vertical plane, swing to miss under the ball (don't change swing mechanics; simply change the target). We can't allow this guy to entice us to hit 6-3 ground-ball outs.
- Left-handed hitters should not pass up first-pitch breaking balls that are up and over the plate (his get-ahead deuce). Typical fastball action will run in on you; therefore, work hard on staying stacked and use an aggressive upper-torso rotation to keep your hand route inside the pitch.

The key is to relate swing mechanics to the other three components of hitting. Besides our main playing field, we have a practice infield and two full hitting tunnels, each used to simulate part of the pitching arsenal of the previously described left-handed pitcher.

In tunnel number one, we set up a curveball machine on a six-foot-by-six-foot wooden platform that is 18 inches high, simulating the height of the release point from a six-foot pitcher throwing with a three-quarter-arm angle. Typically a left-handed pitcher will throw from the first-base side of the pitching rubber and release the ball 57 feet from the plate at a point 2 to 2 ½ feet to the first-base side of a straight line from the center of the rubber to the center of the plate. This is where we set up the machine and adjust it to create rotation on the ball that simulates the trajectory and velocity of an average deuce throw by a left-handed pitcher. Exact simulation of particular pitches is important when using machines. (When using pitching machines, it is important for the person feeding the machine to establish a rhythm in showing the ball and inserting the ball. This enables the hitter to establish his rhythm just as he would when facing a pitcher.)

In tunnel number two, we set up a second machine exactly as we did the first machine but adjust it to throw an 83- to 84-mile-per-hour fastball to the outer third of the first-base side of the plate. The height of the pitch will be knee to midthigh, and the rotation on the ball will create some sink and tail action.

Station three will be on the main field with a lefty BP pitcher alternating fastballs to both sides of the plate at a 7-to-3 ratio to the hitter's weakest zone—in or out. The pitcher will throw from the rubber, but to decrease read-reaction time for the hitter and increase the accuracy of the pitches, we place a temporary throw-down plate five feet in from home plate and hit from there. We want the pitcher on the mound so that we simulate the true trajectory of the pitch while shortening the distance by five feet.

Station four is on the practice infield. We have our left-handed position players throw fastball strikes from the mound. The hitters work to push bunts to the four hole, and we time them to first base on their third and final bunt of each round.

The fifth station will be in the bullpen. We coordinate the bullpen workouts of the entire staff of left-handed pitchers with the five-station batting practice geared to left-handed pitching. We believe accurate pitch recognition and rhythm and timing are the most important attributes of a good hitter. Therefore we will always try to have hitters tracking pitches in the hitting box during bullpen work. The hitter focuses on timing his hitting trigger with the pitcher. He is equally concerned with using correct visual technique to pick up information as soon as possible so he can quickly recognize the pitch. If the pitch is in the strike zone, he physically addresses it (begins to initiate the swing) and mentally produces the stroke he would have used to hit the pitch. When a hitter knows he is not actually going to swing at a pitch, he will be better able to focus and gain feedback on his visual technique and his ability to get in rhythm with the pitcher. From the standpoint of pitching instruction, we believe it is important in bullpen work to have hitters always in the box addressing pitches.

We set up similar five-station BP for other types of pitchers we frequently face. The primary reason we face a particular type of pitcher in our five-station BP is to give our hitters a plan to hit different types of pitchers. When they see this kind of pitcher in a game, they feel familiar with his repertoire of pitches.

To simulate sidearm and submarine pitchers, we use short sets of legs for the pitching machine but keep the machine on a platform, a portable mound, or the pitching mound. We move the protective screen to the side of the machine. We always use our radar gun to make sure the pitch velocity is what we want.

Team Batting Practice

It is not as difficult for collegiate programs to find and develop BP pitchers as it is for high school programs. Collegiate programs usually have large rosters, adequate staff size, and former players still in school finishing their degree work or starting graduate studies. The challenge for the high school coach is to develop a few BP pitchers among his players. He should also seek out capable individuals in the community who would enjoy throwing BP. We have been very successful in getting former Lewis-Clark State College players or other ex-collegiate players in our community to volunteer to be on our BP staff. These guys work to get in good shape and are dependable about being on time.

The BP pitcher always throws off the rubber because we want a true trajectory (down-flight angle) on the ball. We put a throw-down plate 5 feet directly in front of home plate and hit from 55 feet, 6 inches. This cuts down the hitter's reaction time, making an 80-mile-per-hour fastball seem like an 84-mile-per-hour pitch. We expect our BP staff to throw in the 80- to 84-mile-per-hour range. (We usually have two guys throwing the same round and alternating every 30 to 40 pitches.) Velocity and location are a must for a productive batting practice.

We usually have four to five players in each hitting group. We set up a batting-tee drill on the warning track in front of a dugout and have players hit into a screen. A bunting station is in the bullpen. Members of the hitting group rotate through the field hitting station and the other two stations.

Every swing at a BP pitch has a defined purpose that varies from round to round and hitter to hitter. Hitters should understand specific hitting routines, and the coach should enforce them emphatically.

Defensively, our goal is to make a play on every ball hit in BP. We have three outfielders playing shallow at their positions to give them plenty of work going back on balls. They follow a few rules that are absolutes to playing defense in BP:

- Always be willing to make diving catches. Show no fear of the fence.

- Play all ground balls and fly outs full speed, simulating footwork and arm action for throws home or to an appropriate base.

- Communicate to infielders that they catch Texas League fly balls. (By always playing shallow in BP we could take away opportunities for infielders to practice the tough Texas League fly-ball catches they would have to make if the outfielders were playing deep in game situations.)

- Once you read and react to a fly ball and realize you have no chance to catch it, return to your position. Don't waste time chasing balls you can't get to. After you make a play, sprint back to your position and get ready to make another play. The coach will make a point to recognize the best catch of the practice.

Infielders will vary their depth round by round through BP but will always play at least one round on the infield grass for a play at home. Infielders play the balls off the bat at game tempo and throw to first. Infielders always leave their feet to keep the ball in the infield. If the ball is not hit to them, they follow their rotation order for fielding fungoed ground balls. (We are very specific with the fungo hitter about simulating difficult ground-ball plays. A good level of expertise by the fungo hitter is a necessity. Every fungo not perfectly placed is a waste of time.)

Base runners occupy every base and follow specific base-running situations. We expect them to assume a secondary lead on the pitch and execute a three- to four-step reaction to the ball off the bat every third pitch. The runners at first and second react as if the next base is unoccupied. All runners react to pitches in the dirt. The runner at third focuses on reading ground balls he could score on when the infield is in. Base runners rotate up one base when a hitter finishes a round. Our catchers work hard on receiving and blocking techniques during BP and always catch as if runners were at first and third. In pregame BP the starting catcher will catch for 15 minutes.

Structure for Teaching Defense

From a defensive standpoint our practice goals are to develop sound fielding and throwing skills while establishing an active, aggressive, and efficient approach to playing defense. We want our players to have an intellectual appreciation for defensive positioning and game-situation response to any offensive action. The defensive drills we use in practice are explicitly designed to achieve these goals. We usually do drills for fielding and throwing skills with small groups in pre- or postpractice. The primary drill we use to help achieve the balance of our defensive goals is our team defense-offense execution drill.

The drill starts with a defensive team on the field and a pitcher on the mound, no outs, runner on first, top of the first inning. We create nine innings of game-specific offensive situations. Then the defensive group will switch with the players who were base runners. Base runners line up near the left-handed hitter's box. A coach stands in the right-handed hitter's box with a fungo bat. The pitcher throws home from the stretch, the runner at first takes a normal secondary lead, and as the pitch clears the plate the coach fungos a ball to create a defensive play. The first runner in line at home waits one count after the fungo is hit, becomes the batter-runner going to first base, and responds to the fungoed ball. Base runners perform at game-level effort. We expect them to execute according to our base-running philosophy. This is a full-intensity offensive base-running drill besides being a defensive execution drill. We do 80 percent of our base running in this drill.

Extra pitchers line up between third and home in foul territory. Pitchers rotate in on every play. If the defensive situation calls for the pitcher to back up home, he does so while the first pitcher in line (ball in his glove) sprints to the mound while staying out of the way of the play. He prepares to pitch within four or five seconds after the defensive players have sprinted back to their positions. It helps to use two catchers, rotating in on every other pitch. The coach can orchestrate any defensive situation at any time during the nine-inning simulated game. He should be very adept with a fungo bat so every fungoed ball fulfills its purpose. Every three outs we begin a new inning with a runner on first.

At the start of every inning we give the base runners and defensive players a hypothetical score and the offensive team's hitting order—leadoff, four hole, and so on. We take a three-minute break every nine innings. Early in the season we sometimes use this drill for our entire practice, simulating as many as 120 innings of baseball over a three-hour period. After the drill we will use walk-through sessions to review poorly executed aspects of our game drill.

Controlled Scrimmage

A controlled scrimmage can be an excellent teaching structure if some creativity is applied to the methodology. One of the negatives of scrimmaging is that many players are standing around, but the resourceful coach can eliminate that to some extent. We establish a two-minute break between innings during which we run defensive drills for the entire team. Defensive players have 30 seconds to assume their positions following the third out.

A fungo hitter follows a specific routine for types of double-play ground balls, and each infielder will have time to field and start three double plays, for a total of 12 double plays every inning. A manager will time the middle infielders with a stopwatch to measure their efficiency in turning the double play. The elapsed time from the moment the ball touches the middle infielder's glove until it arrives in the first baseman's glove should be in the 1.1 to 1.3 range for shortstops and 1.2 to 1.4 for second basemen. When we time middle infielders on the double play, they strive harder to execute correctly. The middle man becomes more assertive toward the infielder starting the double play, demanding that the throw be in optimum position to complete the play.

Outfielders go to center field for a 90-second fly-ball drill. A fungo hitter follows a specific routine for the types of fly balls the outfielders will work on. The outfielders should each make three tough catches between innings.

Pitchers have a two-minute warm-up period. They sprint to the mound and follow a predetermined warm-up. The routine should include a pitchout and two off-speed breaking balls in the dirt.

Catchers will warm up pitchers with a physical stance and a mentality as if runners were at first and third. In other words, they always work hard to simulate catching in the most difficult situation for a catcher. The catcher's throw to second is timed during games and scrimmages. Catchers throwing to second between innings in game or scrimmage situations should note these key points:

- Always throw in a simulated first-and-third situation. Check the third baseman for his hands-up signal if the runner at third can be back-doored as you're completing your footwork for the throw to second. In scrimmages, a hitter should be in the box, swinging through the pitch.

- Never allow an infielder to be standing at second base when you release the ball; you should throw to an open base to simulate a game situation.
- Make the pitcher throw a breaking ball or change-up.

Scrimmaging the final three innings of an 0-0 game can be beneficial because both teams will incorporate the short game to score a run. (Most teams don't work enough on this part of the game live.) Pitchers are challenged knowing that one run could beat them. To increase the challenge, start each inning with a runner on first. Finishing the final three innings of six games can often be far more beneficial than playing two nine-inning games. The goal of any scrimmage is to play with big-game pressure and intensity.

A Closing Note

Coaches should strive to eliminate the "could have, would have, should have" hindsight of the game by consistently conducting efficient practices. Lost opportunity for player growth and development cannot be replaced. Time is the most valuable tool we have as coaches. Use it wisely.

CHAPTER ELEVEN

Using Practice Drills Effectively

Danny Litwhiler

The old adage "Practice makes perfect" is not true unless practice sessions are instructive, enthusiastic, purposeful, executed correctly, and fun. One hour of organized practice, in a game atmosphere, is worth more than two hours of unorganized practice. Unorganized practice sessions accentuate faults instead of correcting them.

Over the years I learned to adapt old drills and create new drills for certain players. Not all drills are correct for every player. I enjoy discovering new ways to solve problems. This inspired me to develop new gimmicks or ways to teach individual players. Such inspiration improves the whole team and piques interest in the game. Often I took problems to bed and dreamed about them. Sometimes the answer appeared in my dreams or while meditating or even while daydreaming. Sometimes the answers came from the players themselves.

You must coach with good drills. Look for the magical key that is a part of hard work—drills that simulate game conditions and solve specific problems.

Conditioning

Baseball conditioning should take place throughout the year. Therefore, we divided our conditioning program into two phases: (1) off-season or winter conditioning and (2) spring training and pregame conditioning. Similar drills can be used through both phases.

Besides using off-season drills, players should participate in other sports or activities. One of the best is handball or paddleball, using the glove or paddle to hit the ball with the fielding hand. This develops dexterity with the glove hand of baseball.

Running, tennis, Ping-Pong, soccer, jumping rope, and swimming are all good activities for maintaining physical condition. Swimming develops the shoulder muscles. Using the overhand stroke develops muscles almost identical to those used in throwing a baseball. But players should keep throwing a baseball between swimming sessions. Tennis and Ping-Pong are good for the batting eye. Basketball, tennis, and running are good for developing leg strength and lateral movement. Many major-league players were good basketball players. Football as a conditioner for baseball is not recommended because of the obvious possibility of injury, which could damage a baseball career.

At Michigan State some outstanding football players played baseball. Ty Willingham, quarterback and wide receiver, was baseball captain and played outfield. Ty is now the head football coach at Stanford. Dick Kenny, an outstanding barefoot punter, was offered a major-league contract. He turned it down to go back home to Hawaii and be married. I believe that the strong kicking leg muscles that powered his drive off the pitching rubber developed his pitching arm. Kirk Gibson, an all-American wide receiver with great speed and strength, played outfield. With the Dodgers and Tigers he could hit and run but his shoulder never loosened up for throwing a baseball. Steve Garvey, a defensive back in football and my third baseman, played first base for the Dodgers and Padres. He sustained a football injury his freshman year that made it difficult for him to throw from third to first. Garvey's throws were weak and erratic, but he swung a powerful bat. I could not move him to first because I had a good-fielding left-handed power hitter there. The Dodgers put Garvey on first, and he became a Gold Glove winner.

Preparation for a baseball season requires players to work on their own, physically and mentally, from the last game of the previous season until the first day of official practice. At a minimum, players should work on their own for at least a month before the spring-training opening.

Off-season work can be divided into five categories: (a) stretching, (b) running and leg development, (c) throwing, (d) lightweight work for flexible muscles, and (e) bat swing.

The best way to avoid pulled muscles is to do stretching exercises before and after workouts. Stretching helps eliminate fatty tissue and strengthen muscles. A 15-minute stretching session is good for the whole body. Keeping muscles stretched all winter helps prevent sore arms and legs in early practice. Muscles such as those used for throwing during the season are fully stretched and extended by the end of the season. If those muscles are not exercised and stretched during the off-season, they will contract and become weak. Unfortunately, the tendency is to throw too hard too soon. Sudden stretching of the muscles can cause harm.

This chapter includes the drills I believe to be the best in creating interest, productivity, and satisfaction. As a precaution, you should try all the drills personally to evaluate them and make sure they will not cause injury to your players.

Special Hitting Drills

Through my years as a professional baseball player and college coach, the question always came up about whether the front arm or the back arm was the power arm in hitting. The answer in the clubhouse was usually split 50-50, although many said they didn't know.

Mike Marshall, the first major-league relief pitcher to win the Cy Young Award, was a graduate student in kinesiology at Michigan State. He attended school after the baseball season. Mike was a minor-league short-stop in the Phillies organization. He had a good arm with average fielding and hitting ability.

I asked Mike the power-arm question, and his answer was, "I don't know, but let's find out." As a result of his study of muscles used in hitting, we settled on the front arm. He devised a drill to develop the front arm for power and distance. After studying high-speed movie pictures of his swing we noticed two muscles in his upper body stood out and puffed up. These muscles were the triceps of his front arm and the deltoid on his front side.

To prove our theory and before developing a drill, I threw batting practice to Mike, a right-handed hitter. Field dimensions were 340 feet to left, 380 to left center, 400 to center, 390 to right center, and 315 to right field. Mike hit nearly 30 well-hit balls from left to right center but only two over the left-field fence and one over the left-center-field fence.

Mike carried out the drill during the winter and left for spring training. Because of his strong arm, the Phillies began to develop Mike as a pitcher. During the season he had opportunities to pinch hit and take batting practice. We did not count on his right arm, his pitching arm, getting stronger. Nor did we know that strength transfers from one limb to the other through exercise. After the season he returned to school and came to see me. I asked, "Well, how did it work?" He answered, "Come on down on the field and I'll show you."

I threw batting practice, and he hit balls over every fence with ease. From that time on Mike developed amazingly as a pitcher, playing 14 years in the majors. In a season of 162 games he set records in Montreal pitching in 98 games and for the Dodgers pitching in 106 games. Do not use this drill with the throwing arm. For example, right-hand hitters who throw left-handed and left-handed hitters who throw right-handed should not use this drill.

Overload for the Quick Bat Drill

The purpose of this drill is to develop a powerful swing, a quicker bat, and better bat control. The following list outlines the method and equipment used in the drill:

- We want to simulate the baseball swing versus gravity.
- High school players use a 7 1/2-pound barbell.
- Increase at 2 1/2-pound intervals.

- Remain at each weight for at least four days.
- Move to the next weight only when the weight becomes easy to throw through the repetitions.
- The ceiling weight is 25 pounds.
- For high school the ceiling should be 15 to 20 pounds, depending on the physical size of the boy.
- Use an 18- to 20-inch-high bench, long enough for a person to lie down on, for this exercise.

The hand barbell is a single unit. For high school age use two 5-pound weights, two 2 $^1/_2$-pound weights, two 1 $^1/_2$-pound weights, a hand bar with clamps, and a wrench to secure the weights. College players use the same equipment but add two 10-pound weights. Use a pad on the floor under the barbell to prevent a sudden jar to the arm and harm to the floor and barbell. The following guidelines outline the procedure for the drill:

- Lie on your side on the bench, with the front arm of your baseball swing upward. For example, right-handed swingers lie on the right side and lift with the left arm. Left-handed swingers lie on their left side and lift with the right arm.
- Support your head with the opposite arm by resting your elbow on the seat of the bench (see figure 11.1a).
- Lock the bottom of the leg to the side of the bench with your toe and lock the top leg on the other side of the bench with your heel (see figure 11.1b).
- Position the barbell directly in front of the shoulder, resting on the pad. Hold the bar portion of the barbell parallel to the body line (figure 11.1a).
- Use three slow repetitions to loosen the area being stressed. If you feel any pain, drop the weights and stop weight training for the day.
- After three warm-ups, attempt to explode the barbell upward. You will gain nothing if you move the weights easily or slowly.
- If possible, do seven of these explosive movements. After you extend the weights upward, lower them to the pad easily. When they touch the pad, explode them again (see figure 11.1 c and d for the path of the barbell). The barbell moves directly vertical from its original position on the pad. The barbell never extends up over the body to the arm's maximum height (figure 11.1e).

Figure 11.1 Procedure for the Overload for Quick Bat Drill.

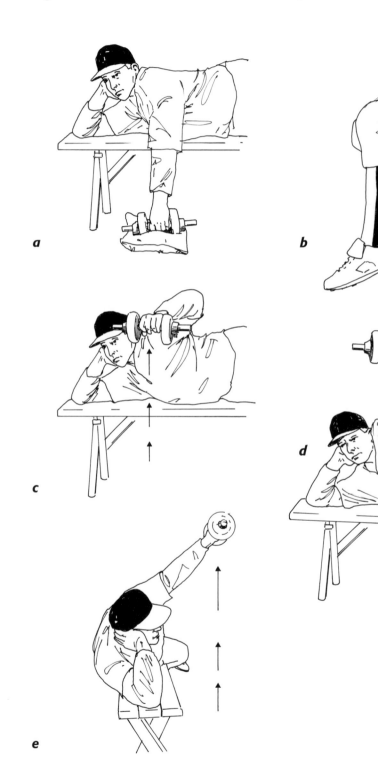

a

b

c

d

e

Do only one exercise of 10 repetitions during a four-hour period. We recommend doing the exercise no more than twice each day, once in the morning upon rising and once upon retiring.

If soreness develops, discontinue the weight training immediately and let your coach or trainer know the location of the soreness. Don't confuse stiffness with soreness. Any good exercise may cause some stiffness.

The total procedure takes no more than a minute once you are on the bench with your hand on the barbell. Do not lift other weights with the same motion.

Batting Tee Drill

I once had little faith in teaching hitting with a batting tee, using it only to loosen up. When I began working with the Cincinnati Reds, Ted Kluzewski showed me the value of the batting tee. The purpose of this drill is to increase power, teach location of bat-ball contact, and improve concentration. The player stands in the batter's box and takes a healthy swing with the bat. Notice where his front foot lands and pivots. Pay no attention to home plate with this swing. Place a tee with a ball directly in front of the front foot and in line with the outside corner of home plate. This is where the batter should meet the outside pitch with the sweet part of the bat to supply power. From that outside ball, on a 45-degree angle toward the pitcher, place the ball in line with the center of home plate. This is

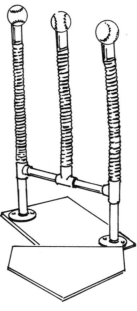

Figure 11.2   Triple tee.

the area where the sweet part of the bat should meet the ball that is down the middle. Now place the ball on the tee on the same angle in line with the inside corner of home plate. This is the area for the sweet part of the bat to meet the inside ball squarely.

These three areas—outside, down the middle, and inside—can be hit with power using the same swing. So I developed a triple tee (see figure 11.2) that holds balls in those three positions. Each ball is a half inch higher than the one outside it. In other words, the inside ball is one inch higher than the outside ball. In the swing the head of the bat will always rise that much from outside contact to inside contact with the ball.

Start work with a ball on the outside of the plate for a number of swings. Then move to the center for more swings and finally to the inside. Now put a ball on the outside of the plate and one on the inside tee. Notice that players will nearly always hit the outside ball but miss the inside ball until they swing correctly. After much practice you will see improvement.

The theory is "from the top, out in front, up the middle," which means the bat comes down on the ball, not up. To hit the ball with power, the batter must meet the ball in front of the striding foot. Hitting the ball behind that foot invariably produces a ground ball to the opposite field. "Up the middle" means that the batter should not try to pull the ball but instead hit it at the pitcher. With the proper swing, the three balls will shoot off the tees on the swing—one to the left of the pitcher, one to the right, and one at the pitcher.

Hip Rotation for Power Hitting

Hall of Fame player Paul Waner used to say, "Throw your belly button at the pitcher." Much later Ted Williams told me, "You hit with your hips." Both meant the same thing, but I never realized what made the hips or belly button turn. I saw a 5-foot, 7-inch, 150-pound professional golfer hit golf balls farther with an iron than I could with woods, at five feet, 10 inches and 195 pounds. I asked him where he got his power. He was a right-handed golfer, and he reached down and slapped the inside of his right thigh between the crotch and the knee and said, "From this muscle. It turns my hips to drive the ball."

Now I had the answer to get more power into the baseball swing, but I had to prove it. Working for the Cincinnati Reds near the close of the season in Cedar Rapids, Iowa, I worked with two players. I asked the first player to set up a tee and a ball at home plate and see how far he could hit it. Left field was 340 feet from home plate and center was 400 feet away. The best he could do was about 320 feet. Then I showed him how I thought he was hitting. The best I could do was just over short-stop. Then I hit again, this time concentrating on the muscle on the inside of my thigh, keeping my hands closer to my body, and rocking back. I hit the ball farther than he did. He said, "This is embarrassing. Give me the bat." Concentrating on his leg muscle, he hit a ball that bounced against the fence. The next one hit the fence. On the third try he hit the ball over the fence. He continued to hit balls over the fence. The other player heard the discussion, saw the results, and after a few swings, he too was consistently hitting the ball over the fence. He asked to try the center-field fence and hit balls over it as well. If I were still coaching, I would be looking for ways to develop that leg muscle for hitting.

Instructional Bunting Bat

While teaching a baseball class at Florida State, I was discussing the theory of bunting. I was explaining how you want the top half of the ball to meet the bottom half of the sweet part of the bat and that you do not want to bunt on the end of the bat or near the trademark. Ron Fraser, later a Hall of Fame coach from the University of Miami, was in the class. He asked, "Skip, if you don't think you should bunt near the trademark, why can't you cut away some of the area on a bunting bat?" I said, "Good idea, why not cut away the top half of the bat also." After class Ron and I went over to the maintenance shop and had them cut away the areas. The bat was too light for bunting, so we bored a three-quarter-inch hole six inches deep into the end and filled it with lead. Now we had a real instructional bunting bat. Worth Sports Company makes the bat from heavy wood.

Casey Stengel bought nine bunting bats. Al Lopez and Fred Hutchinson each bought six bats. That year Casey won the World Series, Fred won the National League Championship, and Al finished second in the American League. Florida State went to the College World Series. I think the instructional bunting bat helped all of us (see figure 11.3).

Figure 11.3   Instructional bunting bat.

Special Pitching Drills

Over the years I also developed a few ideas that could help pitchers with specific problems. Adapting one of the hitting drills was responsible for the first. I suppose it was a combination of curiosity and plain luck that helped me with the other two.

Overload for the Fastball

For years I had been looking for ways to increase throwing velocity. I saw what could be done using weights to improve bat speed and power. I was curious what might be done using weights to improve throwing speed.

I asked the Worth Sports Company if they would make several baseballs in various weights. For the experiment we used one regulation 5-ounce ball, one 7-ounce ball, one 9-ounce ball, one 10-ounce ball, one 11-ounce ball, and one 12-ounce ball. We threw the balls against a net. Do not throw a ball heavier than 7 ounces to a catcher. The heavier balls could harm hands or ruin gloves.

I once had a fine-looking pitcher with excellent control. The professional scouts liked everything about him but his velocity. During the winter he went on a 10-week program with the weighted ball. The next year he improved greatly and had a great senior year. The White Sox signed him, and he played some major-league ball. The important point was that his velocity increased and he kept his control.

Quite a few pitchers used the weighted-ball drill with success. For example, Sonny Seibert was a successful major-league pitcher for 12 years. In 1973, in the twilight of his career, he wrote and asked if the weighted-ball program might improve his fastball. Time had taken some of his velocity. I gave him the 10-week program for his winter workouts. After the 1974 season I read that he had won the Comeback Player of the Year Award. He said that he went on the program as directed and developed a good fastball and a super curveball. I was curious about how he could develop a super curveball with the weighted balls.

Sonny said he used the weighted balls until spring training. Then he used only the 7-ounce ball with his warm-ups. He thought the heavier balls might wear him down during the season. When his arm was loose he would begin working with the 7-ounce ball and spin it, as he did when throwing a curve. This strengthened the muscles in his wrist and forearm. He used the 7-ounce ball until the All-Star Game, when he stopped using it to save his arm strength for the second half of the season. He said he wishes he had stayed with the 7-ounce ball all season because he had a great first half but a so-so second half. He believes he would have finished stronger had he stayed with the 7-ounce ball all season.

Fastball Overload Drill

The purpose of this drill is to develop velocity yet retain control. This is a 6-, 8-, or 10-week program, depending on the maximum weight you wish to use. Throw three times a week with at least one day's rest between throwing days. Use each ball for two weeks, beginning with the lightest ball (7 ounces) and ending with your heaviest for the last two weeks. Once you reach the maximum weight, throwing twice a week or at least once a week should keep your arm in good shape, staying at that top weight. Should you miss a week, drop back an ounce and work back to the maximum weight. High school players should stop at 10 ounces. College players can go up to 12 ounces.

Do not throw a curve with any weight over 7 ounces. Never snap a curve at maximum exertion; three-quarter speed is the proper speed. Throw the weighted balls at maximum distance of 60 feet, 6 inches. Begin throws at a shorter distance and move gradually back to regulation distance.

1. Warm up by throwing a regulation ball (5 ounces) until you are ready to throw hard.
2. Make 10 throws at submaximum exertion with a 7-ounce ball. As the weight goes up, throw 5 times with weight you previously used before making your 10 throws with the new weight.
3. Make 20 throws at maximum exertion with the regulation (5-ounce) ball or until control returns. This completes the weighted-ball program for the day.

Outfielders, infielders, and catchers can use this program. Players should toss the heavy balls against a net. When throwing heavy balls, it is important to concentrate on proper wrist movement. This is a snap throw, not a push. Make certain that players use the same arm and wrist delivery that they use when throwing a regulation ball. Most players tend to push a heavy ball.

This drill can be harmful to the thrower, so players should *never* throw at maximum effort.

Using an Eye Patch to Impove Control

Early in my career as the baseball coach for Florida State, I learned a new drill that helped some pitchers with their control. We had a left-handed first baseman with average skills but a great arm. I thought I could make a good pitcher out of Tony Avitable. But his control was nonexistent, and our players didn't even want him to throw batting practice. He not only missed the catcher but often threw the ball over the batting cage or behind the batter.

Late in our last game, I told Tony to warm up so he could pitch the last inning. The umpire asked me to turn Tony away from the playing field because his wild pitches in the bullpen were delaying the game.

When Tony came in several warm-up pitches ricocheted off the screen. The apprehensive batter moved deep in the batter's box, and I believe he prayed. But prayer didn't help—he struck out on five pitches. The next batter was out on six pitches, one of which soared against the screen. The final batter ducked bravely, never took the bat off his shoulder, and was out on four pitches. I would guess Tony's velocity was in the middle to high 90s. The radar gun had not yet been invented.

During the winter, I tried to figure out how to get Tony's pitches near the plate. His speed was terrific, but the batters, the umpire, our catcher, and the backstop were all in danger. Finally a psychology text gave me a clue.

There is a conjecture called dominant eye theory. The dominant eye is pertinent to aiming and control, whether using a gun, a bow and arrow, darts, or a ball. I thought that Tony's problem was perhaps that his nondominant eye was affecting his control. So why not put a patch over his nondominant eye to allow his dominant eye to take over and perhaps improve his control.

At spring training, I had Tony wearing the patch on the nondominant eye every time he threw a ball. Gradually he improved his control while maintaining speed. When we played our first game, Tony was my starter.

In the first inning, Tony filled the bases and had a full count on every hitter. With many more pitches he then struck out the side. Although Tony threw plenty of wild pitches, he continued to strike out hitters. In nine innings, he struck out 24 batters, an NCAA record that still stands. Tony's pitching helped Florida State go to its first College World Series.

After college, Tony signed a good contract with the Kansas City A's. In spring training a batted ball hit him in batting practice, injuring his throwing arm. Tony never pitched again.

The nondominant eye problem sometimes occurs in pitchers who are left-handed and left-eye dominant and in right-handed pitchers who right-eye dominant. As such a pitcher turns his head in the windup, both eyes attempt to aim the pitch, confusing the brain. The catcher's glove appears to move two to three feet and sometimes disappears. Thanks to Tony, I discovered the nondominant eye problem and was lucky to devise the eye-patch drill to bring control to pitchers who had this problem.

Using the Speed Gun for Pitchers

One of my best discoveries was using a radar gun to check the velocity of a thrown ball. I was always looking for ways to see if my drills to develop arm speed were working. In 1973 I saw a photo of the campus police using a radar gun. I wondered if such a gun would track a baseball, so I called the police captain and asked him to bring the gun over to the baseball field. We had two pitchers throw but we noticed that readings did not always appear. I didn't know what speeds we were getting. They were throwing 75 to 80, so we drove the car over to the mound and had them throw. Now we saw 83 to 85. I called CMI, the radar company, who said we were getting the speed of the throw but that the radar gun was not tuned for a baseball. They said if I would send the gun that they would be happy to fine-tune it for baseball. The new gun clocked about 90 percent of pitches.

I called Bowie Kuhn, the baseball commissioner. He was interested and said he would notify every major-league team. I began to get letters, phone calls, and telegrams asking about the gun. I contacted John Paulson, CEO of JUGS, Inc., to see if he was interested. So the JUGS radar speed gun was born. That original gun is now in the Hall of Fame Museum in Cooperstown. The new gun clocks about 99 percent of the pitches, at an accuracy of plus or minus 1 mile per hour.

The radar gun is invaluable in developing pitchers. A slight change in stride or delivery changes the speed. I am convinced that regardless of what velocity a pitcher throws, he must come close to the following changes of speeds. Also, a good pitcher does not have to throw at 90 or more miles per hour. He has to understand change of speed and location.

Drop 10 miles per hour off a fastball for the slider, 15 miles per hour off a fastball for the curve, and 20 miles per hour off a fastball for a change of pace. For example, if you throw a 79-mile-per-hour fast ball, your slider should be at 69 miles per hour. A curve should be 64 miles per hour, and the change 59 miles per hour. Rudy May used these speeds successfully with the Yankees, pitching a two-hitter after a session on the day of the game.

When a curve or slider is too close to the velocity of the fastball, you lose the effect of the change of speed. If the change of pace is slower than 20 miles per hour off the fastball, the hitter has time to regain his balance and hit with power.

A Closing Note

If drills don't work, you always have superstition. I never saw anyone in baseball who was not superstitious. Four-leaf clovers always work if you believe they do. Do anything that gives you confidence or a positive image of yourself. Always see yourself to be successful in the mirror of your mind. Never see yourself fail. This is a drill of the mind.

CHAPTER TWELVE

Maximizing the Value of Indoor Practice

John Winkin

I have handled preseason practices for baseball teams in an indoor setting for over a half century. What is more, rain or snow has sometimes forced the entire preseason practice indoors. Each year our first time

> **A coach always must prioritize.**

outdoors has been in a warm-climate setting during our spring-break vacation or spring-trip games, often at the site of opponents who had prepared outdoors and played several games outdoors. We have often gotten off an airplane or bus and that day played our season opener. And just as often we returned home to poor weather or poor field conditions that forced us to continue practices indoors.

What generally complicates planning indoor practice is a mandated time limit. It might be 90 minutes, 120 minutes, even 360 minutes, yet baseball practice is always scheduled in a facility that also schedules many other activities, such as softball, basketball, lacrosse, track, spring football conditioning, intramurals, whatever. Therefore, a coach always must prioritize. Practice goals need to be planned, organized, and implemented to get the most from each practice session.

Besides time constraints, coaches conducting indoor practices also must deal with space limitations in meeting the goals planned for each practice. I always depend on (1) establishing priorities for getting a team ready, (2) being well organized for each practice session, and (3) using the available space effectively for each planned practice.

I have always worried about two matters in preparing for preseason and planning indoor practices. First, can I give a fair tryout indoors to players wishing to try out for the squad? I long ago concluded that I cannot do that. I feel that at the college level tryouts are best accomplished in fall baseball. In a high school, where many of the key players are multisport athletes, one has to count on summer baseball (summer amateur league games, clinics, and so forth) to accomplish the "tryout."

Second, I never have adequate time in indoor practices to accomplish all the needed teaching experiences. Again, I work hard at planning and working to accomplish needed teaching experiences at the college level in fall baseball. For the high school level, I have had greater success teaching needed baseball skills in summer clinics and camps and other planned summer baseball experiences.

My basic premise in preseason has been (1) to know which players I needed to focus on to get ready for the season ahead and (2) to focus on correcting each player in each practice experience.

A coach will obviously spend time evaluating who is coming along in preseason practices to see who is ready and to make necessary personnel adjustments. On the first day of practice, you have to know which players you need to get ready for the season. You will likely have to correct, adjust, and make changes to prepare each player and the team itself within the time and space constraints of the indoor setting.

What follows is a summary of how we run indoor practices—our priorities, our planning, our organizing philosophy, and how we use limited space in our drills. We have drawn some of what follows from our book *Maximizing Baseball Practice,* published by Human Kinetics in 1995, which was written with Jay Kemble and Michael Coutts. This book details our blueprint for developing practice sessions to meet the needs and goals of a team.

Our philosophy of practicing baseball indoors is to plan each practice to (1) maximize use of time by identifying priorities, allocating time, and dividing practice; and (2) maximize use of space by defining available space and dividing space.

Maximizing Time

I always spend 60 to 80 minutes a day developing a daily practice session. The best way to prepare a baseball team is to spend the time necessary to plan practice so that players know exactly what to do and when to do it. Players know that every minute will be filled with a drill or routine that will help them develop as a team.

The National Collegiate Athletic Association (NCAA) restricts weekly team practice time and the number of days each week a player can practice. Many of you face similar restrictions, especially high school coaches who are allowed just three weeks of preseason practice and no Sunday practice sessions. Because of these restrictions you must continually evaluate your use of time.

Identifying Priorities

You never seem to have enough time to be as good as you want to be. If you plan well, you reduce the potential for wasting time (and you can use any time left at the end of practice to repeat individual skill work or practice specific game-situation drills). Prioritize your available time to satisfy your needs in developing your team. A quick, organized practice that involves every player is the most effective way to do this. Always keep your players active. Having players stand around is not only boring for them but also can distract the entire team.

The first step in prioritizing is to analyze how you use your time. Our practices run between two and two and a half hours each day; any time beyond that is usually nonproductive. Identify your goal for the day and what you must do to accomplish it. Our top priority in preseason is to develop endurance of our pitchers. Pitchers require the most time to get ready, are the most vulnerable to injury, and require the most attention, so first we organize our practices around building their endurance. In-season, the goal is to maintain endurance. This is what we plan to spend the most time on in every practice.

Our next priority is preparing our hitters. In preseason we require our pitchers to throw a specified number of pitches each day. As the season draws closer, we increase the number of pitches. Regardless of the number of pitches, we have the same goal every day—to build the endurance of the pitchers so they can comfortably make their pitch counts each outing. This usually involves about an hour of practice. Meanwhile, the infielders, outfielders, and hitters are involved in drill work. During live hitting, we schedule basic skills for the everyday players. We emphasize that the live pitching and hitting schedule is that day's game experience for each pitcher, catcher, and hitter. Thus we plan each indoor practice around this priority philosophy.

Allocating Time

Once we know time limits for each practice (90 minutes, 120 minutes, 150 minutes), we then fit into the remaining slots the practice for the other players—fielding drills, team defense, base running, and so forth.

It has always been a priority with me to schedule 60 minutes of pitching and hitting at the same time by having live pitching throw to live hitting. The next priority in allocating time is to work on basic skills for each position.

We allot about 15 minutes a day for each position player to perform drills to develop the basic skills of his position. We spend 15 minutes each with infielders, outfielders, catchers, and pitchers on developing individual skills such as fielding, throwing, footwork, and the double play. This takes about 60 minutes of practice. When practice time limits permit, we allot 30 to 60 minutes for team defense, such as developing knowledge of game situations and reacting properly to any batted ball, attempted bunt, attempted steal, or emerging rundown situation.

We have been fortunate to have a practice facility large enough to allow all our players to get the necessary repetitions. Dividing our facility into two sections allows us to focus, plan our practice, and develop situations in which our players can master the necessary skills within the time available. When we allot time for the basic skills area, we can concentrate on building the team as a unit. We focus on individual skill work for a set time and then bring the players together to develop them into a team.

Dividing Practice

When 120 minutes are available for practice, we divide the time into two segments. In the first hour of practice we focus on practicing basic skills as planned. We organize each area of basic skills within a time frame. Each time frame runs 10 to 15 minutes with emphasis on pitcher drills, infield ball handling, outfield drills, catcher drills, and team defense.

In the second hour we focus on endurance pitching and hitting in the designated pitching and hitting area. We concentrate on developing skills through game situations. Pitchers and hitters battle one another in the hitting area, and the everyday players continue to work on infield ball handling, outfield, and catcher drills in the basic skills area.

If a specific hitting and pitching area is not available, you will have to plan all drills within the 120-minute period. While one group is hitting and pitching, another can work on basic fielding skills. The players continually rotate until all players have completed their repetitions.

Maximizing Space

Although time is a factor in developing effective practice sessions, space is just as important, especially for teams that must practice indoors. Well-developed practices must make full use of all available space and involve as many players as possible.

Defining Available Space

You should develop practices that can fit within the framework of your facility without causing you to compromise your philosophy.

Gyms and practice facilities come in all shapes and sizes. Most high schools have a facility the size of a gymnasium basketball court. The larger the facility, the easier it is to prioritize practice and develop realistic game situations involving most of the players at one time. In small facilities, the need to prioritize is greater. If you have a basketball-court-sized facility, you may be able to do only one or two drills at once, so fewer players will get the ideal number of repetitions. In such a case, you should devote the most attention to your most critical priority in preparing your team.

The better you use space, the more involved each player can be. The more repetitions a player gets, the better he gets. Our goal as coaches is to involve every player for every minute of practice and create game situations involving a complete infield with live pitching and hitting. Many programs, unfortunately, do not have the necessary space and must adjust accordingly. Many teams that must practice indoors do not have the opportunity to practice on a regular-size infield until their first game.

As coaches, we often do not realize how much space we have. Yet, you must use all available space. Use part of the gymnasium's stage to do a hitting drill, use the hallway for base running, use a classroom to do basic skills, and use a chalkboard to teach situations. Many coaches are surprised at the amount of space available once they choose to be creative and resourceful.

Dividing Your Space

It is a priority with me to divide time into two segments—a hitting and pitching period and a basic skills period. Divide space in the same way. Have your pitching and hitting space available at a moment's notice so you can develop practices that focus on live pitching and hitting without taking time away from basic skills drills. This allows you not to rush building your pitchers' endurance, and you can spend as much time as you need on pitchers and hitters.

Using two areas also allows your players enough space to complete the necessary repetitions for proper development. While one group of players, say the infielders and pitchers, work in the live hitting and pitching area, the outfielders can work in the basic skills area (see figure 12.1). Once the first group completes their repetitions, another group of pitchers and outfielders can get their repetitions in the hitting and pitching area while the infielders get theirs in the basic skills area.

Pitching and Hitting Area

A separate area for pitching and hitting allows you the flexibility to concentrate on developing an effective batting order while you also build the endurance of the pitchers. This area also allows you to move the pitchers and hitters into different near-game experience by working the top pitchers against the top hitters. Again, if possible, the pitching and hitting areas should always be available to you and should include an area for pitchers to warm up. This area may be one edge of the gymnasium, a vacant classroom, or an unused stage. Regardless of its location, the area should be well lighted, netted, and at least 70 feet long and 10 feet wide. Two hitting cages are ideal.

If you coach in a program with limited practice space, try spending three days a week, perhaps Monday, Wednesday, and Friday, developing pitchers and hitters. Designate one area just for hitting and pitching and develop stations to keep the players involved in these two activities. You can designate Tuesday, Thursday, and Saturday for basic skills and team defense. On those days, incorporate drills to develop the skills planned for that day.

Again, develop a system that allows your top players and top pitchers to get the quality repetitions they need to prepare for the coming season.

Basic Skills Area

The basic skills area is a large facility with ample room for your players to master pitchers' fielding, infield ball handling, outfield communication, catching, and team defense (see figure 12.1). Likely, this will be a gymnasium or common area to which each in-season athletic team has time allocated each day. The larger the area, the easier it is to make the drills gamelike and place your fielders at real distance when working on individual and team drills.

For safety, the basic skills area should be well lighted and, if possible, completely netted to keep balls from getting away and hitting nonparticipants. Any glass areas should be covered or screened and walls should be padded to protect the players.

Dividing Space in a Single Area

Most high school facilities are small and do not allow for two separate practice areas. If this is your situation, you need to analyze the space available and develop a way for your team to take advantage of it. Prioritize your space to fit your needs. Figures 12.2 through 12.6 show ways to divide available space based on different needs and facility sizes. Most coaches in this situation will have only one major area to work in. This area is commonly a large gymnasium with a batting cage extending from one end to the other.

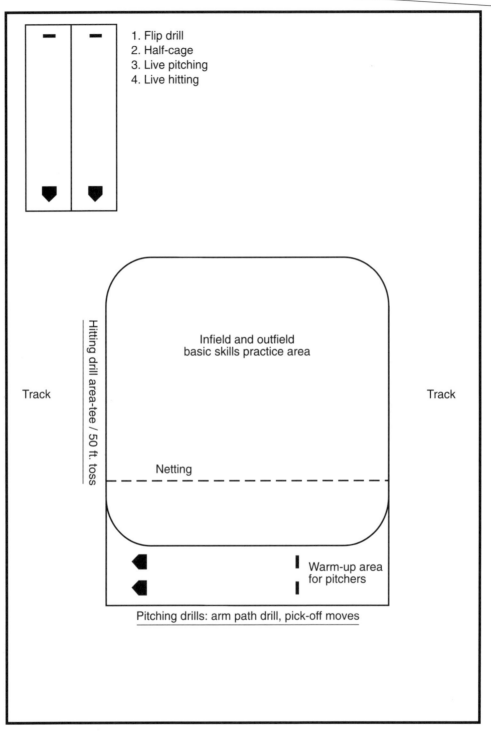

Figure 12.1   Sample indoor practice set up with areas for pitching, hitting, and basic skills.

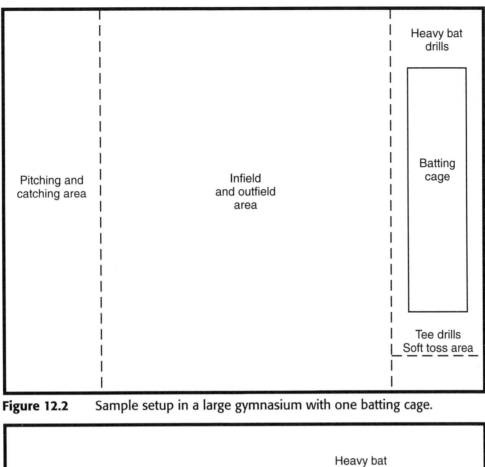

Figure 12.2   Sample setup in a large gymnasium with one batting cage.

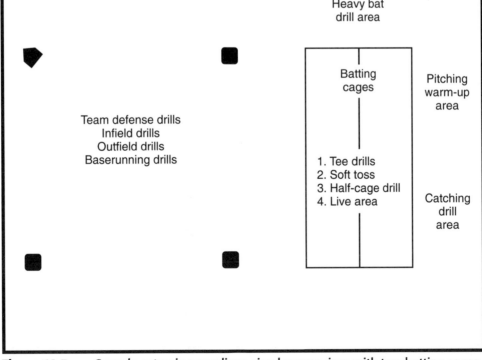

Figure 12.3   Sample setup in a medium-sized gymnasium with two batting cages.

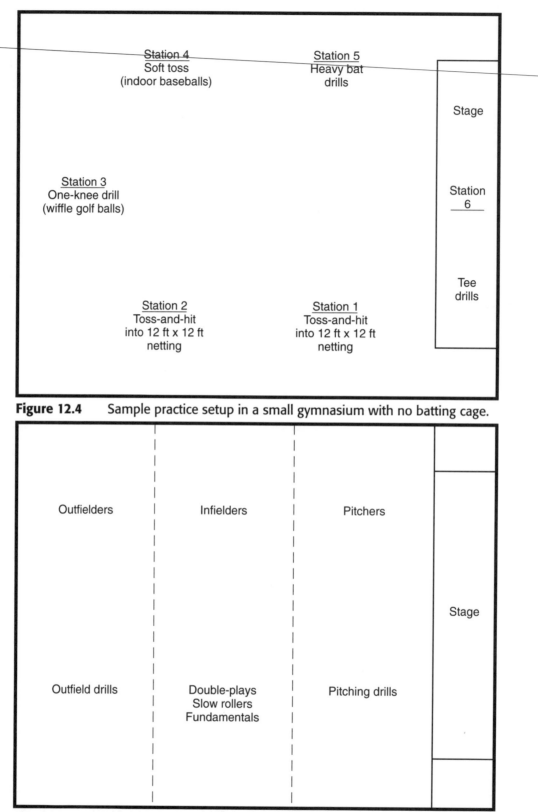

Figure 12.4   Sample practice setup in a small gymnasium with no batting cage.

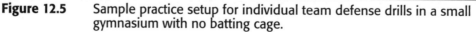

Figure 12.5   Sample practice setup for individual team defense drills in a small gymnasium with no batting cage.

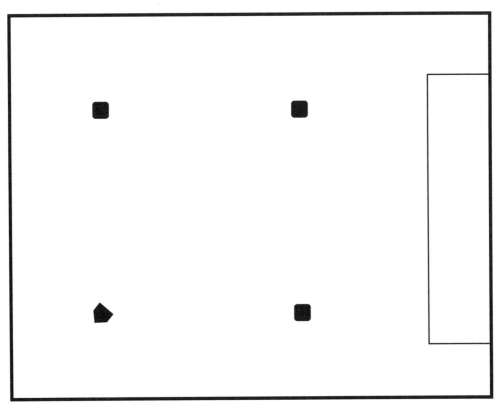

Figure 12.6   Sample practice setup for team defense drills in a small gymnasium with no batting cage.

Maximizing Productivity

As a coach, I have focused my planning, organization, and implementation of each practice on using the most effective means of practicing basic skills. Our drills and routines for position practice are designed, scheduled, and focused to accomplish proper execution of basic skills, mechanics, and technique. Although it is impossible in this chapter to outline and detail everything one can do, what follow are some of our priority considerations and planning in each area.

Six Steps to Proper Pitching Mechanics

As I stated earlier, our pitchers are our top priority in preseason. Pitchers require the most time to get ready, are the most vulnerable to injury, and require the most attention, so we organize our practices around them.

In indoor practices we use a six-step routine to help pitchers master mechanics that will reduce potential for injury and develop consistency. A pitcher who develops a consistent routine and delivery is also likely to throw strikes consistently. We felt this six-step routine was especially helpful to Billy Swift in making the transition from an outfielder-pitcher to a pitcher who won 20 games in the major leagues.

The six-step routine allows a pitcher to warm up carefully by slowly increasing the distance between each step. Each step is a new drill that focuses on an aspect of pitching mechanics, making the pitcher's delivery more consistent. The drill also serves as a starting point in building endurance. The routine has five goals:

- To allow the pitcher to safely stretch out while concentrating on specific mechanics
- To develop a routine for the pitcher to warm up properly
- To practice and make a habit of using proper pitching mechanics
- To allow 10 repetitions in each step that focus on certain aspects of the pitcher's delivery (with each step in the progression relying on each of the earlier steps)
- To complete, in 15 to 20 minutes, a progression in which the pitcher gradually works back to the full distance of 60 feet, 6 inches from a beginning distance of 15 feet

Step 1: Two-Knee Drill

The pitcher kneels about 15 feet from, and squared to, the catcher. With the ball in his throwing hand, the pitcher rotates his upper body so that his nonthrowing shoulder and elbow point to the catcher as he brings his throwing arm and the ball up to the cocked position.

Once the arm and hand are in the cocked position, the pitcher gains momentum by uncoiling his upper body. He then spins the ball at half speed to a location as he stretches out. As the pitcher releases the ball, he protects his arm and shoulder with the proper follow-through: armpit over the knee, elbow by the knee, and a complete sweep of the fingers.

For steps 1, 2, and 3 the best location is low and inside to the opposite hitter: right-handed pitchers to left-handed hitters, and vice versa.

Step 2: One-Knee Drill

The pitcher and catcher position themselves about 20 feet apart. The pitcher kneels on his drive-leg knee with his stride leg bent toward the catcher. The stride leg (or landing leg) is in the ideal landing position.

While in the cocked position, the pitcher focuses on location. As he throws, he transfers his weight from the back leg to the front leg by pushing off the back foot. He rises from a kneeling to standing position while uncoiling his upper body to allow for the explosion and travel of the arm, elbow, shoulder, and hip. Again, as the pitcher releases the ball, he must concentrate on proper follow-through: armpit over the knee, elbow by the knee, sweep of the fingers, and rotation of the hips.

Step 3: Hip Drill or Chair Drill

For the hip drill, the pitcher stands on the mound about 30 feet from the catcher. The pitcher must measure off his stride line, ensuring that his toe and knee are pointing toward the catcher. Once the pitcher is at cocked position, he will simultaneously transfer his weight from the drive leg to the front leg, begin rotating the hips toward the catcher, bring the arm and shoulder through the proper throwing path, and end with the correct follow-through.

This drill develops powerful hip rotation. Upon follow-through, the pitcher should not bring his drive foot forward. He merely turns the foot over so that the outside part of the ankle points toward the ground and the inside of the knee points toward the opposite knee.

The chair drill uses the same concepts as the hip drill but may be used when a mound is unavailable. Use the chair to simulate the mound's downward slope.

As in the hip drill, the pivot foot rests on a chair and rotates on the chair as the pitcher executes the drill. The push-off foot does not leave the chair. The pitcher should concentrate on turning the foot over and rotating the hip. His weight should not shift forward until his arm is up and in the cocked position.

Step 4: Balance-Point Drill

The location for steps 4, 5, and 6 are five pitches inside low and five pitches outside low. This step, along with steps 5 and 6, should be done from the pitcher's mound. The catcher positions himself about 45 feet away from the pitcher. The pitcher marks the point at which his stride foot should land. This makes it easier for you to verify a correct landing spot.

With all his weight over his drive leg, the pitcher raises his stride leg until his thigh is parallel to the ground. The stride toe should be pointed down to allow the pitcher to land on the front half of his foot. The glove and throwing hand should be at the break point. The pitcher focuses on the catcher's mitt, breaks his throwing hand down and out of the glove, and brings it quickly to the cocked position. At the same time, he strides toward the plate, transfers his weight from the back leg to the front leg, begins hip rotation, and brings his drive foot off the ground and forward as he moves his arm and shoulder through the proper throwing path. He should end with the correct follow-through.

Because this is the most important step, the emphasis must be on being in balance before the pitching explosion. We use the expressions "Lift and throw" and "Throw up-down."

Step 5: One, Two, Three Drill

Step 5 brings together steps 1 through 4. Here we break the delivery into three stages, stopping after each stage to ensure that the pitcher is in the correct position. Stage 1 focuses on addressing the rubber and beginning the delivery, stage 2 emphasizes the balance point, and stage 3 concentrates on the release of the ball.

The catcher positions himself about 50 feet from the pitcher. In stage 1 of this drill, the pitcher addresses the rubber, gaining momentum by stepping back with his stride leg and turning his pivot foot in front of the rubber. As he begins this rocking step, it is important for him to keep both his wrist and the ball completely hidden in his glove. At this point, the pitcher should stop and check his position.

Stage 2 concentrates on the balance point and cocked position. As the pitcher reaches the balance point, make sure his wrist and the ball are concealed from the batter's view. Remember to stop at this phase to check that the pitcher is in proper balance, with hands breaking from the middle of his body to go to cocked position.

Stage 3 is the throwing and follow-through stage. With the arm in the cocked position and weight over his back leg, the pitcher aims his hip and front shoulder toward the target. He drives with the back leg and strides toward the plate. As the stride foot lands, he transfers his weight from the back leg to the front leg, rotates his upper body so that the throwing shoulder replaces the nonthrowing shoulder, opens his hip toward the catcher, brings his arm and shoulder through the proper throwing path, and ends with the correct follow-through.

Step 6: Stretch Drill

The stretch is from full distance—60 feet, 6 inches. In developing the slide step, the pitcher quickens his delivery home while least influencing his proper pitching mechanics. From the stretch, the pitcher comes to set position.

Once the pitcher completes step 6, he should be adequately warm and stretched. He is now ready for the rest of his throwing experience, whether it is his long or short throwing day. At this point, gradually add other pitches to the fastball, such as the curve, slider, or change. Once he is comfortable with his pitches, let him complete his throwing for that day. We do this by throwing three sets of spins—2-2-2 (two fastball spins, two breaking ball spins, two change-up spins).

Building Endurance in Pitchers

Developing the endurance of your pitchers and carefully monitoring them are as important as teaching proper mechanics. Like any athlete in training, a pitcher needs time to develop the muscles required to throw a baseball. For programs at the college level, we've found that pitchers can safely build endurance in seven to eight weeks. This allows them enough time to build their endurance to the point where they can throw 100 pitches every four or five days.

Because of restrictions on their programs, high school coaches are lucky to have four weeks to prepare their teams for the approaching season. But even if you are restricted to three, four, or five weeks, it is critical that you do not rush your pitchers. The safest and most effective way to build endurance is on a four-day rotation. Remember, our goal is to build endurance slowly while concentrating on proper mechanics and location.

The four-day rotation was designed as a guide to developing pitchers' endurance (see table 12.1). By following the four-day rotation, you will afford your pitchers sufficient rest while building their endurance.

- Day 1. The first day is the long throwing or endurance day. On this day, emphasize adding pitches to your pitcher's throwing experience. For example, if your pitcher threw 60 pitches on his last long throwing experience, he should throw 75 pitches on his current long throwing experience and 90 on his next long throwing experience. Begin counting the number of pitches thrown after your pitcher has warmed up (use our six-step warm-up routine).

- Day 2. The second day is conditioning day and always follows the long throwing day. This day is also the pitcher's drill day. On this day the pitcher will work hard to help get his arm and legs back into shape.

- Day 3. The third day is for short throwing. This is a stretch throwing day. Once the pitcher has completed the six-step warm-up routine,

TABLE 12.1

The Four-Day Rotation

Long day	Conditioning day	Short day	Rest day
1. Endurance pitching experience	1. Endurance running	1. Short throw	1. Light throwing
2. Endurance running	2. Interval running	2. Endurance running	2. Endurance running
	3. Weight training	3. Fielding drills	3. Interval running
	4. Pappas routine		4. Pappas routine
	5. Two-ball		5. Two-ball
	6. Fielding drills		6. Fielding drills

he throws 12 to 15 pitches from full distance. He should concentrate on proper mechanics and location.

- Day 4. The fourth day is a rest day, with no live throwing to a catcher. The pitcher may play some light toss to stretch his arm, but that is the extent of the throwing.

Here are some other guidelines to follow with the four-day rotation:

- If your pitcher throws 60 or more pitches, he should have at least three days of rest before the next long throwing experience.
- If your pitcher throws between 45 and 60 pitches in a day, he should have two days of rest from long throwing. The 45- to 60-pitch range is a gray area. The more pitches he throws, the more rest he needs.
- If your pitcher throws fewer than 45 pitches, he should have at least one day of rest before throwing again.

Pitcher Progression

Arm problems and injuries can result not only from improper mechanics but also from overuse and improper handling of pitchers. To give your pitcher the greatest amount of protection from injury, monitor his endurance progression during the seven-week pitch progression. The seven-week progression allows for full development of all your pitchers (see figure 12.7).

Week 1 is a stretch week. All pitchers are to use the six-step routine

	Sunday	Monday	Tuesday	Wednesday	Thursday	Friday	Saturday
January vacation; stretching at home	5	6 Short day	7	8 Long day	9	10 Short day	11
6-step stretch week	12 4 pitches	13 Stretch to distance (60 ft, 6 in.) 7 pitches	14 All groups 10 pitches	15 13 pitches	16 17 pitches	17 Groups 1 & 3 B.P. round 13 pitches (½ speed)	18 Groups 2 & 4 B.P. round 13 pitches (½ speed)
Batting practice week; rotation starts	19 Groups 1 & 3 Batting practice 20 pitches (½ speed)	20 Groups 2 & 4 Batting practice 20 pitches (½ speed)	21 Groups 1 & 3 Batting practice 26 pitches (½ speed)	22 Groups 2 & 4 Batting practice 26 pitches (½ speed)	23 Group 1 13 pitches (½ speed) 13 pitches (¾ speed)	24 Group 2 13 pitches (½ speed) 13 pitches (¾ speed)	25 Group 3 13 pitches (½ speed) 13 pitches (¾ speed)
Rotation; live hitting	26 Group 4 13 pitches (½ speed) 13 pitches (¾ speed)	27 Group 1 15 pitches (¾ speed) 15 pitches (full speed)	28 Group 2	29 Group 3	30 Group 4	31 Group 1 39 pitches 13F 13F 13F	1 Group 2
	2 Group 2	3 Group 4	4 Group 1 45 pitches 15F 15F 15F	5 Group 2	6 Group 3	7 Group 4	8 Group 1 Indoor game; 60 pitches; 4 sets of 15
	9 Group 2	10 Group 3	11 Group 4	12 Group 1 75 pitches 15-15-15-15 F	13 Group 2	14 Group 3	15 Group 4
	16 Group 1 Indoor game; 90 pitches; 6 sets of 15	17 Group 2	18 Group 3	19 Group 4	20 Group 1 Indoor game; 105 pitches; 7 sets of 15	21 Group 2	22 Group 3
	23 Group 4	24 Group 1 Indoor game; 120 pitches; 8 sets of 15	25 Group 2	26 Group 3	27 Group 4	28 Group 1 vs. LSU	29 Group 2 vs. LSU
	1 Group 3 vs. LSU	2 Group 4 vs. LSU	3	4	5	6	7

Figure 12.7 A pitcher's seven-week progression chart.

until they are back to full distance. Once a pitcher is at full distance, he throws the required number of pitches. All pitchers involved in the program will throw the first five days. The number of pitches thrown increases each day:

- On day 1, the pitcher throws 4 pitches.
- On day 2, the pitcher throws 7 pitches.
- On day 3, the pitcher throws 10 pitches.
- On day 4, the pitcher throws 13 pitches.
- On day 5, the pitcher throws 17 pitches.

After he has completed the required number of pitches each day, it is important for the pitcher to cool down. The cool-down will vary from day to day. On day 1, from half distance (30 feet) and at half speed, he should throw two sets of spins, including forward (the spin of a fastball), backward (a curve spin), and change (the spin of a change-up). As a cool-down on day 2, he will throw three sets of spins, on day 3 four sets of spins, and so on until he finishes day 5 of practice. As he spins the ball to the catcher, he must concentrate on proper mechanics and stretching.

The goal of rotation and each pitching experience is twofold. First, the pitcher must master the strike zone and concentrate on mechanics. Second, the pitcher will increase the number of pitches thrown every fourth day through game experiences.

To build endurance and strength, the pitcher will increase the number of pitches he throws on the long throwing day by 15 pitches each time. Have your pitchers throw these extra 15 pitches at only half to three-quarter speed. They continue with that way until they reach the desired number of pitches for their role. Starting pitchers and long relievers will progress to 120 pitches. Middle relievers will work to 80 or 100 pitches, and closers will work in the 45- to 60-pitch range.

If you have only four or five weeks of preseason, you obviously cannot use the seven-week progression. Having less time to develop your pitchers means you have to develop more pitchers who can throw longer. If you have four or five weeks to prepare, your starters will be able to throw 60 to 90 pitches, depending on the routine. In a five-week progression, your starting pitchers and long relievers should be able to throw in the 70- to 80-pitch range. In four weeks, they should be able to throw in the 60- to 70-pitch range. This will get you through only four or five innings. Consequently, you need to have more pitchers prepared to get you through the game (see figure 12.8).

Sunday	Monday	Tuesday	Wednesday	Thursday	Friday	Saturday
	12	**13** Stretch to distance (60 ft, 6 in.)	**14**	**15**	**16**	**17**
	10 pitches	13 pitches	17 pitches	Rest	B.P. round 13 pitches (½ speed) 13 pitches (¾ speed)	
18 13 pitches (¾ speed) 13 pitches (full speed)	**19**	**20** Short day	**21**	**22** 15 pitches (full speed)	**23**	**24** Short day
25	**26** 30 pitches 15-15	**27**	**28** Short day	**29**	**30** 45 pitches 15-15-15	**1**
2 Short day	**3**	**4** 60 pitches 15-15-15	**5**	**6** Short day	**7**	**8** Game 60 to 75 pitches

Figure 12.8 A pitcher's four-week progression chart.

159

The Daily Practice Schedule

Daily schedules keep your practices running smoothly and your players involved. When players understand their daily responsibilities, practice becomes efficient and focused. We believe in keeping all players involved in practice at all times. While pitches do pitcher drills, outfielders may be hitting off the tees.

Tables 12.2 and 12.3 outline a daily practice session. Table 12.2 shows the time frame and responsibilities of the players involved in drills. These drills take place in the basic skills area. Pitchers are involved in pitcher drills from 3:00 to 3:10. During this period, they practice throws to each base, covering first, squeeze plays, wild-pitch drills, and holding runners on. From 3:10 to 3:50, they learn how to cover bunt, steal, rundown, and batted-ball situations with a runner on first.

Table 12.3 outlines the responsibilities of all pitchers and players involved in live pitching and hitting. This takes place in the designated pitching and hitting area. This particular schedule assumes that the pitching and hitting area has two cages. If your pitching and hitting area has only one cage, you should use a different chart.

TABLE 12.2

A Daily Practice Schedule

Time	Activity	Time	Activity
2:50	Team stretching	3:30	Defense versus rundown, runner at first
3:00	Pitcher drills: D'Andrea, Novio, Nadeau, Thomas, Dryswak, Hewes, Beaudet, Dillon, Johnson A. Throw to first, second, and third B. Cover first, squeeze, squeeze C. Wild pitch D. Holding runners	3:40	Defense versus batted ball, Little League
		3:50	Square drill: Delucia Knox Seguin Scott Sweeney Tate Slicer Hartung Johnson Small Wild Wilson Beal Duff Tall Kelliher
3:10	Defense versus bunt, runner at first	4:00	Outfield drills: Sweeney, White, Beal, Lucas
3:20	Defense versus steal, runner at first	4:10	Infield drills: Knox Seguin Delucia Scott Slicer Willey Thompson Trundy
		4:30	Bunting, baserunning

┌─ TABLE 12.3 ───┐

A Daily Schedule for Live Pitching and Hitting

Area 1	Area 2
4:00 **P** Higgins (15) **B** Thomas **C** Kelliher **H** Knox, Seguin, Scott	4:00 **P** Burlingame (15) **B** Dryswak **C** Ender **H** Delucia, Hartung, Slicer
4:08 **P** Brenner (15) **B** Smith **C** Thrasher **H** Knox, Seguin, Scott	4:08 **P** Dillon (15) **B** Therrien **C** King **H** Delucia, Hartung, Slicer
4:16 **P** Burlingame (15) **B** D'Andrea **C** Delaney **H** White, Kelliher, Tobin	4:16 **P** Higgins (15) **B** Hewes **C** Taylor **H** Sweeney, Ender, Taylor
4:24 **P** Dillon (15) **B** Brown **C** Tobin **H** Knox, Seguin, Scott	4:24 **P** Brenner (15) **B** Small **C** Thrasher **H** Sweeney, Ender, Taylor
4:32 **P** Higgins (15) **B** Novio **C** Kelliher **H** White, Tobin, D'Andrea	4:32 **P** Burlingame (15) **B** Nadeau **C** King **H** Sweeney, Taylor, Ender
4:40 **P** Brenner (15) **B** Kelliher **C** Tobin **H** Knox, Seguin, Scott	4:40 **P** Dillon (15) **B** Radulski **C** Ender **H** Delucia, Hartung, Slicer
4:48 **P** Burlingame (15) **B** Slicer **C** Kelliher **H** Delucia, Hartung, Scott, White	4:48 **P** Higgins (15) **B** Domenick **C** King **H** Knox, Sweeney, Seguin, Ender
4:56 **P** Dillon (15) **B** White **C** Delaney **H** Kelliher, Tobin, D'Andrea, Hewes	4:56 **P** Taylor (15) **B** Knox **C** Thrasher **H** Slicer, King, Rajotte, Duff
5:04 **P** Higgins (15) **B** Rajotte **C** Kelliher **H** Delucia, Scott, Hartung, White	5:04 **P** Burlingame (15) **B** Hewes **C** Ender **H** Knox, Seguin, Sweeney, Taylor
5:12 **P** Dryswak (15) **B** Seguin **C** Thrasher **H** Kelliher, Tobin, D'Andrea, King	5:12 **P** Beaudet (15) **B** Sweeney **C** Delaney **H** Ender, Taylor, Slicer, Ballard
5:20 **P** Burlingame (15) **B** Thrasher **C** King **H** Delucia, Hartung, Scott, White	5:20 **P** Higgins (15) **B** Delaney **C** Tobin **H** Knox, Sweeney, Seguin, Ender

Numbers in parentheses = number of pitches; **P** = pitcher; **C** = catcher; **H** = hitter; **B** = charts pitches

└──┘

In the outline shown, the time frame of each sequence is in the left-hand column. Each session designates an inning. The first inning begins at 4:00 and runs to 4:08. The second inning runs from 4:08 to 4:16 and so on until the required innings have been fulfilled. The pitchers (P) designated for assignment are placed at the top of the inning, followed by the number of pitches for that particular inning. Higgins and Burlingame throw 15 pitches the first inning. Brenner and Dillon throw 15 pitches the second inning. Burlingame and Higgins throw another 15 pitches the third inning. This continues until all pitchers have completed their long throwing. On this day, Higgins and Burlingame will throw 90 pitches over six innings.

The catcher (C) should be labeled under or next to the pitcher. During the first inning, Kelliher catches Higgins, and Ender catches Burlingame.

TABLE 12.4

The Pitchers' Weekly Practice Schedule

Monday	Tuesday	Wednesday	Thursday	Friday	Saturday	Sunday
Group 1	Group 2	Group 3	Group 4	Group 1	Group 2	Group 3
Endurance 45 pitches	Endurance 45 pitches	Endurance 45 pitches	Endurance 45 pitches	Endurance 60 pitches	Endurance 60 pitches	Endurance 60 pitches
Pitcher drills	Pitcher drills	Pitcher drills	Pitcher drills	Game	Game	Game
Situation: Man on 1st	Situation: Man on 1st	Situation: Men on 1st and 2nd	Situation: Men on 1st and 2nd			

Underneath the catchers should be the hitters (H). In the first inning, Knox, Seguin, and Scott will hit against Higgins; Delucia, Hartung, and Slicer will hit against Burlingame. Each inning someone (B) is needed to chart the pitches thrown. Thomas and Dryswak will chart pitches the first inning.

Providing Live Pitching Opportunities

A pitcher needs the chance to become both mentally and physically prepared for his game-day duties. Throwing to a batter in a game is completely different from throwing to a catcher in practice. By providing live pitching situations, you give your pitchers a chance to develop mechanics, endurance, confidence in throwing strikes, and mastery of the strike zone. Table 12.4 provides an example of a pitcher's weekly practice schedule.

Four Productive Pitching Drills

Any team with visions of a championship season should have its pitchers spend time on all facets of the game, including fielding ground balls, covering bases, understanding plays, and becoming comfortable with the players behind them. We usually focus on pitcher drills four times a week, incorporating them into our practices Monday through Thursday.

In designing pitcher drills, try to provide as many repetitions for as many pitchers as possible as they learn to field bunts, cover bases, and hold runners. We strive for all pitchers, catchers, and infielders to become accustomed to working with each other. Each of the following pitcher drills may be used in limited space and can be completed in 15 to 20 minutes.

- **Drill 1: Fielding bunted balls.** Pitchers field bunts and throw to each base. The first baseman and the third baseman make the call on who fields the ball. The catcher makes the call on where the ball is thrown.

- **Drill 2: Cover first, squeeze, squeeze.** Pitchers practice fielding squeeze bunts and covering first. Catchers practice tag and double-play throw.

- **Drill 3: Wild pitch.** This drill emphasizes the call made by pitcher to catcher after a wild pitch. They direct the catcher to go right, middle, or left depending on where the catcher needs to go to retrieve the ball.

- **Drill 4: Holding runners.** Pitchers practice holding runners at first base and second base.

Hitting Indoors

Ted Williams, former Boston Red Sox standout and the last major leaguer to hit .400 in a complete season, once said, "To be a good hitter, you must be quick with the bat and get a good pitch to hit." Our philosophy concurs and advises the hitter to look at the ball, develop a level shoulder-to-shoulder swing, rotate the hips, and gain momentum toward the pitcher.

When working with hitters, we aim to develop a simple hitting routine that enables hitters to gain quickness with the bat and master the strike zone. The routine is scheduled to give hitters a chance to improve hand quickness through a number of mandatory repetitions and work on eliminating any problems that slow the swing. The routine also provides live hitting opportunities so hitters can master the strike zone and develop mission hitting.

In developing hitters indoors, we schedule two types of hitting—batting practice and live hitting. In batting practice drills, hitters take 250 swings through heavy-bat drills, batting-tee drills, toss-and-hit drills, and half-cage hitting. Live hitting provides game experience though live pitching. We put hitters in situations such as a 2-1 count with a man on first. We use game-situation live hitting to maximize the productivity of our hitting approach.

Mission Hitting

In developing team offense philosophy, we keep things simple. We believe the best guide to follow is mission hitting. For every at bat, the hitter has a challenge and a mission. That mission may be to get on base, to move a runner, or to drive in a runner. If no one is on base, the hitter must try to get on. If a runner is on base, the hitter must find a way of advancing him and keeping the inning going. If a runner is in scoring position, the hitter must find a way to drive the runner home or at least extend the inning so someone else can drive him home.

In practice we always create game situations that allow hitters to practice and become confident in mission hitting. Live hitting provides experience with different hitting counts and game situations.

Mastering the Strike Zone

As a hitter, one of the toughest mental flaws to overcome is swinging at balls out of the strike zone or chasing pitches that are hard to drive. As a coach, we seek to develop a routine that makes hitting good pitches automatic. The easiest ways to master the strike zone is through simulated game situations. This is how hitters learn to get good pitches to hit for each mission.

Hitting Drills

Our hitting drills emphasize four key factors:

- Chin—for the look at the ball
- Shoulder—for the shoulder-to-shoulder swing
- Knee—for gained momentum and shift off the weight
- Heel—for proper hip drive and follow-through

Players practice these four factors as they develop the correct swing through a number of mandatory repetitions. The repetitions should include (1) using heavy or weighted bats, (2) hitting-tee drills, (3) toss-and-hit drills, (4) half-cage swings, (5) batting practice, and (6) live hitting. These are the productive indoor drills.

Marc Sweeney, who played in the 1998 World Series for the San Diego Padres, worked indoors tirelessly on these drills. It certainly developed him as a hitter preseason and in-season.

Six Heavy-Bat Drills

We believe that heavy-bat drills help to get quick with the bat. The heavy-bat routine is a set of drills designed to strengthen and quicken the wrists while developing good hitting mechanics. There are six drills, each consisting of 10 repetitions.

- **Drill 1: Hip drill.** Holding the bat behind his back, in the small of the back, the hitter assumes his stance. As he takes his stride toward the pitcher, he shifts his weight from the back leg to the front knee, rotates his back heel to make use of the hips, and finishes with his back knee pointing toward the front knee. In the finished position, the barrel of the bat should be at the point of contact.

- **Drill 2: Ax Drill I.** With the bat in both hands and arms extended at chin height, the hitter raises the bat over his head, touches his backside, and brings the bat back to the starting point, as though he is chopping wood.

- **Drill 3: Ax Drill II.** With the bat in both hands and arms extended at chin height, the hitter moves his wrists up and down, taking the bat from the starting point and, moving his wrists only, bringing it to his hitting shoulder and then back to the starting point.

- **Drill 4: Shoulder, Contact, Shoulder.** Assuming his stance, the batter places his hands at the starting point of the swing. The bat is even with his back shoulder, and his hands are even with the armpit and back knee. The hitter gains momentum in the plane of the swing, going from the back shoulder to the contact point, with arms extended. He finishes the swing, emphasizing the look at the ball, the shift of weight to the front knee, and rotation of the back heel and hips.

- **Drill 5: Top-Hand Drill.** This drill is performed the same way as the shoulder-to-shoulder drill, except the player uses only the top hand. This drill develops coordination of the top hand in rotation with the hips and back heel. The hitter then performs this drill using the bottom hand pulling the bat shoulder to shoulder.

- **Drill 6: Shoulder-To-Shoulder Drill.** This drill is similar to drill 4, but here the hitter doesn't stop at the contact point. The hitter should assume his proper stance with the bat at its starting point of the swing. The hitter strides to the simulated pitch and practices a full swing, ending with the bat against his front shoulder. The emphasis of this drill is on driving the top hand and pulling the bottom hand simultaneously.

Other Productive Indoor Hitting Drills

We feel that the best batting practice drills indoors are batting-tee drills, soft-toss drills, and half-cage hitting drills (figure 12.9).

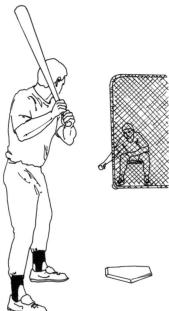

Figure 12.9   The half-cage hitting drill.

These drills, more than most others, force the hitter to look at the ball and recognize the need to avoid moving the chin. It is my view that these drills best serve the hitter when they become a daily part of the hitting routine. In the batting-tee and soft-toss drills, we recommend doing this with both the top and bottom hands to develop concentration in looking at the ball.

Base Running and Bunting

Base running and bunting are skills we try to combine in planning a practice. We aim to accomplish base running when our full squad is present. It is ideal to do this at the beginning of a practice session, but class schedules and afternoon labs often make this difficult. When labs or class schedules create problems, we schedule combination bunting and running at the end so everyone gets the experience and conditioning involved.

We always do form-running drills first. From that point, we create situations for the use of a sacrifice bunt, bunt for base hit, run and bunt, and so on. We use base coaches and various kinds of base running and leads. We normally like to conclude with the four-bases drill.

• **Drill: Four bases.** The pitcher works from the stretch, and the base runners take their leads. The first two hitters each have a bat and take their stances at home plate. The pitcher comes to the set position and simulates a delivery to the plate.

The base runners run to their designated destinations. The hitter closest to the plate takes a full swing and runs out a double. The hitter farthest from the pitcher bunts for a hit-and-run to the outside of first base. Once at first, he moves to the inside first base and takes his lead. The runner who was originally at first runs to third. The original runner at second scores, running to the farthest plate and going to the end of that line. The original runner at third scores at the first plate and goes to the end of that line. Once this has been completed, all bases should be full of runners, and the next two hitters step to the plate.

Again, the pitcher comes to the set and simulates pitch delivery. The drill continues. If the runners go to the correct bases, they will continually rotate and get repetitions at each base.

Fielding

In planning the defensive phase of practice, the focus is on basic skill opportunities and drills that practice execution of proper throwing, catching, getting momentum, and so on. Your team must execute basic fielding and throwing skills.

Drills for Infielders

Infielders need to develop agility, acceleration, and quickness to increase infield range. They must be able to field a batted ball hit at them, to their glove side, or to their throwing side; be able to get in proper throwing position to make the baseball throw; be able to make the appropriate feed to the base required; and be able to execute the turn and completion of the double play. To be a good team, you must execute basic skills and be able to make the double play. You should work on these skills daily.

In double-play ball handling, infielders must execute appropriate feeds and be able to redirect the ball. Practice ball handling each day with drills.

To work on individual skills, we especially like to use the square drill, which we can practice in almost any indoor area with space. It allows players to practice fielding and throwing on balls hit at them, to their throwing side, and to their glove side. We schedule this drill as an everyday priority (see table 12.2).

The multiple ball-handling drills we present are among the best for practicing ball handling in limited space and time. We schedule them each practice day as part of the infield drill section.

• **Drill: Square Drill.** An open area the size of a basketball court is most beneficial. Four coaches or players hit ground balls, and four receive throws from the fielders. Four to 12 players field ground balls.

The fielders set up in their normal positions around the infield. Reserves and outfielders fill in behind the infielders, three at each fielding position. You need one hitter and one receiver opposite each fielding position. When all fielders, hitters, and receivers are in position, the configuration will look like a square.

Each hitter hits a ground ball to his respective fielder. Once the fielder has received the ground ball, he throws to his respective catcher. After the fielder finishes taking a ground ball, he goes to the end of the line until his turn comes again. Players rotate in their respective lines.

This drill takes about 15 minutes (5 minutes per fielding angle). The first 5 minutes are designated for ground balls hit directly at the fielders. The next 10 minutes are for fielders to work on lateral movement (fielding ground balls to their left and right). You can also shorten the drill to 10 minutes—4 minutes straight at the players, 3 minutes on the glove side, and 3 minutes on the throwing side.

• **Drill: 6-4-3 and 4-6-3.** Shortstops, second basemen, and first basemen work on the 6-4-3 and 4-6-3 double plays. Hit double-play balls directly at, to the left, and to the right of the shortstop and the second baseman. Spend 5 minutes a day on each angle.

Catchers, third basemen, and first basemen work on the slow roller, dead ball, and squeeze. First and third basemen will be at their respective positions about 70 feet from the catcher. You will be about 5 feet behind the catcher. Devote 5 minutes to each fielding section—slow rollers, dead ball, and squeeze plays.

• **Drill: 5-4-3 and 3-6-3.** Divide into two groups—third, second, and first basemen for the 5-4-3 drill and first basemen and shortstops for the 3-6-3 drill.

The square drill and multiple ball-handling drills prepared Mike Bordick of the Oakland A's and Baltimore Orioles for multiple infield roles in the major leagues. Mike is known best as a fine shortstop, yet his first starting chance with the A's was at second base. He has also started at third base.

Drills for Outfielders

Getting outfielders ready indoors is obviously a concern because space. It's helpful, when possible, to involve outfielders in some of the basic throwing and fielding skills scheduled for infielders (for example, the square drill).

Building arm strength has always been our priority in preparing outfielders. Drills include one-knee throwing, long toss, hip drill, and momentum throwing. It is important to work on arm strength daily.

Making good reads on balls coming off the bat and getting the best jump and angle (first step with the outside foot) are things we try to accomplish with indoor drills. The following three drills can serve this need.

• **Drill: Angled ground balls.** You'll need two coaches and a group of outfielders. The coaches stand about 20 to 25 feet apart. Two lines of outfielders are 10 feet in front of and facing the coaches. Coach 1 rolls a ball straight toward the wall. Outfielder 1 opens, chases, and fields the ball. After fielding the ball he turns and throws the ball to coach 2. Coach 2 rolls the ball straight toward the wall. Outfielder 2 opens, chases, and fields the ball. After fielding the ball, he turns and throws the ball to coach 1. The outfielders switch lines continually, practicing from both angles.

• **Drill: Fielding angled fly balls.** Drills for fielding fly balls are designed and run the same way as drills for fielding ground balls. Coach 1 lofts a fly ball. Outfielder 2 opens, chases, and catches the fly ball. After catching the ball, he turns and throws to coach 2. Coach 2 lofts a fly ball. Outfielder 1 opens, chases, and catches the ball. After catching the ball, he turns and throws to coach 1. The players rotate lines.

- **Drill: Fielding fly balls directly overhead.** If you are practicing indoors, a normal-sized gym is sufficient. Two coaches and two lines of outfielders are needed. The lines of players are about 20 feet apart, with a coach at the head of each line. Each coach tosses a ball over the head of the outfielder. The outfielder opens glove side and chases and catches the fly ball. After catching the ball, he arrests his momentum and throws to coach 1.

Catchers

In our practice planning, we divide the catchers' practice day into two parts. First, as noted in table 12.3, each catcher is scheduled to catch several assigned pitchers in the live pitching and hitting section of each practice. Second, depending on the nature of the other drills scheduled, catchers normally have a daily 10-minute drill period during the outfield drill period.

In the live pitching and hitting part of our practice, catchers get game-day experience in handling each pitcher. We emphasize (a) mastering communication with each pitcher, (b) working on framing borderline pitchers for strikes, (c) learning the strength and weaknesses of each pitcher, (d) learning each pitcher's repertoire of pitches, (e) learning what each pitcher can throw for strikes, and (f) learning each pitcher's out pitch. Each game-day experience is invaluable in developing the pitcher-catcher relationship.

In the drill phase catchers work daily on (a) grip drills, (b) receiving drills, (c) framing drills, (d) bad-ball drills, and (e) swing drills. Catchers usually work in pairs on each drill.

We emphasize that the catcher's most challenging duty is handling the pitching staff and getting the most out of the pitching talent we have.

Team Defense

We work to have an organized system for preparing our team to react to and to master all emerging defensive situations. Communication is essential in teaching and understanding team defense. All players involved must know correct defensive positioning for cutoffs, relays, and base coverages. The best way to learn team defense is by practicing game situations. To be solid defensively, a team must be able to handle all priority calls, cutoffs, relays, and base coverages resulting from batted balls, attempted bunts, attempted steals, and emerging rundown situations (table 12.5).

On every pitch something may happen, so it is critical for all players to understand their roles in defending against every possible situation. Before each pitch is thrown, every defensive player must know what to do once the ball is hit, fielded, and thrown. The following team defense drill is our favorite for reacting to each base-running situation—batted ball, bunt, steal, or rundown.

• **Drill: Little League.** Construct an infield with the bases about 40 feet apart. Place all eight everyday players and a pitcher at their positions. The setup should reflect a particular situation. A coach stands behind the catcher. Place a runner in your desired situation and put a batter at the plate. Simply throw the ball to an area and call out what kind of hit is it—single, double, or triple. Considering your calls (such as man on first, no one out, double to the eight-center gap), the players move to their correct positions, working on calls, relays, cuts, and base coverage. With the Little League set, you may work on all possibilities—batted balls, attempted bunts, attempted steals, and emerging rundown situations.

Indoors, Little League is one of the best drills for helping your players understand the whole defensive scheme. For each day, we schedule a particular situation focus for practicing team defense (see figure 12.9). For example, Monday, the focus is man on first versus batted ball, bunt, steal, and rundown.

Maintaining Flexibility

This chapter has highlighted what has worked for us in our planning and preparation for baseball readiness indoors. I have tried to center on what has been helpful in attaining readiness when getting outdoors is impossible.

The key has been our philosophy about goals, establishing priorities, maximizing space, and being organized. Our teams have always been able to compete satisfactorily after this preparation indoors. Finally, in handling indoor preparation, a coach needs to be able to adjust and maintain flexibility. Being indoors in a confined space with limited time often tests your ability to adjust to the unexpected—emergencies, sudden schedule changes, sickness, absences, injuries, whatever.

It is hard to anticipate these sudden needs to adjust. I have found that maintaining flexibility enables us to handle the many adjustments we have to make. I've always looked at this need to adjust as a game-like

TABLE 12.5

Team Defense Situations

Batted ball:

1. Priority calls: Who fields the ball
2. Cut-offs: coverage responsibility
3. A. Runner at 1st
    1. Hit to left
    2. Hit to center, right
   B. Runner at 2nd
    1. Hit to left
    2. Hit to center, right
   C. Runners at 1st, 2nd, 3rd
    1. Hit at left fielder
    2. Hit to the right or left of left fielder
   D. Runners at 1st, 2nd, 3rd
    1. Hit at right or center fielders
    2. Hit to the right or left of right or center fielder
4. Extra base hits
   A. Hit to the left side
   B. Hit to center or right
5. Coverage of infielders with runners at 2nd, and 2nd & 3rd
   A. Hit to P or 1B
   B. Hit to 2B
   C. Hit to SS
   D. Hit to 3B

Bunt:

1. Priority call: Who fields the bunt? Where is the ball to be thrown?
2. Coverage responsibility
   A. Regular coverage
   B. Trap coverage
3. Runner(s) at:
    1. 1st
    2. 2nd
    3. 1st & 2nd
    4. 3rd
    5. 2nd & 3rd
    6. 1st, 2nd, 3rd
    7. 1st & 3rd

Steal:

1. Priority calls
2. Coverage responsibility
3. Runner(s) at:
   A. 1st
   B. 2nd
   C. 1st & 2nd (double steal)
   D. 1st & 3rd (double steal)

Rundown:

1. Responsibility and execution: runner(s) at:
    1. 1st
    2. 2nd
    3. 3rd
    4. 1st & 3rd

Sunday	Monday	Tuesday	Wednesday	Thursday	Friday	Saturday
12	13 Drill work—week long	14	15	16	17	18
19	20 Drill work—week long	21	22	23	24	25
26	27 Man on (1st)	28 Man on (1st)	29 Man on (2nd)	30 Man on (2nd)	31 Practice games	1 Practice games
2 Practice games	3 Man on (3rd)	4 Man on (3rd)	5 Men on (1st & 3rd)	6 Men on (1st & 3rd)	7 Practice games	8 Practice games
9 Practice games	10 Men on (1st), (2nd)	11 Men on (1st), (2nd)	12 Man on (3rd), (1st & 3rd)	13 Man on (3rd), (1st & 3rd)	14 Practice games	15 Practice games
16	17 Review	18 Review	19 Review	20 Review	21 Season opener	22
23	24	25	26	27	28	1
2	3	4	5	6	7	

Figure 12.9 A sample team defense practice schedule for the weeks leading up to the season opener.

test for me as a coach. My philosophy has been to make the necessary planning and practice changes as I do in an actual game. This approach works with the personnel changes that we have to make for the practice of a given day. Try to stay on course within your game plan yet be ready to adjust. Maintain flexibility yet stay on course toward your goals for getting your team ready.

A Closing Note

What I presented in this chapter has been invaluable for us in indoor baseball activity, preseason and in-season. I have found that by maximizing use of available time and space and by being productive in everything we practice, we get the most from each indoor practice session. Further, by consistently maximizing the value of each practice day, we are confident that our team is ready for the season opener.

CHAPTER THIRTEEN

Putting Science Into Practice

Gary Pullins and Tom House

Coaches and their players are preparing, competing, and repairing in an age of information. Even baseball traditionalists would have to agree that sport science and sports medicine have affected the game. Biomechanics now has computerized a three-dimensional motion analysis to assess a pitcher's delivery or a hitter's swing. Doctors can look inside an athlete's body with MRIs and arthroscopic surgeries in prehab and rehab situations. Strength and conditioning coaches can be specific with physical

Sport science is revealing that what the good coaches have been teaching for the last 125 years *is* biomechanically sound.

preparation, training muscles to handle the precise movements and workloads required by baseball. Metabolisms can be managed with nutritional intake ratios or blood chemistry enhancers. Not surprisingly, a player's thinking can be mentally and emotionally profiled. Performance can be enhanced with conscious and subconscious affirmation and imagery. And if that's not enough, all of it can be accessed on the Internet!

This barrage of information is a bit intimidating, so baseball people tend to ignore it in favor of opinion. Others find that when they share all this information with a player, he acquires a good case of paralysis by analysis. After all, baseball is an art, not a science, right? Well, not exactly. The goal of this chapter is to keep coaches, young and old, from making the game too complex with science while encouraging them use any resource that will benefit their players and teams. The plan is to combine the practical, proven methods of experienced coaches with the new possibilities of contemporary research and technology. The two have a lot more in common than people in baseball would think. Yes, science can meet practicality. The purpose of this chapter is to point out these common denominators.

First let's examine a few facts about information and instruction in today's game. Sport science is revealing that what the good coaches have been teaching for the last 125 years *is* biomechanically sound. Through intuition, observation, trial and error, they have developed teaching protocols to reinforce exactly what computers and digitized motion analysis are now telling us about a throw, a pitch, or a swing. Is this merely a statement of the obvious? Not really, because what the eyes see is sometimes not what's going on in a movement. Successful instructors, with or without technology to back them up, seem to be three-dimensional thinkers.

Do seasoned baseball experts use a different vocabulary? Yes. The *Arizona Republic* sports page does a credible job of following minor-league players from the Phoenix area. After a less-than-spectacular season, I was visiting with Uncle Cliff, who had also played minor-league baseball 20 years earlier. Uncle Cliff mentioned that he had noticed in the paper my rather dismal batting average and asked, "What pitch is getting you out?"

I responded, "Hey, everybody knows the slider is the out pitch."

The old-timer immediately inquired, "What the heck is a slider?"

After Uncle Cliff heard my discourse on the rudiments of a slider and how effectively it could be used, he said, "That's nothing but a nickel curve." Through the years, pitchers who didn't have a good curveball worked on throwing the slider harder and harder. This made many pitchers wealthy, and some people think it made many orthopedic surgeons wealthy too. It may have been the pitch of the 1960s, but it was still a nickel curve! It's a matter of semantics. Nonetheless, your players and you need to speak the same language.

Different terminology? Yes. Publish a vocabulary list. You and your athletes will be on the same page. Different goals? No. Gary Adams of UCLA related a story that illustrates this point. During fall tryouts, all the pitchers were on the mound for a pitchers' fielding drill. To make the drill gamelike, Coach Adams had his catcher put on all the gear and sent hitters to the plate equipped with a hard hat and a bat to bunt strikes thrown by each pitcher. One of the young freshman pitchers, whom Coach Adams seldom gave an opportunity to pitch during scrimmage games, had caused each hitter to flinch when it was his turn to throw.

Chapter co-author and sports scientist, Tom House.

He had an unorthodox delivery, and the hitters were not sure that he could throw a strike. It was apparent that no one was going to dig in on this young left-hander.

The next day, Coach Adams decided that if they could not bunt off this guy maybe they couldn't hit off him either. Adams put him in an intrasquad game, and the youngster proved to be an effective relief pitcher for the Bruins that season. Observing a drill, analyzing the performance, and having some experience paid off. The coaching elite teach empirically what research and development reveal objectively. Historically they've prepared their players to compete with a proper mix of mental, physical, nutritional, and mechanical work. They have always sought to minimize the risk of injury and strike a balance between preparation and competition. For, between the lines, baseball is still played the way it was 50 years ago, even with the addition of metal bats, bigger gloves, high-top shoes, Oakleys, and artificial turf. It's no secret that most of the game's changes have taken place outside the lines.

Today's athletes are less skilled. The talent bestowed by genetics is still present, and better nutrition and conditioning have allowed kids to be bigger, faster, and stronger. We aren't saying they aren't better athletes; we said they are less skilled in baseball. They don't play as much baseball, so they don't develop and polish game sense and physical tools in their youth. Why? The only time youngsters play baseball is in a structured practice or scheduled game. The story goes that a young baseball fan was engaging an old-timer in a conversation about whether Ty Cobb would be able to hit as effectively in the big leagues today. (Cobb had a .367 lifetime batting average over two decades in the big leagues, using his running speed to advantage in the dead-ball era.) When the old-timer was asked what Cobb would hit today, he responded, "About .310."

The younger fan, surprised by the concession, asked, "Oh, and why would it be that Cobb would only hit .310 in the big leagues today?"

The answer came with a chuckle, "He would be 105 years old!"

Cobb knew how to play the game within the framework of his skill because first he had played sandlot ball. Few kids today play catch with a buddy. No one plays work-up, stickball, over-the-line, or simply tries to hit bottle caps with a broomstick. There are too many other things to do—other sports, video games, rehearsals. Fields and sandlots are, literally and figuratively, empty of baseball. What's worse, by some twist of logic, administrators have mandated fewer coaching and playing hours at all levels of the amateur game, from Little League to college.

In the summer of 1993, Team USA was in Sancti Spiritus, Cuba, for a series with the Cuban national team. They were scheduled to play that night in the largest building in the entire town, the baseball stadium, and the players decided they wanted to go downtown to check out the sights. Because the Cuban people either don't have cars or have no gasoline to put in the few they do have, the native children were playing stickball and baseball in the middle of the main thoroughfare. Quick observation revealed that their skill level was very good in spite of the absence of gloves, spikes, and aluminum bats. The player who most noticeably lacked equipment was the catcher, who was behind home plate with a mask, a worn-out glove, and a smile. The ball these young players were using looked like a dried orange but harder, and every now and then the catcher took foul tips that had to smart. These were the Cuban national team players in embryo. They had no coach. Their instruction came from watching their heroes in that big stadium each night. They modeled what they saw and learned from one another. There was nothing really to inhibit their development as players because it was obvious that they were having a great time. Their approach to the game, although much simplified, was technically solid simply because of the number of repetitions and the modeling approach to learning.

Baseball requires repetition and experience to develop skill. If proportionately fewer kids practice fewer hours and play fewer games, then time becomes a critical coaching variable. Look at the equation:

information and instruction + practice + competition =
coaching experience + player development

You'll note that coaching experience and player development depend on information, instruction, practice, and competition. Obviously, less practice and competition puts a premium on the quality of baseball information and instruction. Although contemporary coaches may not have as much time to gain experience and develop players as their predecessors did, they do have better access to more information, which helps facilitate better instruction. They can get the what, the why, and the how immediately. The outcome is that the learning curve of an inexperienced young coach should become shorter. If he gets better faster, so should his players. Is this happening? Yes, but not as fast as it can.

Let's look at some of the critical research being learned and applied by successful modern coaches. Performance during practice involves proper preparation for competition—mentally, physically, nutritionally, and biomechanically. Players absorb energy, direct energy, and deliver energy into a bat or baseball. Performance can be enhanced through dynamic balance, postural stabilization, and equal and opposite joint integrity. Batters can improve by using an efficient axis of torso rotation. Pitchers excel by having both elbows in front of the center of gravity at release point. With workloads, that is, swings and pitches, athletes are only as strong as their weakest sequentially loaded muscle-energy link. They are only as efficient as their worst mechanical movement. In addition, neither strength nor good mechanics can overcome poor blood chemistry or mental and emotional instability. Too much to think about? Don't panic because we're going to discuss each of these points, one at a time, and provide examples. You'll be surprised how simple it is when we translate it into baseballeze, the language spoken by the coaching legends in their chapters of *The Baseball Coaching Bible*.

First, let's quickly review the four performance constants for success in competition: mental conditioning, physical conditioning, nutritional conditioning, and biomechanical conditioning. Each athlete must manage these absolutes, finding a balance in preparation and competition. They can be taught by coaches who possess just a rudimentary understanding of the theory behind these concepts. Here's a brief description and explanation of each, based on contemporary sport science and sports medicine but expressed in baseball vocabulary.

Mental Conditioning

Mental conditioning is really both mental and emotional management, an absolute that starts with persistence. Baseball is a game of failure. If a youngster cannot deal with striking out, making errors, giving up hits, and losing, he'll never succeed in the game. Good coaches intuitively teach (1) managing feelings of failure, (2) not following the path of failure, (3) visualizing success in the face of failure, and (4) affirming the process of success. Persistence is reinforced when a player can identity why he did or didn't do the job and then is given the means by which to maintain good, or avoid bad, performance. The positive psychological, neurological, and immunological feedback that comes with success has to be stronger than the negative feedback that comes with failure. Persistence, which can be defined as mental or emotional toughness, comes when an athlete understands that feelings of failure are temporary and he is confident of his ability to make adjustments and, therefore, be successful next time. In equation form, it looks like this:

preparation + confidence + opportunity to perform = success

The will to win, then, must be stronger than the fear of defeat. In baseball terms, being successful means knowing how to fail fewer times than your competitor, and then mentally and emotionally managing the process to increase your chances of being successful on the field in the next effort.

Reduced to simplest terms, many players fear two things in baseball—failing and being hit by a baseball. When asked if he was ever afraid at home plate, the great Harmon Killebrew answered, "Afraid? No. Terrified? Yes." Even this big strong guy who hit more than 500 home runs in the big leagues was frightened. When defining his fear, Killebrew explained that one was the fear of being hit and the other, and most critical, was the fear of failure. Killebrew learned to manage those fears. Players might deal with fears differently at each level. To combat them, Little Leaguers and youth-league players need the opportunity of fielding and hitting a baseball at a speed that allows them to enjoy success. If the practice pitcher throws too hard, lets the ball gets away from him, and plunks the hitter, positive learning will not occur. And what about the infielder whose coach or dad continues to hit ground balls on a rough infield where it is difficult for the young player to make a play without being injured?

Thus, building success into the practice experience is important when working with youth baseball. The more accomplished player has progressed to the point where he can contend with his fear of failure. The key to training older players, however, is almost identical to that used with youth, although it is a more accelerated version. That is to say, a more accomplished player (high school and beyond) can be put in a practice situation that is gamelike or, when using a pitching machine, may exceed the need of a game. A hitter may build confidence in a batting tunnel with the pitching machine throwing fast enough that it will eventually defeat him. The hitter will learn to make adjustments. He will go away knowing that he can handle a pitcher who has good velocity because he's been defeated in a practice setting and has learned to make the necessary adaptations. The motto here might be "Get beat in practice so you can win on game day." Too few baseball players and teams practice the hard things in a rehearsal setting. We seem to wait until game day to do something difficult when we should manage it daily in practice.

Note here that it's extremely difficult, if not impossible, to be both a hitting instructor and the head coach, to be both a pitching coach and the head coach, or even to teach the rudiments of the game and at the same time be the head coach. Because most of us find ourselves being both a professor and a strategist, it's important to separate these duties. On practice day a great deal of teaching must go on. During a ballgame, when you have posted the lineup and half the team is already mad at you for not starting them, you become a strategist. Some teaching moments may occur on game day, for sure, but you should often reserve the teaching of those concepts for the next day's practice or a meeting after the ballgame. This will contribute to the players' overall psychological success. Most of us who have been head coaches and then found ourselves in an assistant coach's role have been relieved when no one was mad at us after the starting lineup was posted. It was easy then to continue to teach and encourage because players didn't view us as the enemy. Hence, by having a bit of a split personality, you might help your players, and yourself as a coach, to adapt to the difference between practice day and game day approaches.

Physical Conditioning

We do physical conditioning to develop baseball strength, not body-building, wide-body, which-way-to-the-beach strength. Throwing and hitting require functional strength and endurance specific to those movements. While handling large numbers of pitches and swings, an athlete is only as strong as his weakest link, so there must be parity between little muscles and connective tissues (synergists) and middle-size and large muscles (prime movers). Strength is built with resistance training; endurance is built with a combination of light-resistance, large-repetition resistance training, plus actual throwing and swinging. Both strength and endurance training must be specific to the positions and movements of baseball. It's an integration of straight, supinate, and pronate (fastball, breaking ball, change-up) with linear, circular, and angular (stride, torso rotation, bat path). Proper conditioning programs involve flexibility work, body work, joint-integrity work, machine work, and free-weight work to tolerance in year-round cycles involving off-season building, preseason peaking, and in-season maintenance. All this is simply called specificity of training. In other words, if a player wants to be better at fielding ground balls, he should do just that—practice fielding ground balls. To be a better pitcher, one needs to pitch. To be a better hitter, one needs to swing the bat.

Although we haven't completely unlocked the secrets of physical conditioning, experts and rookies agree that building strength requires a blend of these strength-training strategies and a variety of workout bouts throughout the year. Moderation in overload workouts seems to be most effective. Running seems to promote improvement in running form, agility, quickness, and stamina. Throwing a ball seems to promote arm endurance. Swinging a bat definitely promotes bat-speed improvement. Coop DeRenne of the University of Hawaii found in his research that an overload and underload approach to swinging the bat promoted increases in bat speed. He discovered that the best strategy was for the hitter to use a bat a few ounces lighter than his regular one for underload training and only an ounce or two heavier for overload training. Using the large donut and extremely heavy bats showed, if anything, a decrease in bat speed. One would conclude from this that a moderate strength-training and flexibility program is sufficient.

One thing all good baseball people know is that when the conditioning workouts are brief, spirited, and integrated into teaching the skills of the game, they are much more effective. A professional speed and strength coach will certainly advocate that speed drills and strength training occur at the beginning of practice rather than at the end. Try this in your team workouts and you will probably conclude that practicing baseball is the fun part of practice. A player's love and enthusiasm for the game will take over after he has done the speed and strength drills. As John Kruk, former Philadelphia Phillies first baseman says, "I'm not an athlete, I'm a baseball player." The remaining flexibility, body work, and strength drills will be camouflaged in the currency of baseball practice. What a great way to approach physical conditioning!

Nutritional Conditioning

Nutrition is blood chemistry. Blood chemistry is weight management; wound healing; recovery time; aerobic and anaerobic efficiency; fuel for nerves, muscle, and connective tissue; bone to prepare, compete, and repair. To maximize the benefits of nutrition, think food— combining it, rotating it, supplementing it, enhancing it.

Food combining is finding the best ratio of protein, carbohydrates, and smart fats for each meal, each day, around practice and competition. The body needs all three. Protein and amino acids build and re-build muscle tissue. Carbohydrates provide energy, and smart fats supply backup energy and other bodily efficiencies. Optimal ratios are a function of genetics and physical activity, but try 40 percent carbohydrates, 30 percent fats, and 30 percent protein for a starting point.

Food rotating is eating different foods often. A good rule of thumb is to eat three to five meals per day and not to eat the same food prepared the same way twice in 48 hours.

Food supplementing is compensation for the way our food is prepared, preserved, hormoned, enzymed, and free-radicaled. Try megavitamins, minerals, digestive enzymes, antioxidants (vitamins E and C, beta-carotene, selenium, or as many as you can afford), and glucosamines sulphate (for joint-integrity facilitation) in the middle of your largest meal. We also advocate a daily multiple-vitamin supplement. High cost may reduce the sophistication of this supplement program, but almost all players can afford a daily multiple vitamin that contains some of these essentials.

Food enhancers, or metabolic boosters, are legal but controversial, mostly because of misinformation and improper protocol. Think of them as muscle-recovery facilitators. They don't build tissue; they allow an athlete to train harder and recover more quickly, which helps them be stronger, longer in the movements required in baseball (that is, more pitches, more swings, more efficiency, and therefore more effectiveness.) What are these products? Creatine, Pyruvate, Gamma Oryzanol, Human Growth Hormone, DHEA, Androstenedione. Used properly they all work. Note that there will always be some conjecture about nutritional protocols and strategies. New research may bring to bear slightly different strategies. It seems that when coaches get together to discuss nutrition, we all have different points of view. Be assured, however, that when you either provide your ballclub with a multiple-vitamin supplement or encourage your players to buy some for themselves, you will find that they will become more conscientious in all areas of nutritional and physical preparation. They will become more conscious of diet; hence diet protocols will be enhanced. Young players may even contemplate keeping curfew and sleeping at the same hours each night. Anyone who teaches amateur athletes who are enrolled in high school or college would agree that if the players simply slept at approximately the same hours each night they would be more effective in practices and games. By discussing with your athletes what you believe to be the fundamentals of nutritional design, you can achieve a great deal of success without devoting too much time to the subject.

What are the guidelines for nutrition and resistance training in baseball?

- Don't cycle the dosage. Take a uniform daily amount to facilitate a weight gain of no more than 5 pounds per month, 20 pounds in a season.

- Hydrate early and often, especially if your enhancement is powder. Liquid enhancements are proving to have fewer side effects, although they may be more expensive and have a shorter shelf life. For this reason, many high schools and colleges buy the powdered form of these enhancements in bulk. We urge caution, however, because coaches should never compromise health for economics.

- Train small muscles and connective tissue more intensely than prime movers. Ballplayers want muscle density and balance, not bulk. Try to work the synergists first; finish with agonists and antagonists. Most baseball players have been going to the weight room with a strength-training mentality. Baseball players, however, are better served by starting with the light weights first, taking into account that most of their work is repetition involving fast-twitch muscles. Encourage players to use tubes and dumbbells, to do their stretching, and to involve the smaller muscles in baseball-specific lifts early in the workout, finishing up with some of the bulkier prime movers. Your strength-training instructor may think you're crazy, but he doesn't go home at night and lose sleep if you lose a ballgame. You and I lose a ballgame if the player goes down with a connective-tissue injury. Strength training that is specific to baseball prevents injuries.

Biomechanical Conditioning

The mechanics of a pitch and a swing are surprisingly similar. They each have five components, with energy sequentially muscle-loaded from feet to fingertips out into the baseball or bat.

1. The ballplayer should begin with dynamic balance, with the head over the center of gravity (belly button), which is between the balls of the feet. Most coaches will recognize dynamic balance as the instruction they give an athlete to keep his body stacked, to keep knees, hips, shoulders, and eyes level with the head positioned directly between the feet. Think of a player's head and spine as a bowling ball on a broomstick, anchored at the belly button and supported by the hips and legs. If the bowling ball leans too far in *any* direction during a weight shift, muscles stretch out of sequence. Kinetic energy transferred into the arms and out into the bat or ball is adversely affected. Talk and teach balance and center of gravity.

2. Postural stabilization, or finding and keeping a posture throughout a pitch or swing, is critical. Maintaining balance throughout the swing or delivery is not magic. The use of videotape can be very effective in showing a player instability in his posture during a competitive movement. Once the player knows what he really

looks like, he then sees—through the coach's eyes—the adjustments he needs to make to his mechanics.

What are some typical problems and their solutions? If the head moves up or down during a stride, the fix is in the knees. In other words, if the athlete's head pops up with his first movement out of the hitting or pitching stance, straighten the knees until the head stays still with leg lift. Conversely, if the pitcher's head drops down, flex the knees deeper until the head stays tall at leg lift. If the head "tick tacks" front to back with the leg lift, through the stride into the foot strike, the fix is in the abdominals and lower back. This maintains whatever torso-leg angle the player started with. Finally, if a hitter's head misdirects away from the pitcher, or if the pitcher's head moves away from the hitter, the stance is usually too wide. Narrow it until the head stops moving away from the direction of the stride. If you ask an athlete to assume a good athletic position, one in which they would have mobility, almost all players will choose an armpit-width or shoulder-width stance. This is a stance that usually works before making any kind of stride commitment. Think "firm to forward."

3. Players should have equal and opposite forearm-elbow integrity at foot strike and maintain it through weight transfer and torso rotation. There is a caveat with pitchers. Their fix is with the gloveside arm, not the throwing arm. The throwing-arm path is genetic. If the athlete were throwing rocks at rabbits, he would have an arm path specific and natural to him. Pitchers must line up the front elbow and forearm equally. The throwing arm is down and behind the body at foot strike. The glove arm will align with and be in front of the body into weight transfer and initial torso rotation. If forearm-elbow angles change during a swing, the bat path is inconsistent. If a pitcher doesn't get equal and opposite forearm-elbow integrity, accuracy and control suffer and muscular joint strain increases.

4. The axis of torso rotation is 75 percent of stride length for pitchers and 50 percent of stride length for hitters. For throwing, the best position to start torso rotation is *late*, at more than 75 percent of stride length. This allows the arms to get from hyperextension into flexion as the ball is delivered. Premature rotation results in the arms being pulled through the delivery plane, causing excess shoulder-elbow strain and a release point farther from home plate. Rotating late gets the ball closer to home plate with less effort. The most effective way to encourage late torso rotation is to have the

pitcher bounce five fastballs, five curveballs, and five change-ups on top of the plate. By throwing the ball at this lower trajectory, the athlete will rotate later and get the arm out in front. Do you realize that one foot of distance equals three miles per hour to the hitter's eyes and produces later ball movement with all pitches? Hitting is acquired perception, the ability to read pitch and ball path.

Mechanically, the best batters rotate at 50 percent of stride length at foot strike. Although bat speed is genetic, bat quickness is strength and mechanics. Successful hitters integrate perception, bat speed, and bat quickness as a function of genetics, the number of pitches they've seen, and how hard they work on strength and skill.

5. Player should have equal and opposite forearm-elbow integrity at release point (pitcher) and contact (hitters). Motion analysis of elite players at 1,000 frames per second has revealed some interesting things about release point and contact. The best pitchers stabilize their glove arm at the release point with the glove over the landing foot. Their elbow is in front of the center of gravity, and there is no movement or shift in this elbow-glove position until after the ball has left the hand. In other words, pitchers take legs, torso, and throwing arm to their glove to throw the ball. The best hitters do not change the angle of forearm-elbow and bat until after contact. They hit the ball inside with the same arm positioning as the ball away. Contact is made as a function of torso rotation, not quicker hands or different bat paths.

Ballplayers absorb energy, direct energy, and deliver energy with these five movement components. An athlete who is out of sequence or inefficient with any of these movements will negatively affect his performance or risk injury.

After each baseball season, most coaches take time to talk with their players more than they perhaps could have earlier in the year. In one such interview with a college player who had a less-than-glamorous season, I asked the player what might have led to his demise. The answer he gave is relevant to this chapter. The player was from a smaller high school in a rural area of his state and had been reasonably successful at that level. When he made our ballclub and we began to make changes in his defensive and hitting mechanics, his interpretation of the instruction was that he simply was not good enough. Why else would we try to change his play? Tell your athlete that these are new and dynamic concepts, just developed through scientific research. Your player would not want to go back to television of the 1950s. He probably wouldn't go back to black-and-white movies of that era. Athletics are dynamic, not static. Ideas that can shorten the learning curve can help the player be successful, but he must be willing to take a leap of faith. Remember that these teaching moments will be much more effective in practice than on game day.

A Closing Note

Please do not look at this information as anything that conflicts with tried-and-true concepts that coaches have always taught. The objective data simply confirms the traditional approaches and speeds up the learning process for young coaches who do not have the luxury of time for trial and error!

PART
IV

Individual Skills and Team Strategies

CHAPTER FOURTEEN

Handling Your Pitching Staff

Charlie Greene

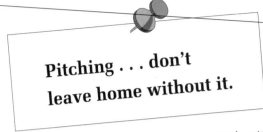

Pitching . . . don't leave home without it.

Regarded by baseball experts as the most important element in a team's success, pitchers are the only players who touch the ball on every play. Developing a pitching staff to its greatest potential is an absolute must. As your pitching performs, so goes your team.

Baseball is essentially a confrontation between the pitcher and the batter. The winner of that battle controls the outcome of the game. Knowing how to develop a pitching staff therefore becomes the top priority for any team.

Identify raw pitching talent (throwing ability) and devise a plan for developing that talent, emphasizing continuity from one level to the next. Rather than developing a reactive approach, develop a proactive one that allows both players and coaches to be creative. An athlete is an artist. Let him put paint on the canvas.

There is a better way of doing everything. It depends on the coaches' creativity. Take something good and make it better. Do not remain stagnant or be afraid to explore unique ideas. Letting new ideas become extinct causes the game to remain too traditional.

We live in a quick-fix society that does not reward patience. Regression is not tolerated, even though doing so could pay big dividends later. Coaches and managers are perceived to have a narrow window of opportunity. The pressure of a quick-result mentality has forced coaches and managers to take shortcuts to attain results. Shortcuts to effective teaching, however, do not exist. But there are smart ways to get the job done.

Principles of Pitching

Pitching is defined by many as the art of refined throwing. Therefore, a potential pitcher must learn how to throw before he can possibly learn how to pitch. Throwing is the basic foundation for pitching, and when properly learned it will lead to rapid development of pitching skill. Pitching skill comes quickly when throwing technique is mastered. Do not accept poor throwing action.

Pitching, unlike hitting, is an action. The pitcher can control all its variables. The skill of hitting is a reaction, involving a series of variables that the batter cannot control, such as the type, speed, and location of the pitch. It is much easier to teach an action (pitching) than it is to teach a reaction (hitting). Time spent on pitching will return quicker, more lasting results.

Pitchers need to be built from the ground up, not continually repaired. While the Band-Aid approach may solve problems on a temporary basis, the long-term effect is minimal. Pitchers need to be built from the ground tip. Having a solid plan will eliminate problems before they occur. A systematic approach is essential to long-range success.

It takes approximately six weeks to make a substantial change in a pitcher's delivery. Pitchers are unwilling to try new things when they are excessively concerned about seasonal statistics. It is difficult and sometimes impossible to make changes during the season. Between starts, pitchers are reluctant to make changes. Relief pitchers find the task even more difficult. The threat of statistical evaluation will always be a deterrent to change. Do not let statistics get in the way.

It is easier to make changes in downtime or the off-season. Develop a plan that each pitcher can implement during this time. Show him the way.

Smooth becomes better, faster. A smooth, flowing delivery is not only more effective but also decreases the chance of arm injury. Eliminate any part of the delivery that inhibits the graceful action of delivering the ball. Maximum effort is not required for maximum results. Encourage about 85 percent effort.

Work smart, not just hard. Develop a systematic approach that the pitcher understands completely. A plan should include daily, weekly, seasonal, and yearly objectives. Keep the carrot out front.

Pitching is part art, part science. Most of the components of the pitching delivery are based on scientific principles. Putting them together is an art.

Ten pitchers working to please one coach produce greater results than one coach trying to please 10 pitchers. You cannot make a pitcher out of everyone; you can only provide players with an opportunity to make themselves into pitchers. Put the responsibility on the athlete. Providing them with opportunities is what coaching is all about.

Do something different every day to make yourself better. You will then have a minimum of 365 somethings at the end of the year. Success does not just happen.

Games belong to the players; practices belong to the coaches. Each pitcher must become his own pitching coach. Trust the players' ability to make decisions, including pitch selection.

Priorities

Establishing priorities with a pitcher starts with the most important priority—making sure the arm stays healthy. Without a healthy arm, all else is meaningless. Overworking the arm is the biggest cause of arm injury. Limiting the number of pitches is a good starting point, but there are many other considerations. And remember, an ounce of prevention is worth a pound of cure.

It is better to pitch too little than too much. Operate on the side of caution. Listen to the athlete. He will provide you with the best X-ray of his fitness. Keep the lines of communication open. If he is hurting, make him feel free to express it. Work him when he feels good. Shut him down when there is an expression of pain.

Once you make every effort to prevent injury to the arm, you can consider other priorities:

- Health of arm
- Proper throwing technique
- Proper pitching mechanics
- Command of fastball
- Development of change of pace
- Command of change of pace
- Development of breaking ball
- Command of breaking ball
- Pitching strategy
- Evaluation of success (statistics)

Unfortunately, we skip to the evaluation stage too quickly. Keep your priorities in order. Make haste slowly. Patience will pay off.

Teaching the Pitcher

In athletics, we learn by what we see, by what we hear, and mostly by what we feel. Developing a kinesthetic sense requires endless hours of repetition, but with pitching we must be cautious that we do not overwork the arm. Devising a proper, safe practice routine requires careful planning.

Learning a skill involves a sufficient amount of teaching plus an enormous amount of practice.

teaching + practice = learning

It is erroneous to think that practice alone will lead to learning. Practice alone leads to permanency. A skill incorrectly practiced is extremely difficult to change. Take the time necessary to coordinate teaching methods with all practice sessions. A true teacher *causes* learning.

A pitcher must first learn how to throw properly. Because throwing is the number one prerequisite for pitching, a player must master it before he further pursues pitching techniques. Without good throwing mechanics, a pitcher will not progress and will find it difficult to learn.

Throwing is the sequential unlocking of body parts to achieve maximum hand speed at the moment of releasing the ball. Hand speed does not continually increase during delivery, and maximum effort hinders the throwing sequence. The ball actually comes to an imperceptible stop before it is released. The pitcher must not rush the delivery.

Throwing action involves

1. swinging the arm back smoothly, with the hand (palm down) close to the body on a line between home plate and second base,
2. transferring weight to the pivot leg,
3. taking a step toward the target,
4. coiling the arm (imperceptible stop),
5. forcefully exploding toward the target,
6. allowing the arm to pronto, and
7. following through.

Learning how to throw requires many correct repetitions. Do not try to get past this stage too quickly. This stage, the most important phase in developing the complete pitcher, should be part of every practice session.

Pitching Mechanics

While a pitcher continues to improve arm action and throwing skill, he needs to work on the fundamental body mechanics that are unique to pitching.

The absolute checkpoints in the total delivery are illustrated in the figures on pages 196 and 197. A picture is worth a thousand words, but a great imagination can create an infinite number of pictures. Take what you see and use your creativity to fill in the rest.

STANCE

- Elbows relaxed and close to body
- Weight over pivot foot
- Ball hidden from batter and base coaches
- Eyes visualizing path of ball to target

BALANCE POSITION

- Weight over back leg
- Eyes focus on target
- Knee at highest point
- Stride forward when hands separate

STRIDE

- Fingers on top of ball
- Stride foot closed
- Shoulders lined with target
- Fine focus on target

EXPLOSION

- Stride knee bent but firm
- Hand pulls shoulder through
- Shoulder follows hand
- Allow pronation to happen

FOLLOW-THROUGH

- Shoulder below chin to target
- Glove pulled into bodies
- Throwing shoulder lower than glove shoulder
- Armpit over stride knee

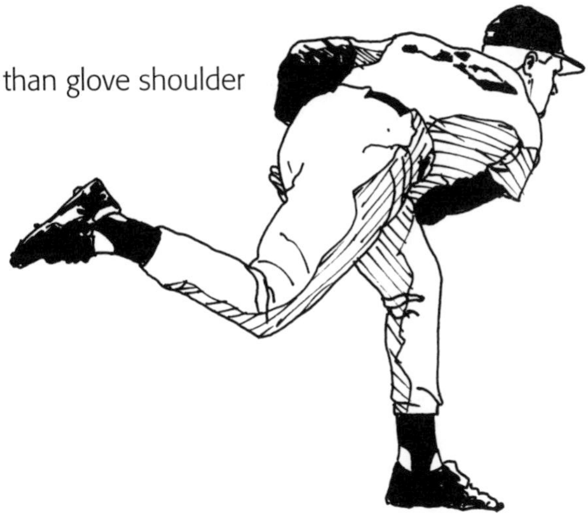

Allotment of Practice Time

Efficient use of time is the cornerstone of any program. As long as time is available, we have no excuse for not practicing. A pitcher can work with or without a catcher, a ball, or a facility. He can work in-season or off-season. A commitment has no limitations; a pitcher can practice whenever he has time available.

Three main factors form the basis for any practice schedule:

- Frequency—how often?
- Intensity—how much effort?
- Duration—length of practice?

If something is worthwhile then we should reserve time to accomplish it. Scheduling that time efficiently produces positive results. Consider the following formula:

$$12 \times 5 > 1 \times 60$$

Spending small segments of time on any drill will often accomplish much more than performing long drills less often. Alternating drills that emphasize heavy usage of the throwing arm with those that are less stressful provides some protection against excessive wear and tear. An hour distributed in short segments lessens the chance of injury and keeps the workload minimal. Finding small amounts of time is practical, especially when a workout requires no special setting.

Drills serve as a motor vehicle in the learning process. Properly designed drills can result in effective learning of a particular skill or part of one. Alternate physically and less physically demanding drills.

I recommend the following drills for making mechanical adjustments. Pitchers can do them with or without a ball, at shorter distances, with less intensity, or with or without a partner. Emphasize creativity.

STAND UP

Purpose
To learn arm action while limiting use of the body

Procedure
Face target, lock feet in ground, turn and throw

GLIDE

Purpose
To learn (closed) stride foot landing

Procedure
Lift hands and foot quickly from set position and throw

TUCK

Purpose
To develop consistent leg lift

Procedure
Lift hands and stride foot, then throw

BALANCE

Purpose
To develop the habit of not rushing

Procedure
Count to three, lift hands and stride knee, then throw

CHAIR

Purpose
To force pitching over firm stride leg

Procedure
Raise pivot foot, use hips when throwing, keep foot on chair

FORM (BALL REQUIRED)

Purpose
To work on mechanics, with no concern with control

Procedure
Throw into a net, observing mechanics (a wall can also be used)

INSIDE-OUTSIDE

Purpose
To develop a feel for locating a pitch on both sides of the plate

Procedure
Alternate throwing to both sides, not throwing strikes

Players can execute these drills by using a <u>wooden dowel</u> two feet long and five-sixteenths of an inch in diameter. Wrap the grip end with tape to prevent the hand from slipping. For safety, do not simulate throwing action with the dowel in the direction of others. Dowels come in four-foot lengths at hardware stores. Because they sometimes break, have extra ones available. The swishing sound provides immediate feedback, demonstrating hand speed. Pitchers should perform a few repetitions of each drill as often as practical. They can work on off-speed pitches when using a ball and be creative by combining drills.

Principles of Throwing Various Pitches

Once pitchers have mastered the foundations of smooth arm action and solid body mechanics, they can easily acquire the various types of pitches. Without a solid foundation, progress is delayed and often unattainable.

Grips for throwing the various types of pitches can be highly individualistic. Pitchers should search and experiment until they find what best suits them. However, certain principles will produce maximum results:

- Pitchers should develop an understanding of the proper rotation for each type of pitch. By knowing the proper spin, they will find it easier to visualize the desired result.

- The tip of the middle finger stays on top of the ball, so the pressure is always exerted from the top to the ground, on all pitches.

- The more the middle finger stays behind the ball, the faster the pitch.

- The farther the middle finger is positioned away from behind the ball, the slower the pitch but the bigger the break. Remember that the tip of the middle finger is always on top of the ball.

- Pitchers should allow pronation to occur, never attempting to supinate (turn the doorknob clockwise by a right-handed pitcher).

- Holding the ball firmly on fingertips produces greater velocity.

- A soft grip decreases the velocity of pitch (effective when throwing change of pace).

- On off-speed pitches, pitchers should use more arm and less body, and take drive out of the pivot leg (shorten stride).

- Forearm position should be established before releasing the ball.

The position of the forearm is changed to throw the various pitches. Have the pitcher face the palm of his hand toward home plate and turn it left and right. The forearm turns with the palm and is positioned for the different pitches. The pitcher should visualize the correct rotation.

Fastball (four seam)—palm directly behind ball, rotation from 12 o'clock to 6 o'clock

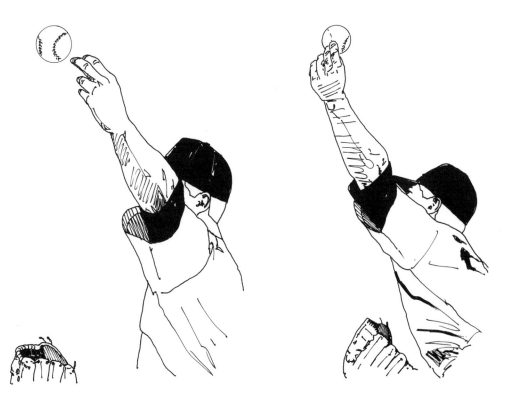

Slider—palm slightly inward, bullet spin or football spiral

Curve—palm farther inward, rotation from 6 o'clock to 12 o'clock

Change-up (not shown)—palm farther outward, softer grip, premature pronation, reverse of curve

Sinker (two seam)—palm slightly outward, reverse of slider

Pitchers should practice the pitches using the previously mentioned drills. Repetitions will help develop a feel for all pitches. Perfect practice makes perfect.

Developing Control

An essential part of being a complete pitcher is having command of all pitches. A pitcher does not really have a pitch until he can throw it over the plate at least 60 percent of the time. Achieving such control requires solid mechanics, smooth arm action, and the ability to concentrate on the target.

Concentration must be total and needs to be emphasized in all workouts. The key to throwing strikes is to fix the eyes on the target at the moment the hands separate, to avoid watching the ball, and to follow through to the target. Although it sounds simple, the pitcher must practice diligently to be able to concentrate.

The ability to throw pitches to both sides of the plate is also an important part of control. This requires not only concentration but a feel for moving the ball left and right. Using the inside-outside drill will help solidify this aspect.

Pitching Strategy

Once the pitcher develops proper pitching mechanics, acquires a variety of pitches, and demonstrates command of them, the game becomes a mental challenge. Having a million-dollar arm and a 10-cent head will not lead to much success. The pitcher must plan each pitch. Present the following principles of strategy to your pitchers:

- waste a pitch or an at-bat, no matter what the score.
- ce patience. Do not be in a hurry to get an out. Stick with your plan.
- away from the middle of the plate when ahead in the count ward the middle of the plate when behind in the count. First-strikes are critical.
- the fastball; get the other pitches over the heart of the plate.
- t try for a swing and miss with fewer than two strikes.
- t worry about the consequences of a pitch. Think of the job at hand. You have no control of other variables.
- Pitch to situations. For example, with no outs and a man on second base, try to stop the ball from being hit to the right side of the field.
- Double up on pitches. Back-to-back pitches stop hitters from guessing, particularly when thrown inside.
- Use the glide step with a good base stealer on first base. Also, change intervals between pitches or hold the ball and step off sometimes.
- Use fastballs when ahead in the count (location) and off-speed pitches when behind in the count (strikes).
- Use an off-speed first pitch with a runner on third base. The batter will be eager to drive in a run.
- Pitch inside when you can afford to hit a batter (open base).
- Use the shake-off signal sometimes even when the correct pitch is called.

- Change the tempo during a long inning. Pick up or slow down the pace.
- Know the balk rule.

Game Preparation

Before any game, the pitcher needs to prepare mentally and physically. He should develop a game plan with his catcher to eliminate any indecision. Being on the same page decreases the need for pitcher-catcher conferences during the game.

Allowing sufficient time to warm up properly decreases the likelihood of injuries. Before tossing the baseball, a pitcher should warm up using his running and stretching routines. This can include jogging, sprinting, stretching, and light weight training. Start with short tosses and gradually increase the distance until the pitcher is long tossing with his partner. Use as few pitches as possible with the catcher down. No more than 50 pitches is sufficient to get ready to start a game. Additional pitches can lead to early fatigue. Pitchers should not waste game pitches in a warm-up routine. Pitchers should strive for rhythm and accuracy, and save velocity for the game.

A relief pitcher should be sufficiently stretched before the game so he will not need as many pitches to get ready. Long tossing and running before the game should suffice. Remember, relievers are allowed eight additional warm-up pitches on the game mound.

Game Situations

Through extensive work in preseason, pregame, and classroom sessions, a pitcher should be thoroughly prepared to meet any situation. Particular emphasis in practice or warm-up should have the pitcher prepared to execute in these situations:

- Pitchout
- Intentional walk
- Pickoff play at any base
- Rundown play
- Covering first base
- Bunt defense
    - Runner on first base
    - Runners on first and second base

- Runners on first and third base
- Runners on first, second, and third base (bases loaded)
- Runner on second base
- Runners on second and third base
- Runner on third base (squeeze play)

- Ball hit back to the pitcher
- Tag play at home
- Backing up the bases
- Intentionally dropped bunt, with runners on first and second base.

A pitcher must be prepared to pitch with an open base, knowing the best times to pitch inside or outside. When executing a pitchout or intentional walk, pitchers often become anxious and are susceptible to a balk call (quick pitch). Pitchers should become more deliberate in these situations and avoid rushing.

Evaluation

Fitting pitchers into a team role requires a constant evaluation of their specific talents. Starting pitchers must exhibit command of at least three pitches and have endurance to throw a minimum of 100 pitches every fourth or fifth day. A starter should be able to pitch effectively for at least six innings on each of his starts. If he pitches fewer innings, a tremendous workload falls to the bullpen pitchers, who are not only asked to pitch more innings but are constantly worn down while warming up to prepare for emergency situations.

Early-inning relief pitchers are usually less experienced and less successful pitchers, commonly young pitchers in the developmental stage seeking game experience. You hope they can pitch some innings and keep the game close.

Late-inning pitchers are those who have exhibited the ability to hold a lead or keep the game close. They should possess many of the characteristics of the starting pitchers and be able to recover quickly from each outing.

The closer must have one dominant pitch, be cool under pressure, and be able to bounce back from an unsuccessful outing. He should be able to pitch on successive days and have no history of arm problems.

Scheduling Workload for Each Role

Starting pitchers should throw lightly every off day, with a solid workout in the bullpen on the second day after a start. The sequence looks like this: game-light-bullpen-light-rest-game.

Relief pitchers, whether early-inning pitchers, late-inning pitchers, or closers, should adopt the following rest routine, which considers the amount of work they have done.

- 35 or more pitches—one day off
- 40 or more pitches—two days off
- 50 or more pitches—three days off
- Two days in a row—one day off
- Three times in the bullpen without being used—sit out the rest of the game

If a starting pitcher is rained out of a scheduled start, he should pitch the next day. If he is rained out two days in a row, he should have his between-game workout scheduled for the next day and skip a start. You may, however, need to make adjustments if you lack pitching depth.

If your team is ahead late in the game, use every available pitcher to maintain the lead if necessary. The next day it may rain or you may not have the lead. Opportunities to win do not come along every day.

Making a Pitching Change

Deciding when to remove your pitcher is probably the most important in-game decision you make. You may want to remove a pitcher

- when he reaches his pitch limit (100 or more),
- when he is ineffective,
- when he is throwing consistently high pitches (due to fatigue),
- when you have a better pitcher available late in the game,
- when you can create a better pitcher-hitter matchup,
- when you want a better fielding pitcher in a bunt situation, or
- when a left-handed pitcher could slow down a base-stealing threat.

Using Statistics

Because baseball is a game of opinions, a coach's gut feeling is probably the best way of determining a pitcher's value. To support or justify your opinion, you might want to use some statistical data to provide some objectivity about a pitcher's effectiveness. Consider evaluating these pitching statistics:

- Percentage of strikes

- Speed-gun reading
- Number of pitches per inning (12 to 15 is considered good)
- Ratio of ground balls to fly balls (ground balls preferred)
- Number of hits per inning
- Number of three ball counts
- Percentage of first pitch strikes
- Percentage of inherited runners that score
- Strikeout-to-walk ratio
- Hits given up with an 0-2 count

A Closing Note

Handling a pitching staff requires much attention to detail. Developing a daily, weekly, seasonal, and off-season plan can pay huge dividends. Once you identify what you need to accomplish, you should set aside time to work out the details. Too often we teach in generalities that neither we nor the players fully understand. Uncertainty lowers confidence, which makes maximum results impossible to attain. Taking the time to work out a master plan that includes frequency, intensity, and duration of workouts leads to positive results.

It is in the best interests of both pitcher and coach to respond to a detailed practice schedule, typed up each day. Daily objectives are like a road map—you know where you are going. Time spent on a daily plan makes every practice efficient. Because pitchers can learn more effectively during the off-season (down time), a detailed schedule for these practices is also beneficial.

A simple rule to follow is this:

- Feel good—practice.
- Do not feel good—do not practice.
- Take what time is available and plan a workout.

I recommend you conduct an exit interview with each pitcher at the end of every season. You should map out a detailed plan for off-season practices, including a video that outlines the specific changes the pitcher should make. Time spent in such communication is a positive motivational experience for the athlete. Ending the season with no off-season plan is a mistake. Have the athlete spend his time wisely. As someone once said, "Give a man a basket of fish and he can feed himself for a week; teach him how to fish and he can feed himself for a lifetime."

CHAPTER FIFTEEN

Developing High-Production Hitters

Gary Ward

There are as many systems for teaching hitting mechanics, drills, and situational hitting as there are coaches. That is as it should be— each coach with a personal philosophy, a set of fundamental practice drills, and an environmentally-based set of terminology with which to communicate to the player.

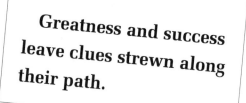

Greatness and success leave clues strewn along their path.

Shortcuts to success are few. Hitting systems that advertise an easy, simple approach to the science of hitting create short-term excitement and long-term failure. Magical marketing phrases that promise the keys, secrets, and hidden recipes to the complex puzzle are voodoo solutions sold to frustrated athletes and coaches. Great hitters make great investments of time and energy as they meet failure, frustration, and pain on the path to self-discovery.

Developing a Coaching Plan

You can achieve greatness as a coach only by taking responsibility for what you presently are and holding yourself accountable for what you will become. Check the reality of your personal coaching goals. Develop your unique style of coaching. If you wish to be great, study those who are great. The eagle does not study the crow. Study, steal, and reformulate others' ideas into usable coaching technique. Refuse to echo others' methods. Be accountable and accept credit for the success or failure of your efforts. Develop your personal coaching plan of teaching hitting by considering philosophy, terminology, and drills.

Philosophy

Do you follow coach A, who advocates linear flow up the middle of the field, giving up power for improved contact? Do you follow coach B, who advocates vertical-axis rotation for improved leg leverage, resulting in turn-arc power? Do you follow what the player brings to the table physically, mentally, and emotionally, and then adjust to that? Take ownership of all material that is presented to your students.

Terminology

You are a product of your environment and will bring a unique set of descriptive terms and phrases to the coach-player relationship. Develop the skill of talking in pictures. Teach the same idea with a variety of methods. Bring your natural sense of humor and the joy of discovery into the learning process. Allow the player input into establishing core goals and the anticipated outcome. Encourage the player to question or reject any ideas presented. Talk the same language. It is their swing that goes to the plate.

Drills

Practice makes permanent. Be precise, creative, and organized because each drill becomes your assistant coach when you are absent. Understand that the player controls the learning environment. The learning process is individualistic and complicated. It takes 30 days to condition a new motor skill into automatic response. The power of spaced repetition requires that the player be repeatedly exposed to a set of information over 15 days before they learn and accept ownership. Most of us have a natural fear of change. Skills normally regress before moving to a higher level.

Working With Players

Encourage player involvement by asking, "Do you understand?" Require the player to rephrase what you say. They understand it when they can teach it. All players learn at an accelerated pace when visual, auditory, and kinesthetic syntax is provided. When the hitter can tell it, the teacher can fix it. Patience is the perfect virtue.

Greatness and success leave clues strewn along their path. They occur as a result of planning rather than at random. Seek from every available source the information you need about skills and drills for hitters. Go to as many professional cages as time and energy allow. Review every film, video, book, article, and picture that you can. Study golf, tennis, softball, and handball for similar skills, drills, techniques, and terminology.

The best source of information, however, remains always the players. Each problem they bring and each obstacle they must overcome provide a learning experience for both them and you. Adversity is the greatest of all mentors for it requires you to introduce new drills, create new approaches, and invent new descriptive terminology.

Luck is the residue of design. Work on yourself harder than you work at your job. Design a plan that challenges you to continue to evolve as a master teacher. Include these seven lucky ideas in your long-term goals:

- No great deeds can be achieved without the investment of passion into a goal that borders on obsession. Great hitters have an undying passion for hitting.

- There is magic in the power of belief. What you believe to be true becomes true when you believe it is possible. Great hitters believe they can hit.

- Create a strategic personal plan that organizes all your resources and those of your teaching laboratory. Great hitters have a strategy.

- Clarify your values. Make clear and specific judgments about what is important to you. Great hitters establish clearly defined, specifically written goals.

- Express an energetic joy for teaching. Bring enthusiasm to the learning environment. Anticipate discovery with each teaching session. Great hitters expend the energy.

- Invest yourself in your players. Develop the ability to bond with players and parents. Great hitters invest themselves in and trust their coaches.

- Prepare to become a master communicator. Your ability to communicate with others will determine the quality of your life and the quality of your leadership. Great hitting coaches are great communicators.

Characteristics of Highly Productive Hitters

The only hitting system that is important is the one you claim as yours. Your system evolves continuously as you add and delete information. It changes as you continue to study, experiment, and evaluate. These dependable dozen characteristics of highly productive hitters will reinforce, alter, and challenge your existing ideas.

Different Strokes

Accept that different folks will use different strokes. Each player brings a unique set of physical attributes to hitting. The player's defensive position capability is a major factor in helping the hitter define the nature of his offensive game. Do not be concerned with your player's initial setup in the batter's box. Take note of hand position, stance, and style as he anticipates the movements of the pitcher. Pay attention to the total athlete—his relaxation, freedom of movement, and vision.

The critical time for observation by the coach occurs when the hitter's stride foot hits the ground. Give latitude to individual nuances and encourage any creative approach that ensures relaxation, freedom of movement, and precise vision. Some hitters have a tendency to swing where the ball is, although it might be a result of a combination of mechanical errors. Be careful not to attempt to fix what is not broken. When the stride foot hits the ground, the bat must be ready to launch, and the hitter must have positioned himself in the most efficient athletic position.

Timing

The timing mechanism for the hitter is lifting the stride foot and placing it back on the ground. The travel time of an 80-mile-per-hour fastball is approximately a half second, timed from the pitcher's release to arrival at home plate. The first half, 25 or more feet, is labeled *information time.* The second half, 25 or more feet, is labeled *reaction time.* Information time allows the hitter to predict accurately the speed, spin, location, and arrival time of the ball. Reaction time allows the hitter to attack the ball aggressively. Film studies show that great hitters may need only 15 feet of reaction time to execute their swings. Any improvement of reaction time will increase information time. The greater the information time, the more disciplined the hitter's strike zone.

Every teaching moment must be spent in providing information and practice drills that allow hitters to increase their information-gathering time while reducing their reaction time. The earlier a hitter can recognize the characteristics of the pitch and its probable arrival time and location, the more relaxed and precise the swing. Any practice that does not emphasize game-speed timing has little value in developing the hitter.

Controlling the Swing

The front muscle system controls the swing. For maximum quickness in swinging the bat, the player must become aware of the speed-enhancing muscles that he must emphasize. This system isolates the kinesthetic feel to the front of the body. The specific areas are the pectorals, the lower abdominals, and the inner leg muscles slightly above the knees. The large and powerful muscles of the shoulders, back, and buttocks are deemphasized. The front muscles control the path of the bat and the speed with which it can be swung. Although the shoulders, back, and buttocks can supply energy and support, when overused they dominate the hitter's swing mechanics, resulting in one giant body spasm. Control in the front muscles guarantees an independent and free movement of the hitter's arms. This provides the player with the ability to both control and manipulate the path and speed of the bat. Using the back muscles locks the hitter's body into a feeling of strength while desensitizing the hand action responsible for bat speed. Using the front muscles can decrease reaction time.

Quick-toss drills with the lead arm and top hand are specifically designed to develop pectoral muscles. Encourage their involvement in the swing. Label it as "Tit-T" harmony. Invite the player to activate the abdominal muscles by making a grunt or hum sound, increasing the volume until he can easily feel the lower abdominals contract. Place a volleyball between the hitter's knees and have him squeeze it with inward leg pressure. Combine these three techniques in executing quick-toss drills.

Quick-Zone System

The quick-zone system allows the coach to monitor three zones visually to guarantee that the hitter will develop the best possible reaction time. The first quick zone is the distance between the knees as the hitter completes the stride step. This power base, the distance between the feet, should be no longer than the length of the hitter's bat. More important, the hitter should hold constant the distance between the knees from this time until the bat reaches contact. Use the volleyball to coordinate quick zone 1 distance with using the front inside muscles slightly above the knees. Quick zone 1 defines how far the bat must travel to arrive at the hitting contact point. The smaller quick zone 1 is, the more the front muscles are activated, the shorter the swing, and the better the bat speed.

The second quick zone is the distance between the elbows at the conclusion of the stride step. Gripping the bat in the fingers rather than in the palms encourages good elbow position. Do not be concerned with quick zone 2 positioning until quick zone 1 is established. Just as the knees work as a coordinated team in quick zone 1, the elbows work as a team, driving the hands toward the ball to start the forward path of the bat. If the distance between the elbows is too great or one hand establishes early dominance, the back muscles are activated, which decreases bat speed and control. Proper quick zone 2 positioning ensures front pectoral muscle control of the swing.

Quick zone 3 is the distance between the barrel of the bat and the hitter's rear shoulder. The shorter the distance and the longer the time the bat barrel remains near the shoulder, the greater the energy collected and stored for hand release. Golf and tennis athletes use this lag to generate superior club-head speed, which results in extraordinary exit speed off the implement at impact. A quick zone 3 distance of one to three inches is ideal. An increase of a few inches in quick zone 3 will activate the hitter's back muscles, locking the swing into an outside path to the ball that can double travel time and halve bat speed.

The hitter executes action in the three quick zones of hitting on every pitch. This occurs during the information-gathering time. If the hitter decides not to swing at the pitch, he is in the take position. The quick zones are coordinated with, and complementary to, the front muscle system. Label this idea "flow to the hole," "function in the junction," or "ride, read, react, and release."

Power

Power is created, directed, and delivered from the ground into and through the lower body. The feet press down against the ground during the swing sequence. Rotation of the legs serves as the rudder, providing directional control for the hitter. This rudder takes the hitter's belly button to a position where the belly button takes a picture of the pitch. The rotation increases as the pitch arrives closer to the hitter and decreases as the pitch arrives farther from the hitter. Quick zone 1 is maintained with an emphasis on the knees working together. The hitter must feel the lower body collect, control, and position all the energy being collected from the ground through the feet. Have the nonbeliever put on some roller skates and swing the bat with the ground's energy source cut off.

The hitter should time each pitch with the legs and then the hands, staying in the legs and positioning the body to hit until he decides to swing the bat. All functions of lower-body positioning improve when the front muscle system and quick-zone system fundamentals are emphasized. If the hitter uses the lower body properly to collect and direct his power source, the upper body will remain relaxed and controlled. This relaxation and control encourage good quick zone 2 and quick zone 3 positioning and result in the bat getting starting on plane. The final phase of the swing is the reaction-time function of an explosive top-hand commitment to the ball from the quick zone 3 position.

Rhythm

Different dancers use different rhythms. The ability to adjust timing rhythm from one pitch to the next is critical to becoming a productive situational hitter. Remember that the stride step and the lower body trigger the hitter's timing while beginning the rotation of the legs. The upper body remains relaxed and unaffected by the lower-body action.

You may now introduce the rhythm adjustment drill. The purpose of making rhythm adjustments is to develop the ability to use the entire field. The hitter will learn to maximize his power potential, execute the hit-and-run, become a confident two-strike hitter, and hit the inside breaking ball.

Place four traffic cones or other clearly identifiable objects at 15-foot intervals from the plate to the mound. Drill rhythm 1 requires the hitter to start the stride step, the timing device, as the pitcher releases the ball. This results in the hitter being early, allowing him to pull the ball for power. Drill rhythm 2 requires the hitter to start the stride step as the pitch passes the 45-foot cone. This tightens the rhythm and results in the ball being hit toward the center of the field.

Drill rhythm 3 requires the hitter to start the stride step as the pitch passes the 30-foot cone. This results in a natural hit-and-run swing. Drill rhythm 4 requires the hitter to start the stride step as the pitch passes the 15-foot cone. This results in a properly timed two-strike swing that would be late arriving and would deflect the ball to the opposite-field foul line. The drill pitcher or pitching machine must simulate an average-speed fastball appropriate for your competitive level. There will be differently timed strokes for different folks. The rhythm adjustment drill will define clearly the individual ability levels of each of your players. It will support and encourage greater understanding of information time and reaction time. It will define the stride step as the primary timing device of every hitter.

The execution of the three quick zones will occur sequentially, with the top-hand release being the final action. These four functions must occur within the half-second limit of pitch travel time and must be executed more rapidly at each drill rhythm 15-foot interval. These four phases could be called the tempo of the swing. The timing mechanism is adjustable to the hitting situation; the tempo changes depending on the timing used in that particular offensive situation.

Zone Hitting

Highly productive hitters have a disciplined swing, knowledge of the strike zone, and knowledge of their individual power zones. Players of modest ability can create their maximum bat speed in a defined zone. The shorter the look, the greater the bat speed. Hitters can reduce their look into an anticipated area of the legal strike zone, about the size of a shoe box, and react only to a pitch in that zone. Great energy can be generated and delivered when the focus is narrowed to a small area of the legal strike zone. This is called zone hitting for power or shortening the look into the P zone. If the pitch does not enter the P zone, the hitter takes it even if it is a strike.

Each hitter can increase his power production by zone hitting until he gets a two-strike count. Rhythm adjustment practice provides the player with a confidence level that removes the fear of striking out. With two strikes, the hitter merely widens the look to the full strike zone and makes a rhythm adjustment. Zone hitting requires the hitter to understand how to adjust the information and reaction times of total travel time of the pitch. It requires that the hitter has practiced automatic response of the front muscle, proper quick-zone positioning, and lower-body systems of hitting. The combination system of rhythm adjustment and zone hitting can make an offensive player of modest talent a valued contributor to the team offense.

Training

The athlete who desires to become a great hitter understands that his body is his business. Developing the needed tools goes beyond the practice of drills and skills. Every hitter needs educated hands. Smart and sensitive hands will know where the barrel of the bat is throughout the execution of the swing. They will be able to manipulate the barrel of the bat during the swing to adjust to the speed and location of the ball in flight to the plate. Every hitter needs to develop great strength in the wrists and forearms. Educated hands are controlled from the elbows down. Players should supplement their baseball training regimen with participation in similar ball-movement games like golf, handball, table tennis, and basketball. They can adapt weight training, swimming, and running exercises to simulate the actions needed to improve hand strength and bat speed.

Encourage your players to engage in a variety of activities that eliminate boredom while training for baseball. They might experiment with plyometrics, agility, dance, martial arts, small-muscle control, quick-twitch muscle development, rhythmic breathing, vision enhancement, nutrition, meditation, solitude, keeping a daily journal of short-term goals, and relaxation techniques. They should emphasize activities that create an athletic body, a body that becomes kinesthetically aware of using the front muscles, controlling the quick zones, and developing lower-body directional power and upper-body precision. Last, encourage players to visualize daily the image of successfully executing their best swings in game situations. Visualization should be lifelike, including weather, colors, and sounds of the game environment. Players should strive to become successful in their visual thought process. Walk the walk!

Dancing With the Pitcher

The hitter-pitcher relationship is not adversarial combat. It is a rhythmic dance of two minds and bodies merging into a codependent athletic action. The pitcher has the ball and the responsibility to lead this dance. The pitcher controls the time, speed, and location. The pitcher is proactive; the hitter is reactive. The hitter ignores the person and personality that provides the cue. The umpire always enters the equation by interpreting the strike zone. The hitter should recognize the role of the umpire without letting that authority become part of the dance.

Powerful and personal positive and negative emotions usually activate large amounts of energy. These are most often counterproductive to the hitter. The hitter should remain close to center and melt down to the most relaxed state of mental and physical awareness possible. The skilled hitter has practiced swing mechanics that produce an automatic response that he can trust in game conditions. The hitter must not allow emotional immaturity to alter this response. He should not take the pitcher's effort to defeat him as a personal affront. A clear and relaxed mind can concentrate and see so clearly that the ball seems to slow down. The hitter should not take the result of the last pitch to the next swing. He should forgive the pitcher, the umpire, or himself for the result of the last pitch.

Encourage your players to develop a 10-second prepitch ritual that they replicate before every pitch. They should defer analysis of previous pitches to avoid paralysis on the next one. The average athlete has an average visual memory of 13 seconds. The hitter should not get ready for the next pitch until he checks the coach for the offensive signal, completes his prepitch ritual to establish focus, and successfully erases the visual and emotional residue of the last pitch. This can be done with one foot out of the batter's box and within a 15-second time frame that does not interrupt the normal flow of the game. The batter must accept the leadership role of the pitcher in this athletic dance but should control the speed of the music.

Working the Pitch Count

Great hitters invest themselves in the team when they bat. Each hitter should treat the starting pitcher as a weapon whose ammunition chamber holds only so many bullets. Each hitter is responsible for forcing the pitcher to use as many of those bullets as possible during each at bat. The team pitch-count rule of 15-90 applies to the total pitches seen in an inning and in a game. It is believed that the most vulnerable time for a pitcher occurs when he reaches 15 pitches in an inning or 90 in a game and is working from the stretch position. The high-production team offense benefits from being patient in getting good pitches to hit within their individual power zones. This disciplined approach can only be practiced if each hitter understands the concepts of information time, reaction time, zone-hitting technique, rhythm adjustment, and the two-strike swing.

Reward the hitter who invests in a team at bat and acknowledge the individual player who sees six or more pitches in a single plate appearance. Keep a running pitch count on the opponent's starting pitcher posted in the dugout near the bat rack. Getting into the opponent's bullpen early reflects success. The hitter who must cripple-shoot early in the count, who cannot take a few bullets for the team, dumps the responsibility of reaching 15-90 on his teammates. Patience should always be practiced without runners in scoring position. Keep records on the number of pitches seen by each hitter per at bat. Your team leader in that category will most often lead your team in runs scored. The longer the game, the greater the influence of pitch count in the outcome. Most championship games are nine-inning games or at least longer than those played in the regular season.

Ten Commandments of Team Offense

Expect every offensive team member to obey these commandments as a commitment to the core goal of winning championships.

1. The walk is the easiest and most productive element of team run production.

2. The threat of the walk allows a modest hitting talent to maximize bat speed and power by using the zone-hitting concept. Each 1-0, 2-0, 2-1, 3-0, and 3-1 count provides you a better look into the cripple zone.

3. You must be able to execute the sacrifice bunt on demand.

4. Advertise the push bunt and drag bunt base-hit techniques to the defense. This advertising results in positioning by the first baseman and third baseman that opens hitting lanes and slows their reaction time.

5. Bunt to avoid the double play. Injury, talent, or weather may overmatch you. Stay positively involved.

6. Avoid the double play. If the runners on base cannot steal and you do not possess exceptional power, make a situational adjustment.

Bunt for a base hit, tighten the rhythm to hit behind the runner, or look up in the zone-hitting concept to get the ball to the outfield.

7. Avoid the fly ball. There are no bad hops in the sky. The ground ball allows the runners to advance more frequently. The ground ball must be caught, thrown accurately, and caught on the base by the receiver.

8. Execute the hit-and-run. Make a rhythm adjustment and hit to the situation.

9. Become a great two-strike hitter. Make the proper rhythm adjustment and hit to the situation. Relaxation and trust learned in practice will help you fight off the rough pitches. Your walks should outnumber your strikeouts by a 2-to-1 margin.

10. Become an intelligent base runner regardless of your innate ability. Know the location of the outfielders, the game situation relative to the score, and the impact of current weather on defensive play. Think your way around the bases.

A Closing Note

I have given you no secret formulas for teaching your athletes to become high-production hitters. What I have shared with you are the discoveries of a coaching lifetime. The success of any coaching career can be measured in ways other than merely looking at the scoreboard. The primary goal of coaches should be to invest themselves, as does the candle, by spending their existence in this world providing light for others to follow.

CHAPTER SIXTEEN

Stopping Opponents With Solid Defense

Jack Stallings

A baseball cliche says, "Fans love offense and seeing a lot of runs scored, but teams win with good defense!" Good defense keeps a team close so it has a *chance to win.* Defense starts with good pitching, and a team will be hard pressed to do well without a good pitching staff (and a catcher who can handle them). But defense also involves the entire team. Playing good defense means players must execute the basic skills well. Learning how to do that will require much effort, hard work, and discipline in practice.

Catching and Throwing

Everything in defense revolves around being able to catch and throw the ball. The biggest mistake in defense is trying to master complicated plays before learning to catch and throw properly; a team can't expect to execute a pickoff or double-steal defense when one guy can't throw the ball and the other one can't catch it! Infielders should spend most of their time on catching and throwing because without those skills defensive play will always be inconsistent. Modern gloves make one-handed catches fairly easy, so today's players have a choice of using one hand or two. But they need to understand the advantages of both and use each at the proper time. They should use one hand when reaching for the ball or reacting quickly and two hands when they must make a throw, when there is a tough play, or when there is danger of the ball bouncing out of the glove.

The key to improving the basic skills of catching and throwing the ball can be accomplished by using proper mechanics when warming up in prepractice. Players should focus on executing five things well in warm-up:

1. Begin the catching-moving-throwing movement as the ball approaches to develop a proper and consistent rhythm, moving the feet to get to the ball rather than standing still and reaching, and catching the ball with the body square to it.

2. When the ball is in the glove, players should begin to "give" with the hands toward the throwing position and shift the feet simultaneously and in rhythm into position for the throw. While the player moves the ball and glove into the throwing position, he should roll the ball for a cross-seam grip that will produce four-seam rotation on the throw.

3. Players should not practice pitches in warm-up! Position players often throw curves or knuckleballs in practice, but players should

practice the skill they need in game action to develop their throwing ability to its maximum, and this means fastball throws!

4. To develop consistent control, players should throw at a target on every throw. People think of control only for pitchers, but catchers who can't throw accurately to second, or shortstops who throw into the dugout as often as they do to the first baseman lack control!

5. All players should overload their arms during warm-up to develop arm strength, using a systematic program of doing a little more each day. Players can overload their throwing arms by increasing either the length of time they throw or the distance they throw. Most players throw only enough to get the arm warm, but that does not develop arm strength. Players can develop arm strength by increasing throwing duration by a minute or so every few days. They can also build arm strength by throwing long toss, increasing their throws to reach their maximum distance using a normal motion, keeping the ball on a good arc rather than a rainbow. Players should start to warm up at a short distance and gradually lengthen the throws to that of the longest throw they must make during a game.

The Catcher

The catcher is second only to the pitcher in importance to team defense. Both are at the center of defensive action. The catcher's ability to throw well is very important in modern-day baseball because of its emphasis on running speed. Although arm strength is helpful, many catchers who do not have a great arm can develop good throwing techniques and be successful. Short, quick steps and good arm and body mechanics can help catchers develop a quick, strong throw.

Blocking pitches in the dirt keeps runners from taking extra bases and gives pitchers confidence to pitch low with runners on base. When the catcher has to shift to the side to block the ball, he should make a special effort to curl the outside shoulder forward so the chest is square to the ball. The ball will then rebound straight out from the catcher's body and shorten the distance to throw if the runner tries to advance. The head should be down and relaxed so a ball bouncing up will hit the mask and not the catcher's throat. Many catchers are poor at blocking pitches because they do not practice it enough, possibly because it is painful. A good drill to teach this skill is for the coach to throw tennis balls in the dirt from a distance of 15 or 20 feet so catchers can become accustomed to blocking with good mechanics and feel no pain when the ball hits their body.

In getting rid of the mask to field a pop fly, the catcher can just flip it off if he has to run for the ball. But when the ball is hit straight up, the catcher should toss the mask away so it will not land near the plate where he might step on it. To be able to catch pop flies well, the catcher must understand the spin and curve of the ball as it comes down. When a batter hits a pop fly, backspin is created. As the ball comes down it will always curve toward the mound. The higher the ball is hit, the more it will curve, but the direction of the curve will always be the same. By understanding the spin and curve of the ball, the catcher can prepare for it even before it occurs by overanticipating and overplaying the curve. With his back to the mound, the catcher should stand so the ball is coming down several feet from his body. The curve will bring the ball to him. If the catcher underanticipates the curve, he will be backing up to catch the ball, which is much more difficult. On a ball popped up a short distance in front of the plate, the catcher should go out and turn around to catch it. The ball will be curving in toward him.

Infield Play

It is obvious that good infield play is essential to team defense. Your team must develop good, consistent infield mechanics. Let's start with fielding position. The feet should be spread for optimum balance and quickness, and the body should be low, square to the ball, with the knees and waist flexed. The feet and glove should form an equilateral triangle with the glove open squarely to the ball. The glove must be on the ground—the hands are three times quicker coming up than going down, body balance is better, and the hands are softer. The bare hand should be near the glove for quicker and better control of the ball with the throwing hand.

On routine ground balls the infielder should field the ball with the glove out from the body to create softer hands. The angle of the glove should be approximately 45 degrees to the ground. The glove and bare hand should begin to give slightly as the ball arrives to help keep it in the glove. The glove and bare hand continue to move into the throwing motion as the hand completes making its grip on the ball. As the arm goes back into the throwing arc, the fielder shifts his weight onto his left foot, takes a short jab step with his right foot, and then steps with the left foot to throw. The stride leg should step directly at the target and be bent slightly to help the arm pull down on release. If the ball takes a bad hop just as it gets to the fielder, he will be much quicker if he keeps his body still and reaches for the ball with only the glove. One hand can move more quickly than two and certainly more quickly than the body.

If the ball takes a bad hop and hits off the infielder's body or the fielder bobbles it and drops it to the ground, he must pick it up with the bare hand. The fielder will be able to throw more quickly without transferring the ball from the glove to the hand, and he will be able to control the ball better in the bare hand. On a bobbled ball the infielder should do the following:

1. Make the play on the first grab. Don't panic! Relax and pick up the ball smoothly.

2. Move the feet to get over the ball and reach straight down for it. This will ensure a good grip with the hand on top of the ball.

3. Bring the ball from the ground to the throwing position without patting the ball in the glove.

4. Move the feet quickly toward the target. The arm should come straight up as the player crowhops to get momentum to make the throw.

Backhanding the ball often affords better balance and body control than trying to get in front of it. It also opens the pocket of the glove more fully and makes it easier to field and throw on any ball fielded even with or beyond the fielder's right foot (for a right-handed thrower). The body should be bent, the ball fielded in front of the reaching foot, the elbow held up, and the forearm held vertical. The glove should give upward toward the throwing position.

Many major-league infielders use the one-handed method for slow-hit balls because they feel they can charge the ball faster. But younger players may need the added safety of using two hands because it allows them to control the ball better in beginning the throwing action. The infielder should charge hard and chop his steps as he nears the ball. This may not be possible on a do-or-die play, and the fielder may have to make that play as best he can at full speed. Smoothness is more important than quickness on this play. If the fielder can circle the ball slightly as he nears it, he will improve his angle for making the throw. It is unrealistic to expect young infielders to field and throw slow-hit balls with specific footwork. It is more reasonable to expect them to get to the ball quickly and make the throw with as few steps as possible. It is better to make the play successfully with two steps (or three) than to fail to make it using only one!

A smash at the infielder is a difficult play because the infielder tends to shy away from the ball and tries to field it off to the side. To avoid this, the infielder should do the following:

1. Get in proper fielding position, glove on the ground and out in front of the body.

2. Do not move the body or the glove. Stay still and let the ball hit the chest, then pick it up and make the throw.

3. Naturally, no one is going to let a hard smash hit the chest, so at the last moment the glove will move to catch the ball. By remaining still, the infielder will avoid shying away from the ball and can let his reflexes move the glove to catch the ball.

Outfield Play

Good outfielders can be a tremendous factor in the success of a team. Becoming a good outfielder requires a lot of practice. The player must not only master the skills of the position but also develop willpower and self-discipline to stay alert and concentrate on the action of the game. The outfielder must be alert to get a good jump on the ball and cover a lot of territory. If an outfielder is playing his position properly, he will be involved in almost every play of the game. He will be moving constantly—backing up a base in case of a wild throw; moving around in the outfield according to the hitter, the count, and the situation; and backing up balls hit to other outfielders as well as infielders. In short, a good outfielder will do a tremendous amount of running during a game. Too often outfielders wait until a bad throw has bounced past an infielder before moving to back up a base. It is then too late. On every throw and on every possible throw the outfielder must break immediately at full speed to get in position in case the throw goes wild.

An outfielder must discipline himself to catch fly balls properly by running hard to the ball, getting his body under control, and catching the ball with both hands above the throwing shoulder. Unfortunately, major-league outfielders often set a poor example for this skill by drifting after a fly ball. Doing this can cause a problem if the outfielder misjudges the ball or the wind blows it a bit. Outfielders must learn to run normally, with the arms pumping in rhythm, until just before they reach for the ball to catch it. If they begin to reach several steps before they get to the ball, they curtail their running speed.

The Double Play

It is vital for middle infielders to shorten up their positions so the pivot man can get to the base before the throw arrives. He can then slow down, shorten his steps, get under control, shift easily on a bad throw, and stay on balance while pivoting. Infielders fear giving up range, but this does not give up range so much as shift it over to the middle of the infield, and it increases the number of double plays. When infielders are in normal position N, ground ball B is a hit and ground ball A is one out. With infielders at double-play depth DP, ground ball A becomes a base hit and ground ball B becomes an easy double play (figure 16.1).

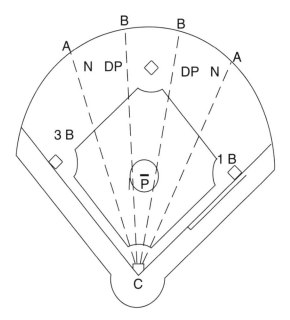

Figure 16.1   Positioning for the double play turns ground balls that are normally outs (A) into hits and balls that are normally hits into outs (B).

The lead throw to start the double play must be a good one. If any hurrying is done it should be on the throw made by the pivot man to first base. The infielders should make sure they get one out. The pivot should be made based on the throw rather than on any preference the player may have on making the play. When one begins the pivot before seeing the location of the throw, he will be off balance on any bad throw. Therefore he must wait to read the throw and let the throw dictate the pivot.

The pivot man must catch the ball with both hands if the throw is accurate because he can get the ball out of the glove more easily and thus throw quicker. Many of the collisions between the pivot man and base runner are caused by the infielder making a one-handed catch. Any infielder who values his life and limbs will catch the ball with two hands on the double play! The steps around the base must be short because they allow better balance, are quicker, and permit the throw to be made while nearer to second base. A shortened initial position helps accomplish this. The pivot man must step directly in to first base to make a strong and accurate throw. Pivot men often try to throw to first base while moving in a different direction. This is difficult to do and often occurs because the infielder approaches the bag so fast that he cannot easily change direction. The pivot man must get his body turned toward first base, make the throw, and *then* jump to avoid the sliding runner.

There is a lot of glamour in the pivot man's leap in the air to avoid the runner's spikes and his bullet throw to first base from midair. But what usually happens is that the pivot man makes his throw normally (from the ground) and then, immediately after releasing the ball, jumps over the sliding runner to avoid the collision. If the pivot man cannot make the throw before the runner slides into him, the batter-runner will probably be near first base and the double play will not be possible anyway.

Infielders should try to complete double plays in four seconds from contact to first base rather than try to make the play as fast as possible. The objective is not how fast they can turn it but economy of movement. Because very few batters can run to first base in less than four seconds, it isn't necessary to make double plays faster than that. Timing double plays teaches infielders how hard and where the ball must be hit to make the play in four seconds, and it also allows infielders to develop a sense of when they have plenty of time on a play and when they do not.

Double-Play Feeds by the Shortstop

To make the underhand toss, the shortstop should pull the glove out of the way to show the ball to the pivot man and to help open up his hips. He should make the toss with a full-arm sweep and release it near ground level for maximum accuracy and velocity. The palm of the hand should be square to the target and accelerate through the release area for maximum velocity (figure 16.2).

Figure 16.2   Underhand toss by the shortstop to the second baseman.

On a ball hit away from the base, the underhand throw is normally not possible, so the shortstop should use an overhand throw with a short arm arc. He should pull his left foot back a little to open up the hips and throw overhand to help improve accuracy. A sidearm throw will usually make a horizontal error if the throw is not perfect, which makes the play more difficult than if the mistake is a vertical one.

Double-Play Feeds by the Second Baseman

The second baseman must have good agility and be able to make short, accurate throws from various positions, often while off balance. To learn which throw is best from what distance and with what weight distribution, the second baseman should practice throws from different distances while leaning both right and left when he catches the ball. The player can work at various distances to determine his range and decide which throw is best according to body lean or whether he catches the ball off his right or left foot.

For the underhand toss the palm should be turned squarely to the target. As the player shifts his weight to the right foot toward the base, he tosses the ball using a full-arm pendulum sweep, releasing it near ground level (figure 16.3). A good weight shift toward the target is necessary. For longer tosses the left foot should step toward the base as or before the toss is made.

Figure 16.3   Underhand toss by the second baseman.

On balls fielded a little farther from the bag, or on balls fielded near the base but with the weight leaning away from the bag, the backhand flip may be the most accurate and quickest throw. As the ball is fielded the hand is turned inward to make it square to the target with the elbow up and the forearm in a vertical position. The player should release the ball with good wrist action to create a proper 12-6 spin. Shifting the weight toward the target as he releases the ball adds velocity and control.

On a ball hit a medium distance to his left, the second baseman can use a half pivot that rotates the body toward second base without moving the feet. The feet need to be fairly close together to ensure easy rotation of the hips toward second base. Having the feet too far apart restricts the turn of the hips and slows the execution of the throw. The fielder turns his upper body toward the bag with the knees bent and the body kept low. He may find the play easier by bending the left knee to the ground; the throw should be made with an overhand arm angle.

A ball fielded while moving hard to the left may require a reverse pivot. The second baseman can reverse by spinning on his right foot, thus moving his body toward second base to make the throw, or he may reverse pivot on the left foot and step away from the base with the right foot (figure 16.4). He must use short steps to help keep the body under

Figure 16.4   Reverse pivot by the second baseman to make toss to shortstop.

control and must try to avoid leaning away from the target while throwing. He should bring the ball into throwing position with an arm action close to the body and use an overhand throw.

Pivots by the Shortstop

The pivots by the shortstop are fairly simple because he is going in the same direction he will be throwing and has the added advantage of easily seeing the runner. The most common problems for the shortstop making the pivot are coming across the base too fast and taking steps that are too large. If he can avoid doing these, the play should be relatively simple. Figures 16.5 and 16.6 show two variations of the shortstop pivot.

Figure 16.5   Dragging the right foot, the most popular pivot for a shortstop, can be used on any throw over the base or to his left. The shortstop should square his body to the throw and take short, balanced steps as he steps past the corner of the base with his left foot. He drags his right foot across the bag, turns his body toward first base, and steps with the right foot to throw.

Figure 16.6 On throws to the third-base side of the base (especially from the pitcher or first baseman), shortstops often prefer to step on the base with the left foot, step toward the mound with the right foot, and then step directly toward first base with the left foot to throw.

Pivots by the Second Baseman

Many second basemen like to circle as they approach the bag so they are moving slightly toward first base as they make the pivot. This is helpful if the second baseman does not posses a strong throwing arm and needs some body momentum behind the throw.

Stepping on the base with the left foot is a popular pivot for second basemen because it enables them to put the same foot on the base every time, regardless of the location of the throw. If the throw is to the left, the second baseman catches the ball, makes a short step with the right foot across the body, and steps with the left foot directly toward first base to throw. On a throw directly to him or a little to his right, he simply catches the ball and throws, either with his left foot still on the base or as he comes off the bag with a short step. If the throw is farther to his right, the second baseman pushes off with the left foot to meet the ball and makes the throw from behind the base.

Straddling the base is another choice. The second baseman sets up with his feet straddling the bag and simply catches the ball and throws without any additional foot movement. This method can be quick and simple to execute for a throw directly over the base.

Priority Calls for Catching Pop Flies

One of the most frustrating things in defensive baseball is a routine pop fly that no one catches. You can minimize this problem by defining a priority system for pop flies and having the team practice it. This is so important in eliminating collisions and mistakes that it should perhaps be the first thing you teach your team each year. Only the players involved should call for fly balls. They should wait until the ball is on its way down before calling it, and they should call it with authority. A common mistake is to call for the ball too quickly and without authority.

Pop-ups down the foul lines should be caught not by the catcher but by the third baseman or first baseman, who must learn to play the fence like an outfielder on pop flies hit near the stands or dugout. The catcher can provide some vocal help. On balls hit between the infield and outfield, the infielder should go back without calling for the ball until either he knows he can get it or the outfielder calls for the ball. Outfielders should catch short fly balls because they are coming in and have a much easier play than the infielder. Once the outfielder calls for the ball, the infielder must swerve off to the side or drop to the ground to avoid a collision. Teams use various words or phrases to call for a fly ball, but we suggest "Mine" and "Take it" because they sound completely different, are short, and "Mine" is a very possessive word.

The priority list, if followed, gives authority on fly balls to those most likely to have the best fly-catching skills and the best angle for the ball. Individual differences in skill on some teams may warrant changing the list slightly (first baseman above third baseman or second baseman above shortstop, for example) but these changes would not violate the basic idea of having the most qualified player take priority over a lesser skilled one and the player with the best angle for the ball having the higher priority. Coaches should establish a priority system based on the skills of the players on the team and the angle each player should have on fly balls. The priority list suggested here is based on how most teams would place their most skilled defensive players:

1. Center fielder
2. Left fielder
3. Right fielder
4. Shortstop
5. Second baseman
6. Third baseman
7. First baseman
8. Catcher
9. Pitcher

Defensive Positioning

Defensive positioning depends on the game situation, such as the score, inning, speed of the runners, batter, and many other game factors. All need to be considered in making alignment decisions. Common sense and following basic strategy dictates alignment, not a "book" of strategy rules. Because every defensive alignment offers some advantages and disadvantages, the coach has to consider many factors before making a decision.

Infield In

Probably the most difficult decision in defensive strategy is deciding when to bring the infield in with a runner on third base and less than two out. Because bringing the infield in doubles the hitter's chances of getting a hit, a coach should not do it unless preventing the run is vital. Unless the runner on third base is the tying or winning run late in the game, the out may often be more important than the run. With runners on second and third, bringing the infield in can be especially dangerous because it may result in giving up two runs on a routine ground ball that gets through the infield. In this regard, the old adage "Play to win on the road and tie at home" is sensible strategy. A tie score in the last of the ninth inning gives the advantage to the home team, so they might be willing to play back with the tying run on third and the winning run on first or second. Then if the visiting team ties the score but does not go ahead, the home team still has the advantage with the last at bat.

When the infield is brought in to cut off a run at the plate, the infielders should come in only far enough to be able to throw out the runner at the plate; as a result, the four infielders will probably play at different depths because of their different arm strengths. A team will be more likely to bring the infield in with a weak hitter at the plate, because a strong hitter will hit more balls hard and make tougher plays for infielders who are playing in close. With none out, the offensive team should not try to score if there is a good chance the runner will be thrown out at the plate, so the defense may bring its infielders in part way. This positioning will keep the runner from trying to score on a ground ball yet be back far enough to have decent range. With one out, when the offense should be trying to score on any ground ball, the infield should come in closer to the plate.

Defensive Alignment When Leading in the Game

When a team is leading the coach must keep in mind the location of the tying run and winning run because they dictate strategy. When leading by two or more runs late in the game, the team's main job is to keep the tying run from coming to the plate. Question: With a two-run lead in the last inning and no one on base, which hurts the defense most—a single, double, triple, home run, or walk? Answer: They all hurt equally because any of them brings the tying run to the plate, and that's all that matters. Coaches must remember that if the tying run never comes to the plate, their team cannot lose. So do all you can to keep the tying run away from home plate!

Prevent Defense

The coach should use a prevent defense late in the game with a lead of two or more runs when trying to prevent the tying run from coming to the plate. Pitchers should challenge the hitters and make them hit the ball to get on base (not let them hit, make them hit!). Corner infielders should be off the foul lines because there is a 5-to-1 ratio of base hits in the hole versus base hits down the line. The shortstop and second baseman should play more to the middle of the field to help balance the infield alignment.

Outfielders should be off the foul lines because they also have a 5-to-1 ratio of hits in the gaps in right center and left center versus down the lines. They should play shallow due to the greater ratio of hits in front of them than over their heads; outfielders should also dive for a fly ball if they have a reasonable chance to catch it. They should throw to second base on a single to keep the batter on first base and keep the force-out or easy play in effect.

All fielders should make the easy play for the out rather than attempt a tough play to get the lead runner. The important thing is getting an out, not where the out is made! The first baseman should play behind the runner on first to increase his range and force the pitcher to concentrate on the batter. If the runner is foolish enough to attempt to steal when he isn't the tying run, the first baseman should put on a pickoff play with the pitcher.

Pressure Defense

When tied or leading by one run late in the game, the defense must try to keep the tying or winning run off second base to make the offense work harder to score. Thus they put pressure on the offense to keep the tying or winning run out of scoring position. The pitcher should pitch normally, challenging the weak hitters and not giving in to the power hitters. In this situation, walking a hitter who is capable of hitting the ball out of the park is not a terrible thing, but walking a number 9 hitter who is hitting .200 with no power would be disturbing!

Infielders should play deeper and closer to the foul lines to reduce the chances of a double down the line. Even though the 5-to-1 ratio of hits means giving up more singles in the hole, in a pressure situation it is worth the risk to cut down on extra-base hits, especially with two outs! Outfielders should also guard the foul lines and play deeper to reduce the chances of a double. Outfielders who dive for a fly ball in this situation run the risk of allowing a double if they fail to make the catch, so they should attempt it only if they have a good chance of success. Outfielders may throw to the plate on a reasonable chance to retire a runner trying to score, but they must hit the cutoff man. Otherwise the batter-runner will reach second base on the overthrow and be in position to score on a single.

CHAPTER SEVENTEEN

Playing Percentage Baseball

Bob Bennett

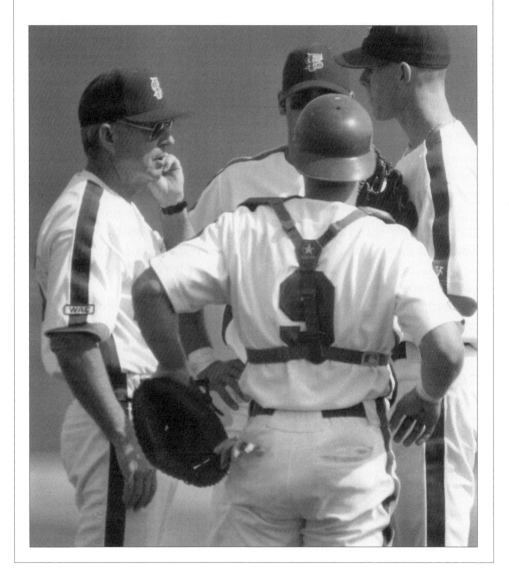

> **Coaching would be a cinch if coaches had a specific formula or an exact answer for making decisions in key situations.**

No precise formula or any other source gives an answer for every situation. Some managers in professional baseball and some coaches in college have an excellent track record of coming up with the right decisions in key situations. Even among these baseball men, none has a perfect decision-making rating. Over the long haul percentage baseball is a good base from which to begin developing sound decisions.

Gathering information from past decisions tells us much about various situations. When you had a choice to bunt or hit, what was your call? Was the play successful? What was the frequency of success? Were attempts to steal executed successfully? More important, did they result in runs or cause the pitcher to lose some effectiveness with the hitters? When you chose to play the infield in to keep the runner at third base from scoring, was that often successful or did it result in more runs scoring? On the hit-and-run, did the hitter make consistent contact? Did that play at least move the runner up one base? When the corners of your infield protected the lines and the outfielders played deeper, did that reduce extra-base hits? Asking and coming up with the answers to these kinds of questions are examples of the process of dealing with percentages.

Statistics can evaluate percentages compiled overall from all teams. They are probably more beneficial when the gathered data are about your team against its opponents. Percentages are important. They tell us what has worked successfully and what has failed. Many variables exist. Decisions based on statistics are reliable to a certain extent. If the statistics are based on major-league players' abilities, it pertains to that group alone. Expecting the same ratio of success with unskilled players is not reasonable. Collecting data from players with like abilities playing against the same level of opponents will produce more reliable information.

Basing decisions on percentage baseball is a good starting point, but it is not foolproof! The game is difficult. Successful results do not occur every day, perhaps because of bad hops, good and bad luck, imperfect players, and execution of challenging plays by coaches. Players have hot and cold spells. They develop mental and physical slumps. Each game is different from all others. Some are like a wild current. Others are dominated by a pitcher or the defense or the offense. Games often have an unusual, unexpected turning point. These are examples of why coaches must use logic with percentage baseball to develop strategies.

The assumption by many is that playing percentage baseball means only one right strategy exists for each situation. To go against the so-called percentage is a quick way to be second-guessed. The person most likely to have information that can support the use of other options is the coach. He knows the skill level of his players and how they have performed in the past. His view of the capabilities of his players is often quite different from that of the observer or partisan fan. Knowing the mental makeup of the team is essential in making strategic choices.

Intuition

Making a decision based on a hunch, on intuition, is another common practice. Some coaches get better results with their hunches than others. Some appear to have an uncanny ability to pull the rabbit out of the hat at exactly the right time. Perhaps more than intuition is at work. These magical, gifted coaches can see details clearly and have a feel for the game. Success comes from the coach's special ability to read the game as it unfolds. Anyone who has coached knows that concentration and heightened awareness vary. Coaches, like players, come with various degrees of skill. The ability to assess the game and its rhythm is a special talent. Coaches can develop some of this ability, but much of it is a gift. Those who have the gift are totally involved with each game, noticing every detail. They are deeply concerned about and interested in those details. They realize that in those details rests the game's outcome. A branch of intuition founded on percentage baseball gets long-term results.

Game Strategy

In the general sense, each game should stand alone as we develop strategy. Each game has its set of circumstances. Because we have not yet played the upcoming game, we do not know how it will turn out. Having said that, unless we have reasons that would dictate special strategies, each game starts with a similar game plan. Until we learn otherwise, the game we are about to play has no unusual factors. Therefore, during the first three innings teams need to be patient and persistent on both offense and defense. On defense, do not try to prevent one run from scoring at the risk of opening greater scoring opportunities for the opposition. On offense, do not try to score just one run at the expense of giving up outs. The objective is to create several runs. Do not allow overaggressive acts to rob the opportunities that the game may offer. For example, if the opposing pitcher has early season jitters, exercise patience. Force him to solve his problem. Until the pitcher shows that he has command of his pitches, the offense should remain patient. Do not help him by swinging at bad pitches or running your team out of the inning. Playing for one run, for instance, means the offense is willing to give up an out to score. At this point, unless specific information says otherwise, it is wise to allow the game to unfold. A disciplined offense often creates more chances to open up the game.

We should not always employ this approach. If the opposing pitcher is extremely good and has a history of pitching low-run games, taking any opportunity to score one run may be necessary. Rain, darkness, time limits, slumps, and hot streaks are reasons why you might play for just one run.

Over time, giving the game a chance to unfold is the most consistent approach. Innings four, five, and six make up the first adjustment phase. After three innings, the game starts to give some hints about its rhythms and challenges. So stick with the original plan or alter it. This is not always an easy choice. Sometimes the information gained from the first three innings suggests a change, and sometimes it does not. If the pitchers of both teams are in complete control of their respective opponents, playing for one run may be the right decision. The same scenario, however, may show good reasons to stick with the original game plan. This would depend on the ability and strength of the offense or the consistency, strength, and confidence of the defense and pitching.

The last three innings of the game are the second and last phase of the game plan. Six innings define more clearly how we might reach a successful outcome. The score of the game dictates the strategy. Earlier we had time to allow the game to unravel. Although the game could change dramatically in any inning, six full innings generally suggest what we will need to win. It may take one, two, or even several runs to win. The strategy employed should fit the score. Obviously, at the end of six innings a 2-1 score requires much different strategy than 6-0 score.

You must consider several variables before making final decisions. The weather, the ability of the players in the particular situation, the tempo of the game, and the competitive conditions of the teams involved at the time are just a few. Add the umpire, the condition of the playing field, and the perceptiveness and approach of each coach. Any of these factors could figure into the decision-making process.

Heightened Awareness

The level of awareness is an important factor in making decisions. If focus and intensity are high and competitors are prepared, higher performance results. Therefore, the coach has a greater variety of plays from which to choose. Some defensive plays give options to the offense. Bunting if the infielders do not charge or slashing if they do is an example. Other defensive plays require the defensive team to make choices. Playing the infield halfway requires the infielder receiving the ball to choose between throwing home and throwing to first base. This is a tough choice for an inexperienced player or a player who is at a low level of awareness.

We all have highs and lows in our daily lives. Players have the same kind of highs and lows in the game. A player who is pressing has great difficulty deciding. The more options we give him, the greater are his difficulties in dealing with them.

Percentages may call for walking a batter to load the bases. The awareness level of the pitcher may suggest the opposite. If the pitcher is unable to compete at a high level, walking the bases to set up a double play may be counterproductive. Knowing how the pitcher reacts to pressure situations is essential in deciding whether to walk the batter intentionally. By adding to the pitcher's psychological shortcomings, we will likely diminish his chance to pitch out of the situation. Eventually that pitcher will need to deal with a wider range of challenges. His emotional state now makes that option too consequential for him to obtain success. The answer is to remove him from the game or chose another option for him.

We should consider the skill level and emotional condition of the team in the decision-making process. Well-honed skills can open many options. A player who is in control of his emotional state can rise to almost any challenge. A player low in either skills or emotional stability is limited. We can say the same of the team.

We may not deal with a given situation the same way every time. Early in the season, we may have limited options with a team. Later in the season the team may have developed more skill, more mental toughness. Therefore, a wider range of options is available. As an example, the coach may choose to play the infield either in or back with a runner on third base. When they play back, they throw to first base. When they play in, they throw home. Later in the season that coach may choose to play those infielders halfway. Now they must decide whether to throw to first base or to home. Because the infielders have confidence, experience, and ability, the coach can give them more responsibility.

Hitting situations are similar. To hit and run successfully, both the hitter and the runner must be consistent. If either player lacks the knowledge or ability to execute their respective jobs, we should not call the play.

To move a runner from second to third, the hitter can either hit the ball on the ground to the right side of the infield or bunt. If the batter is not adept enough to do either, then neither is an option. A steal may be a better choice.

Adjustments are often necessary. The tempo may change suddenly, perhaps from a well-controlled game to one with erratic and unnatural happenings.

Inconsistency may plague a team. Such teams are difficult to manage. Decisions based on percentages are often unreliable in such settings.

When a team is running on all cylinders, more tools are available. Decisions are less difficult to make. A coach or manager can select from a variety of defensive plays. In this environment, we can give the involved players a choice of hitting to the right side or bunting, for example. We should ask only skilled players to make these choices.

If the team does some things well but is limited in other areas, base your strategy on what the team does well. For example, if the runner on first base is the tying or winning run in the late innings with two outs, the steal is a logical strategic move. But if the runner has limited speed and has trouble reading the pitcher, the steal is not a sound option. The next batter or batters must get the job done. The limitations of the player at first base limit the coach's options.

Sometimes players and teams are not physically or emotionally ready to run special plays. At other stages they are ready and can successfully execute very intricate plays. Knowledge of the heightened awareness of each player and the team is essential to making sound decisions.

Moods change. Emotional levels vary. Skill levels of teams and the skill level of each player on that team vary. Consider these variables and match them with strategy. At low ebbs, the team and players are unable to deal with too many options. During periods of heightened awareness the team can deal successfully with all kinds of challenges and options.

Winning is possible when players, or the team, lack high marks in awareness. The team can win provided it uses only the tools it can handle at the moment. A carpenter may have to make cuts with a handsaw instead of an electric saw. His skill may be limited, or he may have no power source. Although the job may go slower, the carpenter can still get the work done. Like the carpenter, the coach should recognize the tools that are available and use the best one for the job.

Batting Order

Design the batting order either to bunch the good hitters or to scatter them throughout the lineup. This places more emphasis on the complete lineup. Another approach is to use team speed by bunching the fast offensive players or sprinkling the speed throughout the lineup.

The ideal lineup is one with power and speed. We want a player with power, good hitting skills, and speed in each spot of the batting order. Much could be done with a lineup filled by players with these skills. Most teams do not have such luxuries. Because we must consider defensive skills, we may weaken the offensive.

Leadoff Hitter

The leadoff hitter should be emotional and aggressive, yet patient. He must be a good starter. Some players play better after they have been to bat once or twice. You should not choose the leadoff hitter from this group. Having a leadoff hitter who seldom strikes out is best. This hitter's on-base average should be high. Good bunting skills are needed in this spot. The leadoff man who is a good base runner with the ability to steal a base is a great offensive weapon. Hitting from both sides of the plate is a bonus. Otherwise it makes little difference whether he is left-handed or right-handed.

Second Hitter

Place a premium on this hitter's ability to make contact and bunt. Speed is important but contact and the ability to hit the ball to the right side of the infield are even more important. We often require that he take pitches to allow the leadoff hitter to get a favorable count on which to steal. We need a mentally tough player for this spot. The opposition will test his patience and consistency. The second batter should be a good two-strike hitter. The second spot best suits a left-handed hitter, but a right-handed hitter who can hit behind the runner may also be effective.

Third Hitter

The hitter in the number 3 spot is generally the best overall hitter in the lineup. Consistency is extremely important. Much of the offense involves the third hitter. Over the season he will come to bat a few more times than the cleanup hitter. He should be a clutch performer. Power is an advantage for any hitter, as is speed. Speed is probably more important than power in the third position in the lineup. A third hitter with both tools mixes well with the first two hitters. He fits in with power hitters in the fourth and fifth spots as well.

Fourth Hitter

The most important attribute to consider in selecting the batter for the cleanup spot is his ability to hit in pressure situations, with men in scoring position. Power is the second consideration. Many will disagree, feeling that power is more important. Consistent singles with men in scoring position will win more games than home runs hit by an inconsistent batter. Power and consistency together make an unbeatable force at the plate.

Fifth Hitter

This hitter should be similar to the fourth hitter. If two hitters on your club have similar attributes, place the more consistent one in the fourth spot. Put the one with the most power in the fifth spot. With consistency from the first four hitters, even inconsistent power in the fifth spot will add strength to the lineup. The fifth hitter will have a chance to drive in many runs. He must be strong enough to garner the respect of opposing pitchers. If he does not, they will put the cleanup hitter on base in key situations. A player who bats in this spot in the lineup should have hitting skills equal to or resembling those of the fourth hitter.

Sixth Hitter

Choose either a batter similar to the leadoff hitter or a batter with power. The choice relates not only to the batter's skills and makeup but also to the skills of the other hitters in the lineup. The offensive approach of the coach is also a factor. Should the sixth hitter mirror the abilities of the leadoff hitter, the offensive strategy will be less traditional. The offensive approach used with a leadoff type of hitter in the sixth spot will be two faceted. The first five hitters initially play for a big inning. The last four batters play for one- or two-run innings. With the two players in the front of this lineup, they can extend the short game from the sixth hitter through the second hitter.

Should the lineup employ a power hitter in this spot, the strategy calls for including the sixth hitter in the group that plays for the big inning. The sixth spot is an excellent place for a hitter with power. Even a player who is inconsistent, or who wavers in some clutch situations, may prosper here. He will have many chances to drive in runs. Opposing pitchers have just faced the toughest part of the lineup before pitching to the sixth hitter, so a hitter in this spot sometimes benefits from a natural letdown by the pitcher. Often the sixth hitter will get more fastballs. A weak hitter cannot be hidden here. But this is a good place for a player with capability to bat higher in the lineup but for lack of experience or another defect that keeps him from batting fourth, fifth, or leadoff.

Remainder of the Lineup

Several factors will determine the remainder of the batting order. Most important is the type of hitter in the sixth spot. The hitting type and ability of the last three hitters and the general strategy of the coach or manager are other factors. We can design the last part of the lineup to make some impact.

If the sixth hitter has power, the seventh hitter should ideally be a leadoff type of hitter. This allows the offense to play for a big inning with the first six batters and use the last three to start anew. The seventh hitter acts as a leadoff hitter. His job is to work the pitcher deep in the count, with a major goal of getting on base. Lean toward the hitter with good speed and good base-running skills. Place the next best available second-type hitter on the squad in the eighth spot. In the ninth spot choose a batter with power or speed. A batter that is not consistent enough to bat higher in the lineup but possesses power and speed is ideal.

If a leadoff type of hitter bats in the sixth spot, the seventh hitter should have some or all the qualities of a second hitter. He should be able to bunt, make good contact, and hit behind the runner. The seventh hitter can help move the sixth hitter up by bunting, taking pitches, or by using the hit-and-run. Evaluate the two remaining players. Place the hitter who makes the best contact in the eighth spot. Place the one with the most power in the ninth spot. Though the ninth hitter may lack consistency, he will have many opportunities to use that power to produce some big runs.

The players who bat in the seventh through ninth spots may be outstanding defensive players with limited hitting skills. Consider each player's best physical assets and incorporate those assets into the lineup. Consider speed or power for the ninth spot in the lineup. Second, try to make the sixth and seventh hitters compatible. The third alternative is to pair up the seventh and eighth hitters. Consider staggering the hitters according to speed, power, or whether they are right-handed or left-handed.

As with many suggestions, the information given begins with the ideal. As coaches, we do not always have a lineup that has an ideal hitter in each spot. Either bunch the good hitters or sprinkle them judiciously throughout the lineup. If the priority is to have the best defensive players on the field, then the coach must use his creativity to make the lineup as potent as possible. Avoid grouping weak hitters. Placing three weak hitters in a row essentially gives the opposition three easy innings in the game.

Player Selection

Who will be your everyday players? Coming up with the answer to that important question generally takes time. In the end the players decide for the coach. The best one or two players on any team can usually be picked from the pack. That leaves the coach with some tough choices. Some players are great practice players but are not so great in games. Others are not standouts in practice but seem to come alive when the umpire says play ball. That is why it takes time to evaluate the total skills of each player. The physical abilities give the coach a good starting point, but he must also look at the mental makeup of the player. Physical ability alone does not make a good player.

Some players have staying power and the temperament to play every day. Others do not. The coach should evaluate not only the physical skills of each player but also the emotional and physical staying power. Identifying those players who possess the durability and enthusiasm to play every day is important. Others become role players. It takes both kinds to win. Some will do well for short stints but have difficulty over the long haul. These players are invaluable to a team if they understand their roles.

Physical skills are easier to evaluate than mental and emotional capacity. Regular contact with the players under different circumstances will help the coaches correctly determine the status of each player. I look for a few revealing signs. I value the player who works on a skill with enough persistence to make measurable improvements. We consider highly those players who are not easily disappointed. Those who easily become disappointed and frustrated are usually short-term goal players. Determination and persistence are both traits of a steady performer. The player who arrives early and stays late should be considered strongly as a long-term goal player. If that player is a self-starter, eagerly seeks information, and diligently puts the information to use, he sends a strong message that he is an everyday player.

It takes an effort to evaluate each player. Some coaches can look inside each player and measure desire, persistence, and competitive strength.

Pitching Changes

Decisions about pitching changes are simply educated guesses. The first guess is the genesis for the second guess. Although almost everyone in the ballpark believes they know when to make pitching changes, the only person equipped to do that is the coach. The coach knows the ability, mental makeup, and idiosyncrasies of each pitcher on the squad. He has information on the opposition, including the tendencies of the opposing coach. The coach uses his game experience and his knowledge of strategy to make the important decisions.

The coach must consider many factors—the pitcher's mental approach, his effectiveness, his ability, and the competitive level of the pitcher in the bullpen. Only the coach can decide about relieving the pitcher. The coach has seen his pitcher in similar situations. His knowledge of the pitcher's competitive makeup is a valuable measuring tool.

In making pitching changes, the depth and strength of the pitching staff become a concern. Often the crowd shouts for the coach to remove the pitcher without considering the alternatives. If the pitching staff is deep and highly skilled, decisions are easier to make. When depth and skills are lacking, the tendency is to be slow in removing pitchers. Because the coach is privy to the temperament and gamesmanship of the pitcher, the call is his. Fatigue and ineffectiveness are reasons for taking a pitcher out of the game. The ability of the pitcher in the bullpen is another reason. Matching the pitcher to the hitter is important.

Fatigue can be measured. Getting the ball up in the strike zone, dropping the arm, getting careless with his delivery, losing the bite on his breaking pitches, loss of speed, and standing upright as he finishes his pitches are a few telltale signs. Occasionally pitchers lose focus. Their concentration drops. A coach's sound evaluation of each pitcher becomes useful at this point.

If trust has developed between the pitcher and the coach, making decisions is usually easier. In some critical situations, I may ask a pitcher for his input. This does not mean I let him make the decision. Someone once told me that the pitcher will tell me what I want to hear. "I would not ask that pitcher," was my reply. Trust means an honest answer. The pitcher may not say a word but may speak volumes with his body language. I often find the information that settles a decision in the eyes of the pitcher.

Each coach should develop a system that the pitchers understand. I have used the following practice in making pitching changes. When I leave the dugout I have often made my decision, and that decision is final. On the occasions when I need more information, I do listen to the pitcher. I also look at his body language and his eyes. His words and actions will help him if he is sincere and positive. If either his words or his actions are negative or insincere, I will replace him.

Knowing when to change a pitcher requires that the coach have a feel for the game. Those who are good at making these decisions watch the pitcher with a fine eye. They notice details of the pitching delivery and carefully observe all the other aspects of the pitcher's game.

A Closing Note

Decision making is crucial for any coach. Some decisions are easy to make. Others are extremely difficult. Often the toughest ones are critical. The outcome of a game, or even the season, depends on sound decisions.

The average fan, or even a baseball expert, sees only part of the scene when the coach or manager employs strategy for a situation. He does not have as much information as the participating coaches. To make decisions without considering the competitive level and skill of the players is not sound. The coaches have data on the players involved. They have empirical knowledge about how their players handle various situations. Strategy is rarely so simple as using a prescribed solution to every situation.

Coaches, like players, experience enlightened periods when their senses are heightened. They also have days when the flow of the game is difficult to find. In games filled with erratic rhythms and inconsistent play, sound strategies are hard to employ. Decisions that cover a given situation in one game may not cover a similar situation in another. Games that are out of control get that way because the participants have lost control of some of their skills and emotions. Textbook strategies are seldom useful in those games. With the variety of challenges in a baseball season, the coach needs a solid base from which to operate. I trust that this chapter demonstrates that percentage baseball is a foundation on which to make sound decisions.

CHAPTER EIGHTEEN

Competing in Tournaments and Playoffs

Cliff Gustafson

Hope springs eternal.

An old saying in baseball is "Hope springs eternal." In the old days this referred to major-league spring training, but it can be applied to every team as it begins its preseason practice. In college baseball, preseason starts in fall practice. Everyone knows that the foundation of an outstanding college team begins with recruiting good talent. But when fall practice begins, you have the players you are going to compete with, and you must begin focusing on the spring season. Developing spirit and attitude to become a playoff-caliber team becomes extremely important at that point.

I have always believed that it is important to set goals for the team and for each player. These goals should be realistic yet attainable through hard work and dedication. It is important that each player accept responsibility to strive to reach those goals.

Fall practice is the time for basics and fundamentals. It is also the time to teach your philosophy so each player will begin to think in your terms. Emphasis should be on earning a position on the team, so that on the first day of spring practice each player is aware of his role.

At the University of Texas at Austin, we were fortunate to have a long tradition of winning baseball teams, and we made each player we recruited aware of the responsibility he would have in maintaining, and even improving, that tradition. We wanted every player to know that team expectations would be high. I felt this would reduce the pressure each player might feel.

Early in my career at Texas each time we qualified for the College World Series, Rod Dedeaux and his University of Southern California Trojans were there. They won five consecutive national titles, yet they were not always the best team. I observed something very important during that period. Seven teams that made it to the College World Series were hoping to win it, but one team that made it, USC, *expected* to win it. With that attitude, losing a game early in the tournament or falling behind early in a game did not faze them. I think Skip Bertman at Louisiana State University has in recent years established that attitude in his teams. In later years at Texas, I heard comments from opposing coaches and players that Texas expected to win every game. That was exactly the attitude I wanted my teams to have. If each player worked hard at fundamentals and conditioning, their confidence would soar, enabling each to perform to the best of his ability.

Scheduling to Develop Depth

If a team is to be successful, it must have quality pitching with depth. When you advance to the tournaments, especially the six-team regional tournament, depth is essential. Knowing this, we provided every pitcher we would need down the road with opportunities to make many appearances in games. If our weekend series did not permit us to use them all, we would schedule a scrimmage outing on Monday or Tuesday with gamelike conditions. For our season in the spring, we divided our schedule into three seasons—first the nonconference schedule, second the conference schedule, and third the postseason playoffs.

We arranged the nonconference schedule to have a balance between very strong teams, good teams, and some weaker teams. With the at-large possibilities for NCAA play, you must always try to establish a good overall record. I never really trusted the Rating Percentage Index as much as I did the number of wins as a measure for playoff consideration. Ideally, the preconference schedule would include participation in a tournament, which would give our players a feel for tournament participation in the postseason. Before conference play, we tried to arrange our pitchers' starts to give them a good chance to succeed and build confidence. It was also important to have a couple marquee weekend series with nationally ranked programs that would pack the ballpark, both at home and on the road, just before opening conference play.

For the second, or conference, season we always had a three-game weekend series, which in a strong conference like the now-defunct Southwest Conference was sure to put a burden on our pitching staff as well as provide a pressure-packed weekend for the position players. This was further preparation for the pressure of postseason play.

It was also important to schedule nonconference games on Tuesdays to allow games for pitchers who pitched only a little, or not at all, in the weekend conference series. This also gave us an opportunity to give playing time and more at bats to early season nonstarters. You will often discover a pitcher or position player you had overlooked who now appears ready to assume a larger role.

We had a junior pitcher who had been a highly regarded recruit but was crude and raw and had not distinguished himself during his first two years or early in his third year. We did not use him at all in our first two conference series. We then had a Tuesday nonconference game and an open week in conference play the following weekend. He pitched well on Tuesday, so we gave him another start on Sunday. He earned a berth as one of our top starters for the remainder of the season. He was first team all-American and a first-round draft pick in June of that season. Jerry Don Gleaton went on to pitch for about 12 years in the big leagues.

Another example of why we like to keep nonstarters sharp through spot starts, scrimmages, and mental preparation occurred with a backup second baseman named Johnny Sutton. During the regional tournament we lost the second game to a great Mississippi State team. What was worse, one of our all-time leading hitters, our left fielder, was injured and would be out for the tournament. Because of Johnny Sutton's intensity and desire, I inserted him in left field. He became the spark who led us back to win the tournament, beating Mississippi State twice. Sutton was named tournament Most Valuable Player (MVP) and continued to energize us through the College World Series to an undefeated championship.

In preparation for postseason tournament play, we were fortunate to have a postseason Southwest Conference Tournament preceding regional tournament play. We tried to switch gears slightly from our pretournament routine. Although we continued to work hard in practice, we shortened our workouts, rested our top pitchers, and provided more fun activities in our practices. We wanted the players to enjoy the postseason experience yet focus on the impending tournaments and stay loose and relaxed before the actual competition. During those few days, we reviewed our early season fundamental drills and continued to practice our special plays—bunting plays, defending bunts and double steals, and all the team plays we might have to execute.

Setting Up Your Pitching

Probably the most important decision entering a playoff tournament involves setting up your pitching plans. In regional tournaments, the first-round matchups were determined by seeding. If your team was seeded No. 1, you played the No. 6 seed. I believe this is the only time you might consider starting a pitcher other than your number one pitcher. Even then this is a ticklish option. If you decide to hold back your number one pitcher, there is a danger that this move would affect both your team's mental approach and the opponent's approach. Your players are likely to feel that this opponent will be easy. Further, your opponent would be aided both by the obvious opinion that you do not respect them very much and by the knowledge that they will not have to face your best pitcher. This means that you would very possibly receive a lesser effort from your team and a greater effort from the opponent.

The other drawback to holding back your best pitcher is obviously that he might not be available later in the tournament. With all these considerations in mind, it is nearly always advisable to go with your number one pitcher in the first game. You might be able to obtain an early lead and remove him after the trend of the game has been established.

To illustrate the importance of this decision, it is important to remember that any team in the playoffs probably has one outstanding pitcher. Baseball is a game where just one man, a good pitcher, can keep his team in the game. I violated my normal practice of starting my great left-handed pitcher, Greg Swindell, in the first game of a regional tournament one year when we opened with Southern University, a team from what then was a weak baseball conference. Our scouting reports indicated that Southern was not a strong team. But they proved to have a great pitcher, and we soon saw that we had our hands full. With a 2-2 score in the sixth inning, we brought Swindell into the game and were fortunate to pull out a 3-2 win in 12 innings. Their pitcher later played in the big leagues for several years. That was a strong lesson to me.

In the 1996 regional tournament we were competing in, the University of Miami was the No. 1 seed and opened against No. 6 seed Sam Houston State University. Miami Coach Jim Morris understandably thought he could save his ace for later, so he started his number three or four pitcher. They lost that game to Sam Houston. Miami proved to be good enough to overcome that loss and came back to win the tournament. I know that Coach Morris experienced many anxious moments as a result of that first-game loss.

An exception to the advised rule of going with your number one pitcher in the first game of a tournament might be if your number one pitcher is a right-hander and you are facing a lineup loaded with left-handed hitters. If you have a left-handed starting pitcher it might be a good idea to start him. You should consider spotting your left-handed starter against a team that is strong on the left side unless you have more than one left-handed starter. This becomes one of the most important decisions you have to make in tournament play, because a high percentage of left-handed hitters are not nearly as good against left-handed pitchers.

One Lefty Who Burned Us

Sometimes the lefty-versus-lefty percentage can backfire on you, as it did against us at the College World Series during USC's amazing run of five consecutive championships. We had a very good left-handed pitcher going and were locked up in a tense 2-2 game in the top of the eighth inning. With two outs and a runner at second, we had a choice of pitching to USC's right-handed hitting three-hole hitter or putting him on and pitching to their number four hitter, a lefty who was 0 for 3 with two strikeouts. We elected to walk the right-hander and pitch to the left-handed hitter. After two weak swings on sliders away, the strategy was looking pretty good. The next slider was up a little, and the left-handed USC hitter hit the ball over the scoreboard. We lost 5-2. That left-handed hitter was Fred Lynn, who went on to a great major-league career.

In my defense, the next day USC flip-flopped their three and four hitters against a right-handed pitcher. Their opponent had almost the same situation and elected to walk Lynn. The next hitter (the one we had intentionally walked the previous day) hit the ball out of the park. USC went on to win their fifth straight championship. Rod Dedeaux, certainly the greatest college coach of all time as well as a wonderful friend, kids me to this day about my decision to pitch to Fred Lynn.

Probably the easiest decision to gamble on with your starting pitcher is for game two of the regional. You have seen your opponent play earlier in the tournament, and you probably have information about their number two pitcher. Because your second, third, and fourth starters are probably not as prominent in your season success as your number one pitcher, holding back your number two pitcher will not have as much of a psychological impact on your team or the opponent.

A significant factor in selecting your starting pitcher, especially after the first game of a tournament, can be the umpire working the plate. If you have seen all the umpires who are working the tournament, you should have observed the strike zone of each one. Though we might want to think the strike zone is constant, we know that each umpire's judgment of the strike zone varies some from that of another. If the plate umpire has a very tight strike zone, you should select a pitcher with good control for that game. Conversely, if you know that the umpire has a very large strike zone, that would be the best time to start the pitcher who sometimes struggles with control. Taking this factor a step further, if you have seen that a particular umpire calls any pitch three to six inches beyond the outside corner a strike, you can take advantage of this by using a pitcher who likes to work hitters away. Your catcher must also observe this tendency and set up out there.

The regional tournaments, the six-team variety, that had existed for the last 25 years were the toughest on your pitching staff because you would be required to play as many as six games in four days. If you could survive that difficult and competitive tournament, the pressure on your pitching staff was much less at the College World Series because of off-days and never having to play two games in one day. Under the format of recent years it became possible to get to the College World Series final game by using only two pitchers. This was in sharp contrast to the regional experience. Tournament play, whether it is early season, conference, regional, or, ultimately, the College World Series, puts renewed importance on conditioning and adequate rest. The trainer's job takes on a new dimension, involving care of the players, treatment of pitchers' arms, and making sure the players receive plenty of rest when off the field. Emphasizing good eating habits to the players becomes an added responsibility as well.

Adjusting to Tournament Schedules

Sometimes you get into situations, even in the College World Series, where you have no control over rest and sleep schedules. This happened to us in a serious way in 1981. We opened against a great Arizona State team, the best offensive college baseball team I have ever seen. ASU put us in the loser's bracket right away, and we started our effort to come back. At that point in College World Series history, the NCAA had a deal with CBS to televise a Saturday noon game, which CBS hoped would be for the national championship. This would happen only if one team was undefeated entering the final game.

In this particular tournament, however, Oklahoma State University had defeated ASU earlier in the tournament. We were to play a Friday night game against an undefeated OSU team, with the winner going to the Saturday televised game with once-defeated ASU. We got into one of those rock'em, sock'em games with OSU that lasted 15 innings. We erupted with eight runs in the top of the 15th and won 14-6. The game ended at 2:00 A.M. on Saturday. By the time we got our team back to the hotel, it was after 4:00 A.M.

Needless to say, we were tired when we arrived at Rosenblatt Stadium at 10:30 A.M. for the noon game against ASU on national television. The ever-gracious ASU coach, the late Jim Brock, met me at the field and offered to give my team a pep talk. He said he would start out by saying, "I know you guys are tired, very tired, and didn't get but two or three hours of sleep, and I know it is going to be really tough to play this game." At this point I stopped Coach Brock and said no thanks to his kind offer. He truly had one of the greatest wits the college game has ever known. By the way, ASU beat us soundly on Saturday and then won the national championship on Sunday by defeating a great OSU team.

Adjusting to the Umpire

On the subject of taking advantage of your knowledge of an umpire's strike zone tendencies, you can use this information offensively as well. I always tried to teach hitters to be disciplined and to teach them a good two-strike approach so that they would be confident when behind in the count. Thus, if your umpire is one with a tight strike zone, you can afford to take more pitches. This is especially true when you are ahead in the count. On the other hand, if the umpire has a very large strike zone, you must encourage your hitters to hit early in the count.

Once in a regional tournament, we drew an umpire who had an unbelievably large strike zone. Our hitters were unable to adjust early in the game and took many called third strikes. I resorted to using a hit-and-run approach every time our hitters had two strikes, forcing the hitter to swing at anything.

You must train your pitchers and hitters to adjust to the umpire's strike zone rather than become upset by it. This is especially true in regional play and in the College World Series because you will get umpires from other parts of the country you have not seen before. They can be quite different in the way they work.

Adjusting to Your Opponent

I believe every coach wants a good scouting report on their opponents. It is important to have as much knowledge as possible about your opponent. But I do not believe in loading down my players with too much information. I told my teams many times that if they go out and play the way they can, they will not have to worry about the opponent.

I was never a big believer in trying to steal signs from the opponent or trying to call the opponent's pitches. Sometimes, though, I thought a pitcher was so good that we needed to help our hitters as much as we could. Two of those instances happened in back-to-back games in the 1989 College World Series when we faced Alex Fernandez of Miami and Ben McDonald of LSU. We were able to pick up a tip in their deliveries and successfully call their pitches, which enabled our hitters to deliver many key hits early and beat both of them handily. They both went on to great careers in the major leagues.

Another instance that became one of the most memorable games of my coaching career was against Florida State University in the 1987 College World Series. Their great pitcher, Richie Lewis, was our mound opponent, and our hitters needed help. During the third inning we detected a difference in his delivery when he threw his hard slider, a devastating pitch that we wanted our hitters to lay off of. We were then able to get some big hits to take the lead in the game. Lewis finally realized we were calling his pitches, and our great catcher, Brian Johnson, a first-round draft pick, became a victim of Richie Lewis's great competitive fire. He signaled fastball to Johnson three straight times, and blew the ball past him. We were fortunate to hold on and win the game.

In spite of these successful results in calling pitches for our hitters, I still do not feel it is a good practice to do it regularly. There is too much danger that a player will be hurt, and I think it is more important that hitters learn to handle all types of pitches.

Preparation and Luck

As in every sport, success in tournaments and postseason play depends on having your team well drilled, in good physical condition, and mentally prepared so they can execute all the plays in all the situations that arise. You must continue to play the style of game that got you to the playoffs, that you have used all season long.

You must have an element of luck on your side as well. This involves being injury free, an area you really have very little control over. Many potential championship teams have been wrecked by one or two key injuries, especially to the pitching staff. I do not believe that you can ever take a cautious route to the playoffs by trying to protect your players from injury. Encourage them to practice hard and play hard always. If injuries occur late in the season you cannot control it. But if you have developed depth by using extra pitchers and position players during the season, you may have someone who can step up and plug the hole, as Johnny Sutton did for us in 1983.

Another element of success in postseason play is the ability of a team to get hot during the playoffs. I believe this is a result of preparation and expectation of the team and coaching staff more than luck. My former boss and legendary football coach Darrell Royal once said, "Good luck happens when preparation meets opportunity." I believe that is why the great coaches in all sports seem to have "good luck" once their teams reach the playoffs. It is no coincidence that the greatest college coaches our game has seen, men such as Rod Dedeaux and, most recently, Skip Bertman of LSU, are successful in postseason play. Their teams always showed sound fundamentals, great poise, and tremendous pride, along with the appearance that they not only hoped to win but expected to win. They appear confident, their coaches appear confident, they display great sportsmanship, and, maybe most important, the whole squad and staff seem to pull together just a little bit more than the teams they beat to win those postseason tournaments.

PART

V

Player Motivation and Leadership

CHAPTER NINETEEN

Establishing Pride and Tradition

Rod Dedeaux

I am pleased to be included as a contributor to this fine book and to have the opportunity to address what I believe are essential virtues for coaching and playing in a successful baseball program. Our USC teams enjoyed many championship seasons, confirming the fact that nothing succeeds like success. And along with that success we developed great pride and tradition in our program. But where did it all start?

Some observers claimed that luck had much to do with it. And I'm the first to acknowledge that we were very, very lucky through the years. But I never wanted our players to feel they could depend on luck. Luck is usually on the side of the ablest navigator. Luck is what might happens after a team has done everything right—to perfection. Then the residue is luck.

Others suggested that we outspent the opposition. For example, after winning a championship game, our athletic director, Jess Hill, was approached by another school's AD, who claimed that, "USC has perenially such a big advantage because of the great amount of financial aid help that is available." Not so! Because USC is a private school, financial aid was very limited. This forced us to develop individuals on our team who were not getting baseball financial aid. It was from this pool of players that individuals were inserted into the lineup as we went along through the season. In fact, a careful analysis of our lineup in that championship game found that the pitcher was the only player who had a full baseball scholarship when he entered the university.

More consistent than luck and more important than money, and the real foundation for success at all levels of amateur baseball, is the effective physical and mental development of every player in the program. When we took the field each game we believed we had better players who were better prepared to win as a team.

Recruiting the Right Players

Let's get down to the most basic ingredient of our success, which is having the best players. My formula in recruiting was to attempt to get players who were better than those of the opposition, and then be sure that neither my assistant coaches nor I did anything to impede their development. We sought players who possessed physical talent but also a strong mental makeup, who wanted to be part of our program, and who had the aptitude to develop.

In evaluating talent, every coach must answer these five questions about the God-given physical attributes of a player:

- Can he run?

- Can he throw?
- Can he hit?
- Can he hit with power?
- Can he field?

If a player has three or more of these physical gifts, he can play in the Major Leagues.

Along with the physical evaluation comes a more challenging assessment of the hidden mental makeup of the player. Many years ago, a brilliant article in the *The Saturday Evening Post* addressed the topic of scouting players on the basis of physical ability. It was titled "You Can't Scout Desire." I never felt that is quite accurate.

We, as college coaches, have the advantage of examining prospects' academic records. These give us a peek at the athletes' desire to make good in the classroom. If the discipline is there to study and accept responsibility in one area, it figures to be there in another—such as on the baseball field. The best student isn't always the best athlete, but the athlete who applies himself academically almost always gets the most out of himself on the ball diamond, as well.

We have a tendency to get carried away looking for the player who can "do everything." I've heard scouts and coaches say disdainfully about a player that, "He can't play; all he can do is hit." To me that's like saying, "All Frank Sinatra could do is sing." Instead of focusing on what the player can't do, let's figure out a place to "hide" his deficiencies where he won't kill us until those skills improve. Meanwhile, he can hit .350 for the team.

Pursuing Perfection

While we should accept imperfection in striving to improve physical talent, mental mistakes by those who have been properly taught and possess the physical tools to perform skills correctly are unacceptable. My personal philosophy was that perfect execution was the goal. Excellence was expected, good was commonplace, and being just mediocre or fair was not tolerated.

In our organization we expected everything to be done correctly all the time, based on the philosophy that you can't exchange good for bad habits at will. One cannot eat peas with a knife at home, then go out to the Ritz and know how to eat them with a fork.

We also believed in one set of rules. I wasn't smart enough to remember more than one set, and this approach reinforced our emphasis on doing everything correctly.

We didn't leave the handling of adversity to chance. We worked at just how we should act. The pressure of tough games, playing before hostile crowds, "breaks" going for the opposition but against you, and fighting to come from behind can all cause unprepared and undisciplined team to fall apart. It is in these situations where discipline and pride really pays off.

One of my favorite stories related to this is about an incident that happened in the Southern League, where the heat and humidity can be overwhelming. The players had been going badly and were consistently complaining about the hot weather, using it as a primary excuse for their misplays. This prompted their fiery manager, Bobby Bragen, to lay down the law: "I don't want to hear another complaint, and the first man who does is automatically fined one hundred dollars" ($100 was a lot of money in those days). The pitcher that particular day was one who liked the "bright lights" and what went with it, but not the searing heat in the South. When the pitcher came struggling into the dugout after a particularly rough inning, he slammed down his glove on the bench and unleashed a few expletives about the "blankety-blank" weather. While lamenting the heat, he was obviously unaware that the manager had remained in the dugout rather than taking his accustomed position on the field to coach third base. When the pitcher spotted the manager and realized his predicament, he hurriedly followed his comment with, "And that's *just the way I like it*."

That in a nutshell sums up our philosophy. When the going gets really tough, that's just the way we like it. The harder the task, the sweeter the reward!

Learning From Mistakes

While constantly in pursuit of perfection, you also have realize that errors of commission, if not omission, are going to happen. So, as we moved through the season, we expected to learn from every game. We'd look beyond whether we won or lost. How well did we play the game? If we did everything right and made fewer mistakes than the opposition, we knew the wins and losses would take care of themselves. I was concerned that we played the way we were supposed to play.

We have all heard mistakes rationalized or downplayed by comments like, "Oh well, even though we made an error in the field, the runner didn't score, so it doesn't make any difference." Oh yes, it *does* make a difference! Whether the results of the play were harmful or not harmful is not the point. The mistake has to be eliminated because the next time it could cost you the game. Keep in mind we're only talking about mental mistakes. The physical mistakes are forgotten. If a player makes a mental mistake (takes a nap in the field, so to speak), then it's all right if he tosses and turns and can't sleep at night. When he learns from the mistake, and resolves that the mistake will not happen again, then he can fall asleep for a peaceful slumber.

I have been asked from time to time, when witnessing an inexcusable error in a championship-type game, what I would've done had I been coaching the team. My answer is that we would not have had that mistake happen, because by that time we would've learned from previous mistakes. Anyone who would still make that mistake in a championship game would not be in the line-up. A team must learn to do everything mentally correct, whether they are playing on a sandlot, or at Dodger Stadium in front of 50,000 people, or for the College World Series Championship.

Developing Pride

When the going gets tough is when the team must be able to reach down and demonstrate pride. There is no such thing as a crash course for pride. It takes time and good habits to instill the goals that lead to pride. Nine women can't conceive a child in one month. It takes one woman nine months. No shortcuts. Patience and dedication must be the virtues to assure that successes will be repeated. The right things have to be done over and over again for the proper goals to be achieved—they must become habits.

Pride and respect have to be earned. It's like the boxer in the ring who is getting pounded viciously, and upon returning to his corner, his trainer, who is attempting to pump him up falsely, says, "You're doing great. He hasn't touched you; he hasn't hurt you." The fighter replies, "Boss, then you better keep your eye on the referee, because somebody in that ring is knocking the heck out of me." Self-respect and pride must be earned the hard way. It won't work to simply have someone tell you that you're doing great. You have to know it in your heart.

Too often, pride is associated with negative behaviors: self-aggrandizement, arrogance, conceit, or an undue sense of one's own superiority. However, real pride is positive and reflects a *proper* sense of personal dignity, worth, and honorable self-respect. Vanity and conceit can be founded upon nothing. Pride, on the other hand, is founded upon something real, upon something that has been done, upon something tangible. Conceit is offensive. Self-conceit is ridiculous. But a proud self-respect is a worthy feeling.

We took pride in our good habits, from our pregame practices, to the way we took our batting and infield practice. They were precisely organized. During infield we put total pressure on every hit ball, just as though it were in the ball game. The outfielders had to charge the ball, get in throwing position, and throw a strike. Everyone had to be in the correct position. We expected every throw to be perfect, and we never allowed a careless catch or a dropped ball (that's mental). Because we didn't permit errant throws or misplays, we fully expected to take infield with one ball.

On quite a few occasions I addressed the team on the first day of practice and told them that I felt we could be real good in the upcoming season—that here sat the best darn baseball team in the nation, and now, starting this day, we were to going to prove it. I would address the newcomers on the squad, "If you can't make the team, don't blame yourselves. Blame us, because we are the ones who made the decision that you were good enough to make this club—and we don't make too many mistakes regarding talent." But we needed a plan to generate victories from this raw talent and prove that we were indeed the best team around. So, on opening day we had a simple but very effective plan: From this day forward, everyone does *everything* right, and with enthusiasm. It makes no difference how large or small the task may seem. We took pride in all facets of our game, from practices and playing the game to picking up a stray ball lying on the ground that might cause a sprained ankle. After all, a sprained ankle could cost us the pennant. So pick it up.

With that plan, we'd practice all through the year and expect total effort. Practice does not make perfect. Perfect practice makes perfect. We strove to do the little things right, as well as the big things. Again, it was a matter of pride. We sought to instill pride in the team, and we reinforced that everyone must be totally committed to the team. And you know what? If you have pride in yourself, you naturally develop team pride as well. Shakespeare said it best: "This above all: To thine own self be true. And it will follow as the night the day, thou cans't not then be false to any man." That's team pride. If you're true to yourself, you'll be true to your team.

Nothing pleased me more than when we would hear opposing players remarking, "Why is it that when we play on various teams against these same players throughout the summer and winter, they're just 'ordinary guys' like all of us, but when you put them together in one bunch, they truly believe that nobody can beat them? And they're usually right!" It all has to do with pride—in yourself and in being part of a team.

As a team progresses and reaches a point where there is pride in the whole team, one of the great pluses is a genuine affection developed between the players and the loyalty to each other that goes far beyond the college years. Our fellows always seem to feel that the lasting association and fun they had playing baseball far exceeded that in any other organization within the university—fraternity, clubs, classes, etc. This was because, as a team, we really did have fun on and off the field.

One of the many instances that displays this type of enjoyment and loyalty occurred in 1978. At the beginning of the season I told the team we did have the best team in the United States, and that what we had to do was to prove it. (They did believe me and they did prove it.) In our annual alumni game that spring, as always, we picked a team that was celebrating a certain period or event and suggested to them that they gather and play again as a team against our varsity. And since this was 1978, we suggested to the 1968 team that they celebrate their 10th anniversary of the national championship by playing our varsity squad in our alumni game. We took it a step further and invited the 1958 team also, because they would be celebrating their 20th anniversary and national championship. And then, we invited the 1948 team to come celebrate the 30th anniversary of their national championship.

There were 23 players on the 1948 team, including the bat boy. Two of them had passed away, leaving 21. Would you believe, without any fanfare other than just passing the word around and telling one another, that 19 players showed up, 30 years later, to actually play in the game, and have a party the day before and again that night? All but one had received a degree, and that one had been successful in his particular profession. Everyone had been successful in a profession, in education, in business, and certainly in life. That also included the 23rd person, the bat boy, who happened to have had a very successful career as a big league manager. He was known to the baseball world as "Sparky" Anderson. We all called him, and still do, "Georgie." Bless his heart, he has always said that the 5-year association with our USC team was the force in his life that led to his success.

Making Every Player His Best

Identification with and pride in being part of the team must be held by each member of the squad. That is why it is essential that you make a strong effort to give currently mediocre players a good chance to develop. At schools where financial aid is restricted, you simply won't succeed without such a player development system.

It is a tremendous asset, of course, for USC to be a prestigious university located right in the heart of Los Angeles. Something is always going on in addition to sporting events, so every weekend is like Homecoming. This has been a big advantage to us, and the university has made its expectations of excellence widely known. But because USC is a private school with very limited financial aid, we were forced to *develop* individuals who were not on baseball scholarships. It was from this pool of players that we inserted into the line-up throughout the season. In practice they had learned all the attributes that we demanded. And when it came time to perform, they were ready.

In baseball at USC, we never let the term "walk on" be part of our vocabulary. That is, we didn't favor the players on a baseball scholarship simply because they had the scholarship, and we didn't discriminate against the walk-ons simply because they didn't have a scholarship. The financial aid an athlete had could never be a determination of his worth, nor a judgement of his ability. The best players had to play, and it didn't make any difference whether they were on a baseball scholarship or not.

For the development of these individuals, there of course has to be a plan. We were handicapped with a very limited area on which to practice and play. There was only one field with no other territory on the outside. Everything had to take place on the field or in the batting cage. Part of the plan was to work at getting these individuals into ball games at the slightest opportunity. This resulted in losing practice games, but our spirit and desire were undiminished. We strived to win with the team we had on the field with the players in those particular positions. But there is also a lot that a young player can learn by sitting on the bench.

The time that players spend on the bench is very important in developing team skills and the mental approach. We expected the bench players to be trying just as hard to win as those players that were in the field, and we expected their presence on the bench to be a learning period by closely observing what was happening on the playing field.

We challenged our players not to say, "I'm just as good as the person in the field, so why am I not playing?" My answer was, "Why should we make a change to be just as good as the person playing? You have to be *better* than the one playing to replace him." A developing player has to prepare himself while sitting on the bench so that when he does get into the game, he will not make the mental mistakes. It is often said "Don't make the same mistake twice." My philosophy is "Don't make the same mistake once." By observing from the bench you have learned what's right or wrong before you ever step onto the field.

After I graduated from USC, where I was shortstop and captain and we had won the championship, I joined the Brooklyn Dodgers, having been signed by the one and only Casey Stengel. The thrill of sitting on the bench at Ebbetts Field was awesome, and the clubhouse meetings listening to the old professor were spellbinding. On one occasion, Casey was giving a powerful lecture on a play that had been incorrectly executed the day before. And at a certain point he looked at me and shouted, "Dedeaux, what would you do if that play comes up today?" And I answered, "Skipper, I would slide down on the bench closer to you so that I could see it better." A strong bench is vital to a baseball program's success. And time spent on the bench—if used effectively—can play a vital role in players' development.

Inspiring Veteran Leadership

While building up the bench it is equally important to be nurturing leadership from returning veteran players. This is made more difficult in our sport because of the routine loss of outstanding players to major league baseball after their junior year. And, typically, the schools that have the better teams and the better ballplayers will lose more high-caliber athletes at the end of their junior year. Even so, there must be an on-going effort to inspire the veterans to take charge of the incoming and younger ballplayers.

There is also great value in having previous ball players continue on as assistant coaches. Because of our perennial limited budget for coaching, we perhaps did this more than most by having ballplayers continue in our program as coaches. Even if they were playing pro baseball in the minor leagues, they did not report until later in the spring, and in some instances there was a prearrangement to permit them to finish the spring school season before reporting.

The 1984 Olympic Team, made up of truly superstars and stars-to-be, was fortunate to have, among others, leaders like Mark McGwire, who in his quiet way led by example. When a player questioned a decision by the coaching staff, he would admonish them and say, "Just do what the rules are that are laid down. I doubt that your opinion on the matter is superior to this coaching staff. My counsel is to do it and do it enthusiastically." Having leaders like this on the team really helps the younger players develop.

"Trojans Never Give Up"

The Trojan baseball teams have always had tenacity to keep fighting and not give up. It was a matter of pride. In fact, our motto was "Trojans never give up." A very warm thought to me is worth repeating. Pete Redfern was truly one of our outstanding young pitchers with a very promising career ahead. He was a sensation in his first two years in the majors, and I was told by none other than Robin Yount that, "Pete might just be the toughest pitcher in the American League." Then Pete was hurt in a fluke accident in the off-season while diving into shallow water and suffered a crippling spinal injury. He was not expected to survive, but he slowly showed signs of possible recovery when the medical opinion was that he had "no chance." Days later when he began to show some signs of recovery, the nurses and doctors said that it was absolutely a miracle that he was still alive. I was then allowed to go in and visit with him. The first thing he said in a voice so low it was barely a whisper was, "Trojans never give up." He is now confined to a wheelchair, but has gone on to do some successful coaching in the high school ranks.

We expect our returning players to provide sterling and direct leadership, both with counsel and by setting the example (we call them "Salty Vets"). With rare exceptions, our assistant coaches have been former players at USC and this has made for total continuity in our ideologies and systems.

Motivating Your Team

In baseball, as in the business world, some people are better motivated than others, just as some are better motivators than others. Veteran leaders and individual players' own initiative certainly help, but in the end, motivation is the responsibility of the coaching staff. And the secret to motivating baseball players, or players of any other sport, is successful salesmanship. The coach must sell the idea so that everyone will want to do it, and do it with enthusiasm.

I believe there are three steps to successful salesmanship:

1. Make the person think the way you think.
2. Make them feel the way you feel.
3. Make them act the way you want them to act.

Tommy Lasorda was a great motivator. Sparky Anderson certainly had that knack throughout his entire managerial career. Casey Stengel was able to convince his players which things were right and which were not. Even though they had different styles of communication, they made sure their messages were clear and motivational.

People used to talk about Casey's "Stengelese" and how impossible it was to follow his dialogue. Well let me tell you, from high school days, I literally sat at his feet by the hour and by the day listening to his discourse, and then would work with him on those principles. He had a way to make you understand, and I've always said I could understand every word he said. (Now I have to admit that sometimes it worried me when I was the only one who seemed to understand him!)

One of the many reasons clinics such as we have at the annual ABCA convention are so great is not necessarily for the new techniques discussed, but because they may give you different ideas of how to present the same facts the speaker has been trying to convey. You then leave the discussion thinking about how you might modify and apply the words and concepts presented to benefit your own program. You think about how to use this new knowledge to motivate your players, using your own words and style of expression.

I often use a phrase picked up from a great former football coach at USC, Howard Jones. He had an expression he would use over and over again in motivating his players. Coach Jones would exclaim, "Ya gotta wanna!" Successful ball players have this desire. They *want* to succeed—it's a matter of pride.

Building and Maintaining a Tradition

Traditions—whether they are beliefs, stories, procedures and other "how to" knowledge—are usually handed down from one generation to the next in an unwritten form. Veteran leadership and continuity on the coaching staff help, but when trying to sustain a winning tradition in a baseball program, it helps to have some trophies or championship rings—tangible evidence of your past successes. But what if you don't have a shelf full of trophies yet? How do you establish a winning tradition?

As emphasized previously, one of the primary ways to establish a winning tradition is to cultivate a sense of pride. Tradition and pride go hand in hand, and I've described some tangible ways to establish the intangible pride into a baseball program. If you do this, you will be sowing the seeds of tradition and becoming a team to reckon with year after year.

Winning is obviously part of that tradition. But the toughest thing in sports is to win *again*. One of the factors is, of course, the quality and the attitude of the returning players. The "To Win Again" mentality reaches down into the true character of the players. Dedication starts with the opening day of the season, and never lets up. Players have to know that they can't merely throw their gloves onto the field and expect to win the ball game. And they sure can't take their scrapbooks into the dugout and have it produce victories.

There is no question that a history of success in sports has a profound impact on a school. Winning becomes a tradition, and the administrators, staff, students, and alumni become family with the teams. They live and die through the ups and downs, and together exude confidence and the will to win. They have pride in their school, just as you have pride in your baseball program. Once you establish pride into your program—pride in everything, from the little details to the pride that comes from knowing you worked hard and did everything right—good things will happen on the field as well.

The difficulty of repeating past successes (what I call the "To Win Again" syndrome) is an on-going challenge not only in sports, but in the business world as well. If a company has a successful year, there is no way the CEO will say, "Last year was a good year, so let's just do everything we did then and we'll get good results." No way! From day one, new challenges are issued to individuals in charge of certain areas. They are expected to set new and improved goals to meet new challenges and reach new heights of success. You can't rest on your laurels; they won't put runs on the scoreboard. It's the old story of climbing a flag pole: If you stop, you'll slide backwards. You've got to have the *pride* to keep climbing. As Coach Jones would say, "Ya gotta wanna!"

A Closing Note

People have been kind to say that we've had some very good teams, but one thing I can assure you, we all loved the game, and we had fun playing. Nobody had more fun than we did.

Chapters in the first part of this book emphasize the need to generate a love for the game and to make it fun for future generations of players and coaches. Let's not allow apathy or misguided legislation to take the joy out of baseball. Share your enthusiasm for the game and help others experience the pride that grows through the development of the mental and physical abilities of players and teams. For what makes baseball truly fun is not so much the winning itself as it is knowing the dedication, teamwork, and competitive effort that produced the outcome. And, in that regard, every season can be a success—part of a tradition.

CHAPTER TWENTY

Inspiring Today's Players

Skip Bertman

The rhythms and dynamics of teamwork are familiar to us as coaches, leaders, and managers. If you have ever put together a group that thinks, acts, and succeeds as one, then you know how rewarding and efficient teamwork can be.

A team is a group of people, usually peers, who combine their talents and abilities to accomplish a specific goal or series of goals. Teamwork is more than what you do; it is how you think. It is rarely perfect, so a good team mind-set is that 95 percent of the team members will do what's best for the team 95 percent of the time.

A commercial aircraft provides an analogy. When flying over a body of water, the aircraft is, technically speaking, off course 95 percent of the time. The navigational system must make tiny, continual corrections to make sure the plane lands exactly where it is supposed to. Building a team is like that. It's OK to be off course, as long as small corrections and adjustments are being made all the time. Teamwork is not a guru-driven, mystical process; it's a political process, it's brokering, adjusting, compromising, and getting others to buy in.

People want to be good teammates, but they don't know how to keep the natural forces of competition from pulling them toward self-serving goals. Teamwork requires individuals to surrender self-interest for the greater good of the team. The mind-set I'm talking about says, "I don't care who dropped the ball. If I can stretch and reach it, I'll put it back into play."

Being a good team member is a skill and, like any skill, a person can improve it. You have to realize that some people are better at it than others. We live in a society in which individual work and achievement are coveted. Sometimes, it's hard to find team-oriented role models outside your family. Most of the kids we're working with grew up in part in the 1980s, commonly known as the decade of greed. Good role models during that time were rare.

Almost all of today's young people are familiar with computers, which may also contribute to a reduced emphasis on team play. Yet, to have excellent team play, no team member can have an individual or hidden agenda. If his goals and ambitions are different from those of the team, the team is less likely to succeed. The question is how we as coaches and managers can get team members on the same page so they trust one another, enjoy one another, and have a mind-set of one.

Achieving a Team Mind-Set

At LSU, we strive for a team mind-set, and this is where I do some teaching. I cover the tradition of teamwork in America, from the pioneers who banded together to travel west in covered wagons, to the quality-control groups during World War II, to the feeling of one we had during the Persian Gulf War, or any other examples I can use to convey the message to my team. I teach them that anything can be accomplished if we can get enough people to care about what we are doing.

I often refer to a line from the Broadway play *Fiddler on the Roof.* You remember how it starts. In a very poor Russian village, the lead actor is on the rooftop trying to play the violin without falling off. Throughout the village, other fathers are on their roofs trying to scratch out a simple tune without falling off and breaking their necks. "We've kept our balance for many, many years," the actor says. "How? That I can tell you in one word—tradition!" Then he goes on to say that because of tradition each of us knows who he is and what is expected of him.

To think as one, as a team—that's the most satisfying part of the game. Actually, it's the heart of athletics—the blending of personalities, the individual sacrifice for group success. Only that kind of thinking can take you to a place where only teams can go.

Let's look at some of the elements of achieving that team mind-set. For example, when changing pitchers, I ask the pitcher on the mound to stay there and hand the ball off to the incoming pitcher and offer words of encouragement. The player may be leaving because he is not performing well, yet he is still going to offer encouragement to the new pitcher. That's a team mind-set.

On the practice schedule every day, I put a meaningful quotation or affirmation from the many I have collected over the years. You can never tell when somebody will be able to use that information. You have to motivate and build your team every day.

One thing we do that's not so subtle is our individual player conference. It gives us a chance to stay in touch with each player, get to know him better, and let him know we care. At least four times each year, I'll meet privately in my office with each young man on the team. We talk about grades, housing, the baseball program, and general topics. The young man may ask me anything about playing time and performance. The player knows that all this information is personal and confidential. I feel it is necessary, however, to involve parents, who are also part of the team. So I send them a report of all the matters we discuss. This keeps parents informed, so they can also be motivators, and it spurs players to take appropriate action because they know their parents are informed.

Here is a great quotation about teamwork from legendary Penn State football coach Joe Paterno: "When a team outgrows individual performance and learns team confidence, then excellence becomes a reality." I often distribute quotations like these to our players to promote the concept of teamwork.

Designing a Team Covenant

The team mind-set is the first thing we must establish. Next is our team covenant. A covenant is a binding, written agreement—a solemn promise. Naturally, we take our covenant seriously. I have everyone on our team—players, coaches, managers, trainers—sign a covenant. We design a custom covenant for each team. We start with our coaches' goals and priorities, which include academics and our moral environment. We carefully define excellence as we envision it. We include the team motto and a list of key phrases we continually use throughout our program:

- Synergy
- The law of averages
- Motivation
- Belief and faith
- Loyalty

Of course, we include a place for the players to sign the covenant. You can create your own covenant, but you must personalize and customize it for your team. That way, your players will know what you expect of them.

Creating Synergy

Next, I build on our team mind-set, our traditions, and our covenant to create synergy, which means working together. But synergism is more than that. It's two or more people working together in a way that their combined power is more than just the sum of their individual power.

Here's a great example of synergy from Pat Williams's book *The Magic of Teamwork*. His example is a horse-pulling contest at a county fair. The first-place horse pulled a sled weighing 4,500 pounds. The second-place horse pulled 4,000 pounds. The owners figured the two horses together could pull 8,500 pounds. But when the owners hitched the horses together, they were able to pull 12,000 pounds, far more than the sum of their individual efforts. That's synergism.

How does that affect your team? You can put together 9 guys who can play like 10, 11, or 12. The trick is to find the best 9 with true synergism. That team will play better than the team with 9 guys with the best statistics. That's why our written covenant contains the statement, "We play our best 9, not our 9 best." I look beyond statistics for emotion, excitement, and passion. I find that other players will often respond better when a particular player is in the lineup. I look for that response. That sends a message that individual statistics are not as important as team statistics.

The Law of Averages

Next I teach our players about the law of averages. It's not a principle, not a theory. It's a real law. So real is this law that insurance companies and the gambling industry put the entire fate of their enterprise into the law of averages. It doesn't predict what will happen on every play, but over the long haul, the law of averages must, absolutely must, work. It's a law! And remember, everything counts. It's in our covenant.

Taking One Step at a Time

In college, I once had a philosophy professor who asked the class, "When I clap my hands, how much does your life change?" Of course, I thought he was kidding, that my life wouldn't change at all, but I found out later that some chemical changes occur in the split-second of a clap. Then he said, "If I was to clap my hands during the entire four years you were in college, how much would your life change?" The answer, obviously, is a lot.

Like a single clap, some things are very difficult to measure. When one of my players visits a boys' club and talks to some of the youngsters, did the team get better? Yes, just as in that single clap. Will an extra round of batting practice win the national championship? Probably not, but if that extra round is just one of a series of claps, it will cause a lot of momentum.

Remember the first line in M. Scott Peck's book *The Road Less Traveled?* "Life is difficult." There's no doubt about that. What's difficult is taking small steps to achieve very large goals. A gentleman named Don Bennett knows a lot about small steps and difficulty in life. He was the first amputee to climb and descend Mount Rainier. After getting up and back down the 14,400-foot peak, a throng of reporters emerged and asked, "Don Bennett, how could you do that?" He looked down at his single leg and said, "One hop at a time."

That's how teams are built—one idea at a time, one practice at a time, one day at a time, one player at a time, and, yes, one clap at a time. A small series of successes causes a wave of momentum. Keep this in mind—your attention to detail will rub off on your players. We pay an awful lot of attention to detail at LSU—the way we dress, the way we fix the field, the way our cages look, and yes, the temperature of the coffee in the concession stand. Every decision you make counts. It's a law. It's in our covenant.

Believing in Miracles

We all need a lot of baseball fortune, but actually, luck has little to do with it. LUCK—Laboring Under Correct Knowledge. Luck is knowing the probabilities and making those continual, tiny adjustments to put your team in position to win. That's all coaches can do.

Coaches can't control the outcome of a game, but they can control probabilities. A football coach can get his kicker closer to the crossbar just before the winning field-goal try. A basketball coach can get his best shooter closer to the basket for that final shot. Of course, a baseball coach can get the winning run to the plate. Here's an example of how good baseball fortune combined with a great team mind-set created the greatest moment in my coaching career.

We were in Omaha in the championship game of the 1996 College World Series. With two outs in the bottom of the ninth, we're down by one run with a runner at third base. Warren Morris stepped to the plate. He had been injured for most of the season and hadn't hit a home run all year. Then, bang! He hit the first pitch out of the park. On the 50th anniversary of the College World Series, on what could have been the last at bat of the season, reality and fantasy merged for one short moment. The CWS had never been won that way in 50 years, but part of our mind-set is that we believe in miracles, in coming from behind, in winning against all odds. We believe in the power of the human spirit. It's in our covenant.

Now having this magic doesn't necessarily mean an athlete will win the Heisman or make it to the big leagues. Some will, and some won't. But it does mean they will be fun to work with and fun to watch. They will make memories and sometimes create victory out of pure dust. Because they perform so well under pressure, people will follow them anytime, anywhere. These people have passion, and that's something that can't be overrated in the team concept.

Every spring day or evening in America, in some league or another, a player will step to the plate with two outs in the bottom of the ninth and hit in the winning run. It's a real possibility, but you have to convince your players that your team can be the one to do it. You have to build on the team mind-set and get the winning run to the plate. Most important, you have to believe that it can happen.

Taking Responsibility

Another area we cover in the covenant is responsibility. In America today, the national pastime is no longer baseball; the national pastime is transfer of blame. Kids learn this at an early age. Democrats blame Republicans, Republicans blame Democrats, rich people say the government takes too much in taxes, and poor people say the government doesn't do enough for them. It goes on and on.

Baseball is a game well suited for transfer of blame. The mound is too high, or maybe it's too low. The field is too hard, or it's too soft. The sun's too bright, or maybe it was too cloudy. You see, parents blame coaches and coaches blame umpires. TOB—transfer of blame—is not allowed in our program. Players must take responsibility for everything they are and everything they are not. For example, I explain to my players that when they pout or show poor body language, they really hurt the team. Remember the hand clap—everything counts!

Playing for Excellence

When a team plays a baseball game, only four things can happen. A team can play well and win, it can play well and lose, it can play poorly and win, or it can play poorly and lose. Naturally, our goal is to play well and let the law of averages take care of the rest. As a coach, I try to reduce the pressure on the team, especially a team like ours for which the expectations are so high. In pressure situations, like championship games, we tend to have polar thinking—either win or fail. It's like choosing between two doors. Door number 1 is marked "Win"—behind it are all the rewards, satisfactions, and pressures that come with it. Door number 2 is marked "Fail," with all the heartbreak and pain that comes with it. But there is a third choice for all of us. Door number 3 is a good choice. It's marked "Excellence." Coming through that door means that you played as well as you can and that you represented your school, your family, and your Maker with the proverbial 110 percent effort.

Players on my team know they are welcome anytime through door number 3, win or lose. Actually, winning can't be the most important thing when several hundred baseball teams suit up every year and only one can win the national championship. Trying to win and being the best you can be, both on and off the field—those are the most important things.

Building Trust

I want to tell you now about one of the most fragile commodities in the world, and that's trust. Without trust, families break up, businesses fail, communities can't survive, and, of course, teams aren't successful. In the Jewish religion, just before the rabbi pronounces the bride and groom as wife and husband, he will ask the groom to step on a wine glass covered by a cloth napkin. The groom steps on the glass, it shatters, and the rabbi says something like, "This is to remind you how fragile love and trust really are. I could never put that glass back together again. Yet, if you take care of it, if you guard it, it can last a lifetime."

The wine glass is a symbol of both fragility and strength. On our team, each player has a crystal ball (actually, it's acrylic). I ask the players to keep the balls in their lockers and in their homes. I remind them that everything that goes on in our program is in that ball. The times they hug and tell one another how much they care for each other, or the times they haven't been the person they should have been, or the times I wasn't as good a leader as I could have been—it's all in that ball, and it must stay there.

If in a selfish moment, a moment of meanness, a player drops the ball and it cracks, then the core of the team seeps out. I could never put the ball back together. Next year, I could get a new team, but I doubt I could put this team back together again.

Besides the small crystal balls, we have a larger crystal ball in our squad room that serves as a symbol of trust. The players sign a cardboard piece that rims the ball, and every time we meet, it is a reminder of trust.

Trust is a purely human quality, and so is distrust. Trust is a lubricant passed from one human being to another. Of course, you can't see it, but it is real. You can't see a germ, but you wouldn't argue that germs aren't transferred from person to person. You know when trust is present, and you know when it isn't present. When trust exists on an athletic team or a business team, people have great freedom to be themselves. An environment is created in which they can risk and disagree and fail, and still feel good about their decisions because they know they will be loved and trusted by their teammates.

Here is what makes trust so difficult. Trust is digital, like a digital clock. The clock either says 12:24 or it doesn't. It can't be halfway. A woman is either pregnant, or she isn't. A conventional light switch is either on, or it's not. A lightning bolt either occurred, or it didn't. A crystal ball either broke, or it didn't. You can't be 90 percent trusting—it's all or nothing. It's been said, "You can only receive what you are willing to give." You have to be trusting to earn trust. Just as love characterizes the attitude of two people in a marriage, trust characterizes the attitude of all people on a team.

When I started at LSU in 1983, naturally I was new to the players. But I had a vision. I had been to Omaha, Nebraska, for the College World Series before. The sights, sounds, and smells were familiar to me. I had explained to the players that anything you vividly imagine, ardently desire, sincerely believe, and enthusiastically act upon must, absolutely must, happen. That first season I told them about TEAM—Together Everyone Accomplishes More, Totally Excellent Alliance for Magnificence. The pledge of allegiance starts with "I" and ends with "All." It takes all of us for any one of us to be successful. I told them about the Boston Celtics, all the titles they had won without ever having the league's leading scorer. Our players had T-shirts on which were printed a large baseball that said "Team" and a smaller baseball that said "Me." We ate together, we worked hard together, we prayed together, and we did all right the first year.

The second year I told them a story my high school football coach had told me. It's a story about holding on to the rope. I called each player into my office and showed him a piece of rope that I threw over the edge of my desk. I asked each player, "If you were at one end of the rope with nothing between you and a thousand-foot fall to certain death, who would you want holding the other end of the rope, knowing that his hands were so strong and that he loved you so much he would never let go?"

Well, Marty Lanoux said Jeff Reboulet, and Reboulet said Andy Galy, and Galy said John Dixon, and so on. I said, "Fellas, when you tell me, 'It doesn't matter who holds on to the other end of the rope, as long as he's a teammate of mine,' then we'll be one. We'll be free to trust one another, make mistakes, and still feel good about our decisions."

That season we did very well. We ended the year in a series at Auburn University, where we had to win two of three to capture the first conference championship at LSU in 10 years. On Saturday we split a doubleheader, so it all came down to Sunday's ballgame.

It was May 1, 1985, and that's when our program turned around forever. The game was tied, 1-1, through nine innings. We scored run in the 10th to go ahead. In the bottom of the 10th, with the tying run at second base, a fly ball was lifted to my left fielder. He ran to his right to catch it—it wasn't a really tough chance—but as I looked down to see the play, I noticed all our players straining their necks, wondering if he was going to make the play. They were transferring a message of nontrust. The ball hit his glove and fell to the ground. Heads went down, spikes started to shuffle. I said, "Fellas, what's important now is to pull together and believe in one another."

We went ahead again in the 13th, and with a runner at third with two outs in the bottom of the inning, I brought in Eric Hetzel to pitch for us. Eric was an excellent pitcher and an excellent competitor, but he had pitched the day before. In looking at the pinch hitter coming up for Auburn, I told Eric, "Let's just use fastballs, get him out here, and we're going to leave here with a championship, right?" He said, "Right." But as I turned toward the dugout, I saw our players with their heads down, spikes shuffling, again transferring that message of nontrust. Several pitches later, the Auburn batter blooped a single over third base, and we were tied again. Of course, the heads went down again. I said, "Fellas, pull together. We need each guy."

In the 14th, we went ahead again. Stan Loewer, who had also pitched the day before, came in to face Auburn in the bottom of the inning. Stan worked himself into a situation with a runner at third base and two outs. He was standing behind the mound, rubbing up the ball. That's when everything changed. A senior pitcher from Miami, Florida, Robbie Smith, stood up on the edge of the dugout and called, "Stan, Stanley, hold on to the rope, hold on!" Marty Lanoux at third base turned to shortstop Jeff Reboulet and said, "Jeff, hold on to the rope!" Jeff shouted across the diamond to first baseman John Dixon, "John, hold on!" I can remember our catcher, Rob Leary, with his fist in the air, shouting, "Hold on to the rope!"

Did Stan strike out the batter with three pitches? No, it was better than that. He worked himself into a 2-2 count against an excellent hitter. Stan delivered a good pitch, and the batter swung, and as the ball hit the ground, our dugout emptied, transferring a positive trust message. With that kind of trust and belief in his teammates, Jeff Reboulet fielded the ground ball, threw to first base, and we were the champs.

As a coach and team leader, people expect you to hold on to the rope. They expect you to hold on to the rope of communication as well. And, of course, people in your family expect you to hold on to that rope of love.

A Closing Note

Edgar Guest wrote a great poem titled "Tomorrow" that I often recite to our team. It goes like this:

> He says he's going to be all a mortal could be, tomorrow
> None would be braver and stronger than he, tomorrow
> A friend who was troubled and weary he knew and needed a lift and wanted
>   one, too
> On him he would call to see what he could do, tomorrow
> Each morning, he'd stack up the letters he'd write, tomorrow
> He thought of the friends he would fill with delight, tomorrow
> It's too bad indeed he was busy today, hadn't a moment to stop on the way,
>   more time I'll give to others, he would say, tomorrow
> The greatest of workers this man would have been, tomorrow
> The world would have known him had he ever seen tomorrow
> But, the fact is he died and faded from view
> And all that he left here when living was through
> Was a mountain of things he intended to do, tomorrow.

Don't wait. Lock on to that new resolve to be the best you can be. Be the best teammate you can be. Remember, the No. 1 team in your life is your family. So tonight, tell everybody in your family how much you love them. And just before you go to bed tonight, thank God you live in the greatest country in the world, the United States of America.

Hold on to the rope!

CHAPTER TWENTY-ONE

Developing Responsible Decision-Making Athletes

Gordon Gillespie

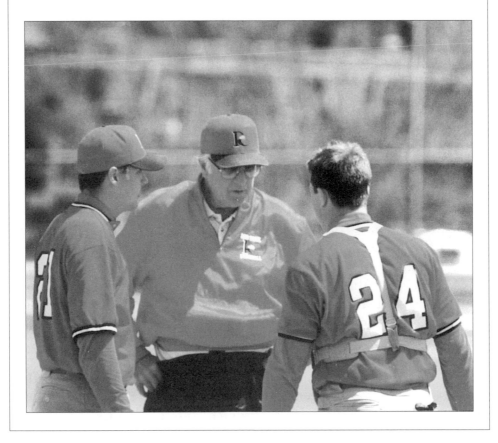

> **Baseball is a mind game.**

Coaches compare baseball with chess, a crossword puzzle, bridge, or any activity that takes a lot of thought and planning. Many observers of the game think that baseball moves too slowly, that it is boring. We who are in love with baseball, fascinated by its strategy, counter this thinking by saying, "Once you really understand baseball, you will enjoy it."

The problem is that most people trying to learn the game cannot visualize all the little battles occurring within the big war of the game—pitcher versus batter, catcher versus batter, runner versus pitcher and catcher, defense versus batter, batter versus third baseman in the bunting game, and so on. The war is offensive strategy versus defensive strategy. Many factors influence its conduct—weather, type of ballpark, who is pitching, type of team we are playing, type of manager we are playing against, and others.

What do baseball strategy, its battles, and its wars have to do with developing a ballplayer into a responsible decision maker? My answer is that the essence of good coaching is giving the game to the players. The more responsibility we give to the players, the better they will play the game and the more they will enjoy it. With that increased responsibility comes the need to make more decisions.

The job of coaches is to encourage players to make decisions. Right or wrong, they will learn how to make decisions and how to apply the game to life situations. If you can't accomplish this, your team has little reason for playing the game. The great coaches are the ones who approach teaching in this way. They help each athlete set goals, and they gain their satisfaction in coaching from helping players attain them. Players for the most part have only short-range goals, what they are striving for this week, this month, this season. The coach has similar immediate goals for each player but at the same time is looking at long-range goals and values—hard work, honesty, integrity, handling pressure and stress, dealing with defeat and victory, having love and respect of teammates, learning never to give up.

These values can be learned on the baseball field. The coach can make all these things possible. The baseball field can be the best classroom a person can experience. It's up to the coach. The buck stops with you. Coaches, you are the role model, whether you want this responsibility or not. If you don't want it, do everyone a favor and quit.

Traits of Successful Coaches

As a coach and role model, you will affect the lives of your players. Through your approach to baseball, you will show your players how to deal with many of the challenges they will face in life off the ballfield. I feel several traits are necessary for you to be successful in coaching.

Taking Delight in Young People

Liking kids has to be number one. Your primary reason for coaching should be to help young people grow, mature, and develop. Sure, everybody likes to win, but if winning is the only thing that counts, you'll never have the pride and satisfaction that comes from watching your kids succeed at life. And it doesn't matter what age or gender you're talking about. "Kids" range from five-year-old peewees to college graduates. College coaches even refer to their players as "my kids."

You have to be in coaching for the right reasons. You must like youngsters and want to teach them proper values. These values include discipline, hard work, conquering fear and tension, having pride in their team and teammates, establishing reachable goals, and most important, developing a burning desire to accomplish those goals.

Some people coach for the wrong reasons, including boosting their ego and being in a power position with young people. Some like the limelight, the attention that goes with winning in today's society. They may like the manipulation of people, parents, and the media, which all goes with the power position. The players become pawns instead of people. Instead of developing players into worthy people, the coach uses them to fan his ego. The wrong person in a leadership position can destroy the confidence of youngsters.

It is a simple formula: If you like kids you will enjoy your life in coaching and enjoy helping your players learn to make better decisions. If you are in it for the wrong reasons, you will not last and will end up having gained little respect from your athletes and little self-esteem. Such coaches end up blaming everyone else for a lackluster career.

Being Organized

A favorite expression of people in all occupations is, "I have got to get organized." Jerry Kindall, a great coach at the University of Arizona, refers to a poll of college baseball players who were asked what they valued most in their coaches. Somewhat surprisingly, high on the list was "organization." I know of no one more organized than Jerry. He has won three NCAA baseball championships as well as being selected NCAA Baseball Coach of the Year on several occasions.

You won't accomplish half of what you set out to do without a concrete, workable plan. Every baseball practice is invariably a race against time. You cannot waste a minute. Every moment is precious and planned. Start with the whole. After you lay out your season goals with your players, determine what you want to accomplish each month, each week, each day, each hour. Last, determine what you have to do minute by minute to accomplish those goals. Make sure every player knows the plan and knows what to expect every day from the start of the season to the finish. When the regular season is over, the players will want a good off-season plan, so that they can get stronger, work on their weaknesses, and return as better players the following year. Again, the good coach has all the facets of this plan worked out in advance after seeking suggestions from the players.

Head coaches have to coach coaches. The staff must know their responsibilities and the way the head coach wants the fundamentals taught. The head coach has the final say-so on all matters pertaining to practice and teaching. He listens to his staff and allows them some decision making, but puts his stamp of approval on all things. It cannot be any other way. The buck always stops with the head coach, who willingly and enthusiastically accepts this responsibility.

Being Enthusiastic

If we could bottle enthusiasm and sell it, we would be the richest people in the world. Enthusiasm is a necessity in coaching baseball. It is a fantastic game to teach, for every one of us! The thought of working with your kids should motivate you and get you excited about what they are doing. Going back to the first premise of being a good coach, caring and liking kids, it would be a complete contradiction if you were not enthusiastic about teaching them the game.

Think of Mr. Cub, Ernie Banks, who always has great enthusiasm for the game and the people he played with. His love of the game was infectious. Ernie's favorite remark, "Let's play two," rings true on and off the field. If you are going to be the best, you must have the gift of enthusiasm. You must treat every kid as if he were Babe Ruth and every practice as if it were the last game of the World Series. You always make sure you bring bats and balls to every practice. It's just as important to bring enthusiasm.

My former pitching coach, Joe Heinsen, was 79 years young when he died in 1996. He was the only man alive who was a member of both the

1945 Chicago Cub pennant winners and the 1959 Chicago White Sox pennant winners. Joe was a bullpen coach on those teams, each of which, incidentally, was the last team that had won a pennant for its organization. Joe, at his young age, was the first one at our practices and the last one to leave. He always had time for any player on the team, whether it be some phase of the game or a personal problem. That's enthusiasm. Joe but will never be forgotten by the players whose lives he touched.

Being Patient

The ability to go over things time and time again, never losing enthusiasm, is an absolute for a great coach. Every great athlete had a mentor, a friend, who had the patience to teach him the fundamentals of the game and allowed him the gift of making decisions at critical times.

Ted Williams, Roger Hornsby, Babe Ruth—all had someone who took the time to teach them to hit. Vince Lombardi, one of the great football coaches of all time, had this vital quality. The Green Bay Packers would run the Green Bay sweep 50 times at every practice, and Vince would be teaching the little things that made it work each time they ran it. That is why they were champions year after year. Vince was a patient man.

One of the greatest joys of coaching is to see the least talented suddenly blossom, all because you never gave up on him. The youngsters will never forget how they became successful and will take the same values into their lives. They will help someone else along the way, becoming a mentor themselves, inspiring their protégés as you did them.

Being Persistent

Patience and persistence are married. It is difficult to differentiate between these two virtues, and they go hand in hand in the coaching profession. You must persist, and you must teach your kids to persist. Yogi Berra's quotation, "It's never over until it's over," is an excellent definition of persistence. Chris Evert Lloyd, the great tennis player, was taught at age four by her dad that every volley was match point. Persistence, in simple words, is never giving up. Each of us fail and at times make wrong decisions. It is what we do after we fail that is important. I believe Abe Lincoln was defeated 17 consecutive times while seeking public office. The beautiful aspect about defeat is that it is a powerful learning experience. We learn from our mistakes and poor decisions and go on from there. Dick Butkus, perhaps the greatest of all linebackers, had this quality of persistence. He genuinely believed that he could make every tackle in a football game. And when you watch films of him, it seems as if he almost did. Persistence is a mind-set that coaches can illustrate and teach. Again, this is a useful value for young people to take into their adult lives—never give up!

Being Sincere

We get back to a coach's most important virtue—caring. You must be sincerely concerned about your athletes, first as human beings and second as players. If it's vice versa, it won't work. Resentment will be the end product of your relationship. Being concerned, listening as well as teaching, sharing decision making—these are not easy virtues to acquire. You have to work at it every day of your coaching career. Each young person wants someone to look up to. Because role models are not easily accessible in today's society, a coach often becomes that role model. Sincerity and concern mean that the game and its results are secondary to the people playing it. Take time to make sure that each person under your guidance is getting your best effort of personal concern. This is your most critical coaching goal!

Being Fair

Being fair goes along with sincerity and concern. Everyone wants a fair chance to show what he or she can do. They want the opportunity! Each day the coach has to evaluate personnel. Each team member must be reviewed and analyzed. Great coaches have the gift of being able to evaluate personnel quickly and get them into the proper position and proper pecking order. But even great coaches can be fooled. A player can come out of nowhere to make a great contribution to the team. An attribute of many excellent coaches is that they spend as much time as possible with the second stringers and make them feel valuable to the team. Many teams win championships because the second team constantly pushed the first team to greater heights.

Never discuss one of your player's abilities with another player on the team, because jealousies can occur over the slightest situation. Instead, you should make positive comments during and after practice and games. It is always easier to compliment the team rather than a few individuals.

In the area of being fair and making evaluations, beware of parental familiarity. Try to distance yourself from the parents of the youngsters you are coaching. It is difficult to maintain objectivity if you are friends with the parents. Be respectful and polite but do not let the relationship develop beyond that. This is especially difficult when you are coaching in a small community.

It is amazing how parents lose their objectivity if their son or daughter is not in the lineup. Your best friends will quickly cease being your best friends if their youngster is sitting on the bench. This is a tough call, and again I caution you to keep your distance and your professionalism. For reasons like these, coaching can become a lonely profession. Let's hope that your players will sense the difficulty of your decisions and apply that fairness to their life decisions.

Maintaining Integrity With Officials and Coaching Peers

Unless you are coaching in the professional ranks, or at a top NCAA Division I program, you are never going to make a lot of money in coaching. Most coaches won't make a million dollars in their lifetime. This is not a critical issue. Your integrity is everything. The one thing you must never jeopardize is your good name. I mentioned salary and money because if you became a millionaire and lost your good name, what did you really gain? With today's pressure on winning, coaches can never give into the pressure of skirting the rules! Your good name is your highest priority. Never place yourself in a win-at-all-cost situation.

Never compromise on right or wrong. It is a black-and-white situation, not a gray area. In dealing with umpires, referees, and those who govern the game, we want the play called right at least 90 percent of the time. Instant replay has proven time and time again that we can't expect more than that. Officials are human and they will make mistakes. The important idea here is that you must support your officials rather than tear them down or ridicule them. Your game and your organization will be only as good as your officials. The more you undermine them, the less confidence they will have. Tension will take over. When people are consumed by tension, they make poor decisions and everyone loses. Don't try to coerce umpires; just try to get the play called right.

Never comment on another coach's lack of ability. The old adage "If you haven't got anything good to say, don't say anything at all" certainly applies. Never give in to displaying anger against the opposing coach in the heat of the game or after the final out. Always keep your cool, especially after a hard loss. Being a class act is easy when you are winning; the real measure of a class act is when things are going badly. The team will emulate you on these matters when it comes time for them to decide how to act. Never set up an excuse for defeat.

Being Human

At some point you are going to become angry and perhaps show it. You might get so emotional that you cry. I'll bet John Wayne even cried. If you care, you are going to cry. It is perfectly OK to show people that you love them. Don't just say it, show it, especially with your wife and family. They are proud of you but they also miss a lot of family time because of your long coaching hours. So you must show your family you love them at every opportunity. This may be the most profound decision you make for your players to observe and learn from!

You will fail and make mistakes. If you offend someone, apologize promptly, especially when you offend one of your players. Your decision to humble yourself will help them make similar decisions at important times in their future.

Handling the Press and Other Media

The media has a job to do, just as you do. Try to make their jobs easier by your cooperation. The coach always feels pressure because everyone wants to know what happened in the game or in the locker room. But guess what? Coaches don't always have the answers. Postgame interviews can be very trying, especially after a close loss. Again, try to remain the class act that you are. Avoid discussing intimate situations with the media about your players. If you are angry with a player, a closed-door meeting with him is the answer. Don't try to motivate your team through the press. Negative public comments cause dissension. All coaches strive to get the right chemistry with their team, which stems from a family feeling and atmosphere. Families don't hang our their dirty laundry. Correct your problems in the sanctuary of the locker room or the coaches' office.

Dealing With School Administration and Faculty

You must be a class act in your relationship with faculty members. It is a two-way street, and the faculty must recognize that you too are a conscientious and concerned faculty member. I have never met an outstanding coach who was not an effective classroom teacher. The great Knute Rockne of Notre Dame was an extraordinary chemistry professor. Vince Lombardi taught physics and math at St. Cecelia High School. The great ones take special pride in their classroom work and in working well with nonathletes.

Approaching a faculty member and asking for an academic break for a player is serious breach of ethics. This puts great pressure on everyone involved, and once word of this spreads among the faculty and administration, the coach's credibility will be zero. Although forgoing such intervention on behalf of a star player may be momentarily painful, your decision to be honorable will make a lifelong impression on your players.

Recognizing Your Support Personnel

Recognize the importance of your support personnel at every opportunity. They are the ones who care the most. Praise them all, including the groundskeepers, the custodian, and the student managers. The groundskeepers are the difference in whether you play or sit on rainy days. They take pride in the field and make it a showcase, your field of dreams. The student managers responsible for the equipment, statistics, and many other functions can make a big difference in the success of your program. They take pride in victories and feel the sting of defeats. They want to be an integral part of the team. If you and your players recognize this and make them feel important, you will give a major boost to your program.

Developing Your Players and Your Team

To develop a championship team, the coach must conduct quality practice sessions, monitor conditioning, understand the mental makeup of his players, and insist on particular behaviors to build and sustain the team concept.

Practicing the Best to Play the Best

When the season begins, the team that plays the best wins the most games. And the team that plays the best is the team that practices the best. In short, the team that practices the best wins! Winning beats losing all the time. The primary considerations for successful practices are intensity and concentration from both players and coaches. Intensity and concentration sometimes lead to a lack of patience from a coach. The coach or coaches may lose control and have a temper tantrum. This is bound to happen on occasion, but it should not be a daily occurrence. Being demanding of the players is paramount, but it should never present itself in the form of screaming, ridicule, or demeaning remarks. Coaches are in a power position and should never abuse it with that kind of behavior.

Conditioning

One of the most important parts of successful early season practice sessions is to have your players report with as little body fat as possible. Again, this requires that each player make a decision. One of our goals is to be the best conditioned team in the country. With conditioning comes strength. It is imperative that our players participate in an off-season strength program and continue to lift during the season to maintain their strength.

A primary purpose of a good weight-training program is to prevent injuries. With greater strength injuries are less likely. Strength also helps speed the healing process when injuries do occur.

Along with strength, successful athletes also need great agility and coordination. A bodybuilder's physique is not good for baseball players. Bodybuilders seek only to have well-developed, muscular bodies and to maximize the weight they can lift. Baseball players don't muscle a ball out of the park; they use total-body coordination and lightning reflexes.

Most players can improve their footwork. Basketball, racquetball, handball, and soccer are great activities that will improve foot movement and agility. The abductor and adductor muscles, those that give lateral quickness, are the muscles we must develop through drills. The majority of defensive drills in all sports deal primarily with lateral action and quickness.

Hustle and Bearing Down

Hustle and bearing down are baseball expressions that originated with Abner Doubleday. Hustle means giving maximum effort, and bearing down means concentrating and making the commitment to hustle. Not for one moment can a coach tolerate lack of hustle. Lack of hustle is like cancer; it must be dealt with firmly and quickly before it spreads. An offending player gets one warning. On the second occurrence, offer a quiet, polite good-bye and excuse the player from practice.

Improving Baseball Thinking

The coach, as a professional, must thoroughly understand the mental makeup of the youngsters with whom he is working. Players can be loosely categorized into three types: the scholar-athlete, the book-smart-only player, and the mentally lazy player.

The scholar-athlete is intelligent and has a good athletic background. Such players are constantly thinking ahead and always have their heads in the game. It is ideal when an athlete has outstanding athletic intelligence. Coaching is much easier when you have a team of players with these qualities. A key for you is to emphasize this aspect of the game by often giving them quizzes and tests, both oral and written. Show your players that you cherish learning and help them make an ongoing decision to keep learning no matter how successful they may become.

The book-smart-only athlete gets As in the classroom but seems to have a hard time translating academic success to the playing field. Often this book-smart athlete struggles with athletic concepts. This type of player takes patience, and coaches strive daily to help them catch up with the others on the mental side of the game. Be ready for a pleasant surprise—this is often the type of athlete who fools you and comes out of nowhere at the end of the season to win key games for you.

The mentally lazy athlete is the player who has an excellent athletic background but doesn't work in the classroom and doesn't concentrate in practice. This kind of player is your most critical challenge. This player may have a lot of baseball experience but continually makes mental mistakes. This type of athlete poses a problem because there seems to be no reason why he or she isn't understanding the concepts. Such athletes may never help the team because their total background has been a lack of seeing the whole picture. In baseball slang, they just cannot bear down and keep their heads in the game. Consequently, they hurt the team through lack of thinking and poor decision making in key situations. Their athletic ability rarely makes up for the harm they do to the team. You must continually work with these players to teach them how to think properly in game situations.

Insisting on Respect for Teammates

Coaches cannot tolerate players being disrespectful to one another. The day of the bully is long gone, and any older player who hazes the younger players on the team is completely out of order. Personality differences are expected; this is the way God intended it. We have one common cause—to be as good as we can be at everything we do. Baseball is a team game, which means we think as a team, act as a team, and place the team first in all decisions. We tell team members that all decisions are based on what is best for the team. After that question is answered, decision making becomes much easier. Everybody must pull together, a principle we recognize as a valuable life lesson that transcends baseball.

Maintaining the Team Concept

It is the head coach's responsibility to ensure that petty jealousies do not develop between players and coaches. We must coordinate our practices so that our drills, whether they are individual, one on one, two on two, or as a team, are competitive and intense. Although the goal of our drills is always individual improvement, we must also continually build team coordination. The coaching staff must strive to be cognizant of the total team and not become locked into individual players they are working with. No coach should be building a little kingdom or surrounding himself with "his boys." This creates problems that could be the undoing of your program. The head coach must recognize this situation and correct it immediately. We are a team—not an offense, not a defense, not pitchers, catchers, infielders. The team wins or the team loses. It's just that simple.

Being Punctual

The head coach is the first one at practice and the last one to leave, and the rest of the staff follows that example. In many situations allowances must be made for coaches who come late or leave early, but they must be for valid reasons. It is important that every coach be at practice and be fully prepared. Never should the players be on the field or gym floor without their coaches. Good coaches and staff members are not planning practices at the last minute. From the first moment of stretching until the last grueling cardiovascular exercise, every player gets the coaches' full attention. Coaches should not socialize on the field with other coaches. There should be no conversation with each other, only total concentration and awareness of the players and the practice drills. Nothing is more irritating to a head coach than an assistant who does not give total attention to the team every moment of practice.

Being Responsible

The head coach is in charge and makes all final decisions. He gives the credit to the players and assistant coaches in victories and takes the responsibility for losses. He corrects players and coaches alike and makes decisions on all team personnel problems. He always listens to his associate coaches and in many cases will agree with their feelings. The staff must understand that the buck stops at the top. When the head coach accepts the responsibility for making decisions, the players will observe that. When their time comes, they will do the same. Loyalty is important on a coaching staff. The coach never asks or pleads for it. If it isn't there, then he has the wrong people working for him. Loyalty is a two-way street, and the head coach must display loyalty to his staff and, of course, his players.

Coaching Protocol With Opponents

Cordiality and respect would be good ways to describe our relationship with other coaching staffs. I would like to list some do's and don'ts for you and your staff on this subject.

The do's are these:

- Respect your opponents. Never underestimate the opposition.
- Treat them with professional courtesy.
- As the host team, go out of your way to make them welcome before the game. Take care of their needs as best you can.
- Go all out on every play, giving your best effort as a coach and as a team. Anything less than your best effort is an insult to your opposition and your integrity.
- When the game is over, it's over! You now resume a normal courteous relationship with your opponent.

The don'ts include the following:

- Never criticize your opponent's performance.
- Never criticize opposing coaches or their strategies. You have enough to do taking care of your problems.
- Never exchange scouting information about another team unless it's a conference requirement. Everyone should do their own homework.
- Never discuss your offensive and defensive concepts with anyone but your staff. You have a certain style of play that belongs to you. Revealing pertinent information can mean losing the close games.
- When speaking of an individual player on another team, use only praise. Never criticize the performance of an opposition player.
- Shoulder your share of conference or organizational obligations, such as tournament play or travel accommodations. Do whatever it takes to make it better for the young people you are working with.
- Always be gracious in winning or losing. Never engage in childish displays of anger during or after a game. Similarly do not tolerate unsporting conduct.
- Coaching your team against one of your former staff members or players is difficult, but they know you and your philosophy. Easing up would be an insult. The respect is already there; you will always be friends, regardless of the results of the game.

Pregame Protocol and Pregame Practice

We adhere to the following rules in our pregame practice:

- Everyone is dressed and ready to go with time to spare. We wear our uniforms with class and dignity. We dress as a team, not to individual whims.

- We run to our positions to take pregame infield and outfield practice. We make it a flat-out race.
- We play every fungo ball as a game situation.
- Every outfield throw to a base must end up on the base, with a tag on a phantom runner.
- Every infield throw is a bullseye.
- Every catcher's throw is a cannon shot right on the bag.

Pregame practice sets the tone for the way we play the game. After we finish infield practice, we zero in on our opposition to learn anything we can about their defensive abilities and what we might capitalize on when the game begins.

Postgame Protocol

After the game our team demeanor can pave the way for either success or failure the rest of the year. The rule is to look for the positive after a defeat and to avoid being too haughty after a win.

After a win, we do not imitate major-league teams with public displays or handshakes or high fives on the field. The older-day pros would cut your heart out to win, but they did not go in for all the baloney of meeting in the center of the field at game's end to give high fives and pats on the back. We keep celebrations like this where they belong, in the dugout or locker room. If we win in dramatic style or someone gave an outstanding performance, we'll necessarily want a little celebration, but we line up promptly to shake the hands of our opponents.

After a loss, our public display will be a handshake with the other team after the game. This is not easy to do, but we want people to know that even though we lost an important game, we are going to go about our lives. Again, this is tough, but it is part of the value system we are trying to instill in our players.

Postgame protocol is for the coaches to congratulate the effort of each player, especially those who did not play well and those who did not play at all. We can always give a kind word. We want each player to have something positive to take home.

For home games, everyone is a groundskeeper for 15 minutes after the game. We try to leave our field more beautiful than it was before the game. Our dugouts are spotless, and our bullpens, main field mound, and batter's area are packed with dirt and manicured. A quick drag of the infield by one of the coaches really helps if it rains during the night. We always try to cover the pitching and batter's area with small tarpaulins, which really helps with spring rains.

If we are the visiting team, we take a few minutes after the game to clean up in and around our dugout. We respect our opponent's field as we do our own.

We don't meet as a team after games. Our routine after games is individual congratulations to every player, field maintenance, and then home to supper.

Final Thoughts on Practice Sessions

Using a stop watch makes everyone faster. There are only two ways to improve speed—a race against another person or a race against time. In baseball we're interested in a player's 30 time, the time it takes to cover the 30 yards between the bases. We find many things to time besides running speed. Release throwing time of defensive players—catchers, pitchers, infielders, and outfielders—is extremely important. Each coach should have a stop watch. We constantly time our players, and on game day we time our opponents.

Create as much competition as you can in every drill. Keep score on ground balls caught, throwing accuracy, bunt attempts, two-strike hitting. Use your imagination to make practices as much fun as possible.

"Gamers" is a term used in athletic circles for those who seem to play especially well on game day. Never let the word "gamer" influence your attitude as a coach toward practice. Some gamers might like to loaf at practice. You will be confronted by workers and nonworkers at practice. The nonworkers must go! On game day let's hope we're all gamers.

The coach has to be a tough guy at practice. I think of the Marine drill sergeant who realizes what it takes to ready his troops for combat and win the war. This has to be the coach's attitude. When practice ends and the drills are over, the team should be near exhaustion and almost crawling to the locker room. This isn't easy on your players, but it is the only way they are going to improve and reach their potential. In time, your players will respect your decision to push them hard. When they become leaders, they will do the same.

As for injuries, some are serious enough that the athlete cannot play, but some are mere hurts that the player can play through. Much of it is psychological and may depend on the player's pain threshold. Deciding whether to play is a tough call for both players and coaches. My suggestion is to use some sort of variation on the rule "If you can't practice, then you can't play." This really helps with the psychological side of it. The player can give the injury a try to see how it feels at practice sessions.

Create game situations you want to work on. The coach can create every possible situation he wishes—the inning, outs, score, home team, count, and so on. The more pressure you create in practice, the better your team will respond in a game. When you have your team well trained to handle pressure situations on their own, then you don't even have to be there. You can fall asleep in the dugout and let them play. The more responsibility we give to the players, the better they will respond with good decisions in pressure situations. A team dependent on its coach in all critical situations will not win championships.

Game Strategy

All your preparation—planning, conditioning, practicing, working with players' thinking and behavior—comes together on game day. Once the players arrive and start their stretching exercises, you, as the head coach, start concentrating on the game. I suggest little conversation and a lot of observation. Who looks ready? Who's injury is still troubling him? What are the opponent's strengths? Do not miss a thing! Here are a few ideas that you will find useful in conducting strategy during the game.

Preparing the Starting Pitcher

After you conduct or supervise infield practice, hustle to the bullpen to observe the starting pitcher. Pitching is 75 percent of the game, and you should spend at least 10 minutes with the starting pitcher. Again, you don't need to say anything—no paralysis by analysis, not a lot of remarks about mechanics. A coaching tip is fine, but nothing more. Walk in from the bullpen with the pitcher and catcher to review any last-minute strategy. You and the catcher should each give the pitcher a positive remark before he crosses the white line and goes to the pitcher's mound.

Handling the Pitching Staff

Handling the pitching staff is your number 1 priority. It is a skill that comes with experience and working closely with the pitchers. A good pitching coach is a valuable asset, but you make the decision on whether to take the pitcher out of the game. You plan the rotation and must have the same knowledge of pitching as the pitching coach. It is a grave mistake in coaching to pass on to an assistant this most important phase of the game. The buck stops with you. Let your pitching coach receive the compliments and credit for the success of the pitching staff, but the head coach must always take the blame for the loss!

More runs are scored in the first inning than in any other. This has been true throughout the history of the game. Why? Game tension! As the pitcher first crosses the white line to warm up, he is trying to concentrate and find his pitching rhythm. It takes some pitchers longer than others; there is no set pattern. It was said that if Steve Carlton could survive the first inning, he'd pitch a complete game. Have patience in those early innings. This is yet another life lesson your decision will communicate to your players.

Don't be hasty in making a decision to remove your pitcher. In tournament play you may be unable to leave a struggling pitcher in the game because you cannot afford to get too far behind. But during the regular season try to go as far as you can with a pitcher. He must learn how to pitch through adversity if he is going to improve.

Use this idea to your advantage on offense. When you are going against a top-flight pitcher, a good strategy in the early innings is to score early because you might not get to him at all. Take pitches in the early innings, trying to draw walks and playing for that big inning. The bunting game is another way to get to the other team's ace, especially in poor weather.

Another critical time for pitchers is the final inning. The last three outs cause a lot of tension, and pitchers tend to try too hard for those final outs. On occasion you will see a pitcher get a little wild. You have to recognize this and react accordingly. On offense you should take pitches until the tying run comes to home plate. On defense you may have to go to the bullpen if your pitcher becomes wild.

Adjusting Hitting Strategy Inning by Inning

As your defense comes off the field each inning, meet with them to discuss the strategy you will use in this at bat. The strategy naturally depends on the score and the inning. You don't have much time, so communication must be quick. We use some short phrases to signify what we want to do in this inning. For example, if I tell the players as they come into the dugout, "Play baseball," I mean we have no special concerns and each hitter is on his own.

You can develop countless variations on this communication system. The idea I want to give you here is that you must work on your system before the season, refining it as the season goes on. You must quiz your players during practice so they know what is expected of them during a game. You don't have time to give them several paragraphs during an important inning, so your system must be in place and understood by everyone before the game begins. Major decisions are made by the coach, but players are required to make right decisions within that context. Here are some illustrations of these brief communications.

- **Play Baseball:** Each hitter is on his own but will still look for signs from the coach in certain situations, like bunt situations, 3-0 counts, steal situations, and hit-and-run possibilities.

- **Plus One:** With plus one our players know that we are to play a catch-up concept and take the first pitch. We won't swing until a strike is called on the hitter. The hitter will take the 3-1 count unless notified by sign that he has the green light to hit away. We use plus one in two situations—when we are behind or when we want to draw walks from a pitcher who has shown some wildness. We may want to open games in plus one to make the pitcher work and get an idea of what kind of pitches he throws.

- **Regular Catch-Up:** We use regular catch-up when we are down three or more runs early in the game. Each batter knows that if the first pitch is a good one to hit, he should nail it. But if it is a ball, he does not swing until he get a strike on him. If the count goes to 3-1, he takes the next pitch if there is no one on base. If runners are on base, he checks the third-base coach to see if the take sign is on.

- **Regular Baseball:** We use this in a close game in the later innings. I stand by the bat rack and tell each hitter what strategy we will use. We might change tactics in the middle of an inning depending on what is transpiring. Because it is a close game, our entire strategy could change from pitch to pitch, so each hitter must keep alert.

- **Look to Drag:** We use this strategy when we have noticed a weakness in the defense and want to alert our players to it. In this case we see that the third baseman is playing deep, the pitcher is slow off the mound, and the weather favors the bunting game. So as the players come in from their defensive alignment we say, "Look to drag." This tells them that they are on their own and that the good drag bunters may want to try it.

Staying in the Game

My primary offensive philosophy is that we never have enough runs. Along with this idea, I teach my players that we can always score enough runs to win. In other words, if we're ahead we try to score more, and if we're behind we know we have the means to catch up. In this sense, we are never out of the game. Vince Lombardi said that he never lost a game—it's just that he sometimes ran out of time. He had faith—and his players had faith in him, his system, and themselves—that they could always come back to win when they fell behind.

I refine this concept by telling our players that when we are behind our immediate goal is to get the tying run to home plate. I make all decisions with this in mind. This means that when we are down by three, we are in the game. All we need are two base runners, and we could have a tie game, or perhaps we take the lead. Teach these concepts in practice during game-condition pitching so your players believe in themselves. In this way they will know what it takes never to be out of the game.

Always Thinking

The great game coach is always thinking; he is always an inning or two ahead. He knows the full capabilities of each player in his lineup. He does not make mistakes in using his personnel. He anticipates all defensive and offensive situations and devises a plan for each possibility. He makes the right calls, anticipating the bunt, the hit-and-run, and the squeeze play. The coach's concentration is so great that he says little, if anything, during the game unless it applies to strategy. Tom Landry, the great Dallas football coach said, "I cannot talk and think at the same time." He could not be distracted during the game. I am offended if anyone breaks my concentration during the game.

Playing Lovey-Dovey Baseball

We must play this marvelous game with sportsmanship, pride, honesty, humility, and respect for our opposition, but they've got to know that we're coming after them to beat them. We can play a great game only if our opponents play a great game, so we want them battling us the same way we're battling them. If you're playing just for fun, please take up another sport.

There is a wonderful quotation by Maury Wills: "Baseball is a take-no-prisoners concept." That's how Maury wanted the game played and managed.

Many have loads of fun at picnics playing what I call "lovey-dovey" baseball. It's a great time but it's not what we as coaches are teaching. In lovey-dovey baseball, you don't dive for balls, you don't score too many runs, you don't offend anyone, you don't break up a double play, you don't bunt or steal if you're way ahead. Those aren't the rules we follow.

My idea is to compete, to bust our butts always! The greatest insult to me and my team is to ease up against me at any time. You'd better keep coming hard, trying to bury me, because I know that we are going to rally and win this game. That philosophy must be paramount in our program. If it is, then we will become a championship team. We will have learned how to be winners even if we lose the game. And the decisions made by players and coaches alike within this context duplicate what is required to succeed in other life matters.

A Closing Note

Let me repeat what I said in the introduction: There is a fine line between winning and losing, and the difference in all sports, not only baseball, is the coach. You determine the way your team plays the game and whether or not your team is successful. And how you conduct your practice sessions determines how your athletes play in the game.

When it's over, it's over! Never lose your cool and hurt anyone's feelings after the game. Choose your words carefully. A childish outburst from the coach can badly shake a player's confidence. If you're at the boiling point, get away from the team until you have cooled down. Do not make tough decisions under a great deal of stress and tension. Think things through and make the big decisions only when you are under control. This is one of the most important lessons you can teach your athletes. Remember, you lead by example, especially after the game.

Teach your players how to be proud but humble in victory, thanking your opponents for their effort. More important, teach your players how to handle defeat, how to be proud of your effort even if it fell short, even if you struck out with the bases loaded or dropped a key fly ball. Champions don't win every game, but they learn from every game.

Remember, coaches, you often make the difference in many youngsters' lives. They learn from you, from what you do and what you say. They will become winners because you are a winner. They will make the right decisions because you made the right decisions. Your philosophy of baseball will teach them how to face adversity and prevail throughout their lives. You will show them how to handle victory with humility and grace, and how to use defeat in a way that they become better persons because of it.

You will live in their hearts long after they stop playing baseball. This is at the core of what you give them.

CHAPTER TWENTY-TWO

Building Character and Loyalty in Players

Andy Lopez

I once read a statement about athletics that I believe is altogether true. It reads: "Some believe that sports builds character. I believe sports reveal character."

In this chapter I will share some concepts, ideas, and stories from my past coaching years, as well as some general philosophies, that I hope will help you as a head coach determine whether you can develop character in an individual and, more important, within your team. More simply put, can you and I as coaches walk the tightrope of making our guys competitively tough yet having them become solid citizens on a day-to-day basis?

I believe you can do this, and it is our obligation as educators to attempt to walk this tightrope with our athletes and our programs daily.

You and I must be realistic. No matter how much you work to establish these characteristics, the final piece of the puzzle will be the athlete himself. In other words, your attempt to help your athletes must be met with an open, receptive, and teachable spirit by the individual athlete. The final and most important ingredient, beyond all the teaching, drills, concepts, and philosophies, is that your athlete must want to obtain the traits and characteristics that lead to the intangible called character. In all honesty, in the 22 years I have coached I have seen many of my athletes go away with much the same character they had when they arrived in my program.

With that statement made, I ask these questions. Do I find myself discouraged in my attempts to teach character? Should I be discouraged in my future attempts to teach character? I believe not.

I truly believe that our most important challenge in coaching, above and beyond the wins, is the attempt to establish the winning character in every young man we coach while always focusing on this statement: "One man with character is going to equal the majority."

I believe that it is our job to find that one man and work on him with the hope that he will spread some seeds, not only among his program, but throughout his walk of life.

Walking the Tightrope

Let's get on the high wire and walk through the balancing act of transforming young athletes into tough, competitive players with that character you know will bring success to you and your program. More important, they will be able to go out into everyday society and represent themselves, their families, and, in a real sweet way, your program and university in a positive manner. Not only will they be solid citizens in the ninth inning of a close game, they will be solid citizens in the classroom and in public.

Remember, it is a tightrope that we will walk. At times, we are going to stumble. We are going to fall. Many times in my attempts to work with young guys in trying to develop this character, I have I felt as if it was not going to work. I see failure staring me right in the eye and become discouraged. This can be disheartening, especially when you are working with a young guy or a particular group throughout a difficult time in your season.

I encourage you to hold on to a statement that I read a long time ago by Wilfred A. Peterson: "In great attempts, it is glorious even to fail."

The attempt that you are going to make, and that I make yearly, to mold and shape character, to build quality young men, will sometimes look like failure. But in that great attempt, even failure can be considered a successful endeavor. I believe that with all my heart. Unless we pursue that attempt, we have failed as educators.

I am beginning my 22nd year as a head coach, including 5 years at a high school level, 6 years at the Division II level, and 11 years now at the NCAA Division I level at Pepperdine University and the University of Florida. I have been fortunate to have had success at each level. I was blessed tremendously in taking over a high school program that eventually played for a city championship in Dodger Stadium. I was blessed to take over a Division II program that was not very successful but would eventually be a group that played in the College World Series. Now I am very fortunate to be coaching at the Division I level. Three of my squads have visited Omaha, highlighted by a national championship in 1992 while I was coaching at Pepperdine.

As I reflect on the teams and players I have coached over the past 22 years, the one common note that continues to ring in my system is they had character. The individuals I considered to be my best players, not necessarily my most talented players, had character. It is an intangible. I could never describe it, but when you see it and are around it, you will realize that it is what you want—not only for that individual player but for your entire program.

Talent is an obvious factor for success. I will not be so foolish to make the statement that I don't want to be successful. We all want success. I love to win. I cannot stand to lose a ball game. Honestly and truly, all of us as educators and coaches must understand the importance of seeking character, trying to develop character, and trying to bring that character out in individual players. I hope the statement that will be made about your club is that it had a lot of character. All of us would like to have that label placed on our programs.

Each of us as a head coach has a center of influence that guides and controls our motivations for teaching and coaching on both a yearly and day-to-day basis. I know that at one point in my career my center of influence was basically to win a ballgame, to win at all costs. I am embarrassed that when I first started at the high school level there were games, days at practice, and stretches in the season when I really wasn't thinking about anything but wins.

I have come to the realization now that if you do it right by building character and establishing the things that are important within your guys, the winning takes care of itself. My center of influence is one in which I want to guide, teach, direct, and encourage all my players to avoid the pitfalls that I had to go through as a young man. In essence, I want to build a program that will challenge every facet of my players' lives. I want to build a program that will help establish a foundation of character that will lead to success for these athletes not only in the current season but for a lifetime. They will go out to be successful businessmen, successful educators, successful coaches. The foundation of their success will be not only mom and dad but also the time they spent at the University of Florida or wherever the program may be.

Creating Confrontations

How do we pursue this great attempt of developing character? For me, I personally design all our practices, all our meetings, every facet of our program to challenge each athlete. I did it as a high school coach and now I do it as a college coach. I want to stretch these athletes to become a little more mature than even they think they can become in the time frame that they are with me.

We always design our practices with competitive drills at the beginning and end of our sessions. At our practices I seek out areas where I can confront an individual or a team. By confrontation, I do not mean that we are looking for a combative showdown. We pursue not a negative confrontation but a realistic confrontation, a realistic confrontation that it is going to relate to what the players are going to be confronted with in a game, in a season, and in life. I have found in my life a series of confrontations that sometimes I don't want but that I must handle and deal with. In essence, I have to take responsibility for the way I handle the confrontations that have occurred in my life. That is what we try to do in our practice situations and in all facets of our program. I want to look for, or even create, realistic confrontations for my athletes and see how they handle the responsibility of those confrontations. I know that those are the types of situations that will come up in games and, more important, are but small replicas of what they will face in real life.

Here are some examples of ways that we create confrontations. We confront our hitters each day by giving them only one pitch to execute on in a practice setting. In early batting practice they will have 25 or 30 cuts in a row. In our practice situation, a hitter will get one chance to execute. He either executes that one chance or he doesn't. After that one chance, his teammate gets his chance. In a hit-and-run drill, the hitter gets one chance to hit and run successfully. That is a confrontation. He has to show responsibility of concentration, execution, and humility to be successful. If he is unsuccessful, he must have the strength to make his next at bat a more positive one.

For our infielders, we do mass ground balls before practice, with our pitchers hitting. All the coaches are grading out the infielders. All eyes are on them. We put stop watches on them to monitor their times in making plays. The confrontation is that we are going to put stop watches on you in practice and evaluate you on every ground ball. That is what they are going to face in a game situation.

Our outfielders never just sit and shag during batting practice. They must play in designated areas in the outfield. On every ground ball hit in batting practice to an outfielder, the outfielder must execute a do-or-die play to home plate. They don't have to throw the ball, but they must go through the execution of a do-or-die play. Every ground ball in batting practice is a confrontation, a realistic confrontation, of a game-winning or game-losing play at the plate that they will encounter during a season. Every fly ball is a tag-up situation. The outfielders must go through the mechanics of getting to the ball and getting in the proper throwing position to prevent a player from tagging up. Again, we just put them in a confrontational situation in practice that they will face in a game the next day or later in the week.

With our pitchers and catchers, we have intense and detailed bullpens in which a pitcher must throw a particular pitch in a particular location. The only way he gets to his next pitch in his pitching sequence (fastball, change-up, curveball) is to throw the fastball in the outer half of the plate for a strike. Some of our pitches never get past a fastball for a strike on the outer half of the plate in the first couple weeks of practice. We present the confrontation and situation in which they must be responsible for their actions in a practice setting daily. We hope we are going to build strong character—character of responsibility, character of execution. It will lead to success in practice, which will lead to success in a game setting, which we hope will lead to success in life.

Our catchers work in three stages under the same premise of creating positive confrontation during the bullpen. In stage 1, with nobody on base, they work on getting pitches for the pitcher by framing pitches. In stage 2, with runners on first or second, they must work every two or three throws to get their bodies in a throwing position for a steal attempt of second or third base. In stage 3, with a runner on third and the game on the line, they must block any ball that would allow a run to score or avoid a passed ball. The catchers are in a confrontation in the bullpen as well.

As a coach, you can designate what stage they are in or allow them to designate for themselves. You are always aware of what stage they are in based on what is going on. If the catcher is just catching, he is obviously in stage 1. You can evaluate that. If he catches a pitch and comes to a throwing position, he is in stage 2. If he has blocked a curveball in the dirt, he has been in stage 3. It is a positive confrontation, a positive area of responsibility that leads to strength and success both on and off the field.

Our goal is to have gamelike confrontational situations so that our players will have a chance to reveal their character in practice rather than in a game. I think that is important. I want to learn my player's strengths and weaknesses in a practice setting rather than a game setting. It is not only for my benefit or the program's benefit, but for that young man's benefit. Once he reveals his character we can either applaud it or start working on some of those weaknesses.

Along this line of positive confrontation, I once heard a statement that I believe very strongly in my heart: Victory is not superior to confrontation. In society we are hung up on victory. We try to avoid confrontation. Again I want to be clear on this. I am not talking about being in a bad mood, about yelling and screaming in a negative confrontation. I am talking about creating confrontations in our lives as athletes and as human beings that make us better and bring out the character in us, confrontations that reveal the character that we need to strengthen.

I think about a young man who was honest enough with some areas in his character that he needed to strengthen. He had that character revealed a little bit and walked the famous tightrope before he decided he wanted to walk to the other side. I think of a man named Josh Fogg.

Fogg was a pitcher in our program at the University of Florida. He just finished an all-American career and was a third-round selection of the Chicago White Sox in the June 1998 draft. He was one of the top closers in the nation, one of just two pitchers in school history to make 100 or more appearances. He ranks second all-time with 103 appearances.

But in his freshman year, Josh ran away mentally from his confrontations. The confrontation in his freshman year was that he was not successful. He posted a 6.29 ERA and was having moments of failure. I felt in the fall of 1997 it was wearing on Josh. I can recall vividly, and Josh would as well, the practice situation when we confronted it. We confronted the issues of the previous spring when he experienced periods when he was not successful.

Either he was going to confront the issue that he had to be bigger than his fear of failure or he would never establish victory in his life. I am happy to say that in the fall of 1997 Josh Fogg finally confronted the issues. That spring he was very good for us, leading to successful sophomore and junior seasons.

In essence, Josh never had victory, but he confronted the character that was lacking. Today he is a solid pitcher with a tremendous future at hand. More important, he strengthened and developed his character by confronting some weaknesses that he needed to confront. He took responsibility instead of running away.

Josh Fogg is a tremendous example of victory not being superior to confrontation. But it is confrontation that leads to victory. He has now been victorious at the college level, and I believe he will be victorious not only in pro ball but in life.

Making a Value Statement

Along with positive confrontations, I believe one of the strongest teaching points we make in our program is teaching our athletes that everything they do is a value statement. Each year at our team meeting I make a statement to our athletes that if you are an all-American in this program, so is your mother, so is your father, so is your sister or brother. If Joe Smith is an all-American at the University of Florida, the whole Smith family is an all-American here.

On the other side of that coin is that if you are thrown in jail, so is your family. If you are flunking out of school or you are drunk on road trips, if you are a bad-character human being, sadly enough, so is your family. Your family comes along in the negative form of it too.

All of your decisions are value statements. What value do you place on practice time? What value do you place on early batting practice time? What value do you place in making sure you get to study hall?

What value do you place on getting in the night before a game? Or going to a party? Everything you do is a value statement. These value statements will eventually decide what type of character you have as an individual.

In my first year at the University of Florida in 1995, we had a walk-on named David Eckstein. He was one of the great examples of this teaching concept. Everything this man did was a value statement. He was unbelievable. He would be at early batting practice every day. He would take extra ground balls every day. He was always around the baseball stadium. He never wasted time. Everything he did was a statement of value. That statement was, "I want to be a better player."

We are talking about a walk-on athlete. Along with that he was a tremendous student. He was a great young man, and on and on and on. He left us as an all-American and is very successful in Double-A ball with the Boston Red Sox. Again, David Eckstein had some characteristic traits that led to success, but he developed those traits because he understood that everything he did was a statement of value. He valued being a good student and a good player more than being a party animal and an average student. He made his statement of value daily as you watched his life.

Characteristics of Success

We teach in our program that every day you make a value statement about what you want your character to be and what you want your life to be. You choose it to be either a success or a mystery.

Let's discuss the characteristics of success. These are the characteristics I believe we need to teach daily to our athletes as individuals.

• Confidence results from being prepared, from paying attention to details, from establishing good work habits. You have the knowledge that you have done everything you can do, so now you should be successful. I believe that when an athlete has inner confidence, he is going to be a lot better not only for us but also, obviously, in his day-to-day life.

• Persistence is a never-give-up attitude. It is always too soon to quit. I think every one of us as coaches understands this idea, but sometimes our young guys do not. It is crucial that we teach our players to enjoy a tough opponent. This gives a competitive greatness to our programs. The confrontation is superior to victory. When you have a tough day ahead of you, it is OK to say to yourself that this is going to be a tough day, but you must add that you are going to get through it. If you get through by the skin of your teeth, you are still going to get through it. You have an attitude of persistence.

• Courage is the ability to be honest with your fears, to face them. Again that confrontation concept comes into play. You need the ability to look at some weaknesses in your life and some fears in your life and confront them. Look at them eye to eye and seek some assistance or help. Maybe it is within yourself to get over an emotional time and just say, "I have had enough of this and I am going to be successful. I am going to deal with these fears and take the steps I need to take." That in itself is courage.

It is just a matter of establishing communications daily with your athletes and being honest with them about their level of courage. Establish that from the head coach to the 25th man on the roster, everyone is battling some fears and concerns. When we run away from them, we lack courage. We can look at them and face them. If you face them, that is the courage we are looking for.

• Poise allows you to balance to success and failure. It is important to show humility when you have been successful and show courage and strength when you have taken a tough loss. From a practical baseball standpoint, poise allows you to slow the game down to play it at your pace. Poise allows you always to be in control of your emotions and your thoughts. Poise is a mature outlook on everyday success and everyday failure.

Coach John Wooden, the tremendous basketball coach at UCLA, said you should make every day a masterpiece and be thankful for everything that occurs in your life. You should be very humble that you have been given an opportunity to compete in an athletic arena.

• By maintaining perspective you don't let the moment identify your life. I make this statement to my athletes constantly. Athletics is a moment-by-moment situation. I have been fortunate that in 1992 we won a national championship at Pepperdine University. It is now 1998. I do not identify with that moment in 1992. I don't go to my home in Gainesville and celebrate the 1992 national championship. If I did that, I have lost perspective. It has been seven years since the event. It was a tremendous moment, but I don't identify myself with that moment. There is another side of the coin. In 1987 I took a Cal State Dominguez Hills program to the College World Series in Montgomery, Alabama, and we had a tough loss. We did not win the national championship. We lost in the College World Series. I don't go home in 1998 to despair and discouragement because of what occurred in 1987. It was a terrible moment. It is a sad way to lose a game as we did. But it was simply a moment.

I try to convey to my athletes that athletics is simply a moment. Do not identify yourself with the moment. If you hit a home run in your first at bat, it is just a moment. Identify with that moment and you might strike out in the next at bat or the next three at bats because you were hung up on the first one. Accept the moment and get to the next one. If you have had a bad at bat, it is just a moment. You are going to have many moments in athletics. Just go moment to moment. Don't identify yourself with or allow your life to be identified by the moment. Have perspective, and it will all work out.

• Loyalty is the backbone to every successful person and every successful program. It is the attitude that keeps every player on the same page of *team* success, not individual success. I believe that every player desires to be successful, but not every player desires to be successful for the team! Loyalty will lead each player to desire team success above all else. It's the characteristic that leads a player to work on his game away from regular practice time. It's the characteristic of a champion, one who forgets himself entirely, and concentrates on the goal at hand. We speak of this characteristic daily in our practices. We point out whenever possible the most powerful truth of all, that loyalty breeds success.

Speaking the Truth in Love

Along with teaching the characteristic of success, we can bring out the best as coaches in our programs by being honest. Speaking the truth in love is a concept I use often in our program. I learned this from my father. If from the first day you meet the club or from the first time you meet a player in a recruiting situation, you work diligently to be honest, you will see those fruits in a big-game setting. The honesty factor is the most difficult factor in my life. I know there are some things I don't want to say to my athletes. It takes ability and courage to be objective with your athletes. It is difficult for me, Andy Lopez, to be objective when it comes to my four children because a lot of emotion is involved. I have a lot of love for those four children of mine. It is very hard to be objective when it comes to my children.

When it comes to being honest and realistic with my children, I have to cross that line and walk that tightrope if I want to grow in character and be honest. I take that into the context of coaching. Your players are going through the rigors of a season, and sometimes we become subjective and emotional. We don't look at situations for what they are and we fail to see the weaknesses some of our athletes or program might have. You need to be objective.

One particular situation reminds me that if I am objective, honest, and speak the truth in love, my program will reap the benefits in a big-game situation. In 1992 at Pepperdine, I was honest with the athletes from the very first day. It was their third year in the program, and they were juniors I had recruited. They came to Pepperdine even though it was a small school that had been to Omaha only once in the 50 years of existence of the program. We talked about some things. We were objective and honest with each other. When they were having great days, I told them they could play with anyone in the country. When they had bad days, I told them they could not even dream about playing on the national realm.

I would tell them, "You can't run this type of defense in practice and expect to be in Omaha. You are living an illusion. You have to run it at a more intense manner and do it at a better pace, more precise and with better execution. If you do that, you'll be in Omaha to play with the best in the country."

The irony is that we got to Omaha in 1992. A special moment occurred as I gave my first scouting report to the team about the other squads in the tournament, teams like Miami, Texas, Cal State Fullerton, and Wichita State. At the end of the report, I glanced at the team, the 25 players in the program in Omaha, the men we had recruited three years before, and I told them we were good enough to win this thing. If I had been deceitful and played mind games with them for the previous three years, I am not sure they would have believed me at that point. I am sure some of them would have walked away saying I was playing head games with them. But they had heard me speak the truth to them in love for three years. When I said I believed we could win if we did A, B, or C, they believed it. I had athletes come back to me and say, "Coach, as soon as you said that we knew that you believed because we had believed too. We felt we could do it, but we just needed to hear it from your voice."

We went out and won four games to be the 1992 national champions. Talent was a factor. Character was crucial. I believe that because I was honest with those athletes from the day I recruited them through those three years that when I said, "Fellas, if we do this, this, and that, we can win a national title," they truly believed it. The fruits of honesty showed themselves for 10 or 12 days in Omaha in 1992.

Setting Realistic Goals

As a coach, it is important to be optimistic. When you set realistic goals and attack them, it establishes something that they can obtain. Optimism is contagious. As a head coach, you need to give it to your athletes. Be optimistic with them as individuals, whether they are a hitter or a pitcher, so that they can be as good as they want to be. You must be willing to follow the steps we will travel over the season.

It is crucial that you don't motivate the impossible. I did this as a young coach. If you go to a pitcher who you know in your heart when being objective is not going to win 10 games, it will not help to motivate him on the idea that he will win 10 or 12 games. In your honest evaluation, he is a 5-game winner. Do not motivate on the impossible because it sets up the player to fail. He will be frustrated.

In 1987 at Cal State Dominguez Hills, we were fortunate to win our conference, go to the College World Series, and finish third in the nation at the Division II level. The next thing I know we are ranked No. 2 in the nation in the preseason. We had a tremendous outlook and a tremendous club, I thought, and a chance to go back to the College World Series and win it.

In January, we had an unbelievable string of injuries, more than I have ever experienced as a head coach. In a two-week period, we lost starters—a center fielder, catchers, and pitchers. On one night, I lost my starting shortstop and second baseman in separate automobile accidents in different locations. It was mind boggling. Before those two weeks, I had motivated the team on the goal that we could get back and win the national championship of Division II college baseball. After those two weeks, I longer motivated on that. It would have been unrealistic, motivating on the impossible.

Someone might say I was selling my guys short. No, I wasn't. When the starters went down, we did not have the depth to come back. It would have put too much pressure on backup people to do something that really they were never geared to do. From that point, our motivation was to be as good as we could be and see how fast we could improve day-in and day-out. How quick can a backup guy turn himself into a starter? Let's take it one day at a time.

Before those injuries, I was motivated, and I was motivating my team on the goal that we were good enough to get back and win it. I encourage you to be optimistic but caution you never to motivate toward the impossible. Set realistic goals, attack them, and let the optimism be contagious with your athletes.

Showing Enthusiasm

Like optimism, enthusiasm is contagious. You have to find the best way to succeed. Not just your way. Not just Coach Lopez's way. Find the best way to succeed with each of your athletes. I have tremendous experience in this area with Brad Wilkerson at the University of Florida.

Wilkerson is one of the best players I have coached. He was a three-time all-American and won Player of the Year honors his junior season. Brad taught me a pickoff move he used as defensive first baseman. He would take a step toward home plate when we put the pickoff play on, trying to deceive the runner that he was going to break toward the plate. It was a tremendous move, and it was the best way.

To show my enthusiasm, I decided we were going to put that play into our defense. It will be something we do as long as I am the head coach at the University of Florida. It was an opportunity for me to seek the best way, not my way, through Brad and the rest of the club. I wanted to establish the idea that we are seeking the best way to succeed.

Using Positive Motivation

It is imperative that we as head coaches establish positive motivation. I admit that there were times in my life when I motivated players through fear and intimidation. That form does not last a season. I believe you must have positive motivation.

The way to do this is share with your athletes your vision and expectations with realistic goals. Teach from those visions. For example, if an athlete does a good job executing the hit-and-run, my vision is the execution of the hit-and-run will lead us to the championship. If you don't do a good job on the execution, it is no longer a vision but a hallucination. We are not going to play for a championship if we cannot execute the hit-and-run. With the pitching staff, we tell them that when they pitch to a location and hit spots, they have the right to believe that they can pitch for a national championship. Without the basic execution, it is again is not a vision but a hallucination.

What you are trying to do to your program is motivate through a positive vision you have for each individual and your entire program. Your goal is that your players will be motivated to strive to do their best because they know you, as their head coach, believe in them. You believe they can do the things that you established and set as a vision. You motivate out of your belief in them, not through fear or intimidation. It is a positive plan of motivation. Sometimes you can motivate when you become upset. For that short moment, it can be a positive thing. If you continue, however, it really starts wearing them down.

The essence of positive motivation it that it will last through the whole the season. More important, it will last in their lives. They will strive to do their best simply because someone believes in them.

I have been fortunate to know what it feels like to be motivated in a positive way, knowing that someone truly believes in me and what I am trying to accomplish in my life. I think of a crucial time in my life back in 1972 when my father used positive motivation to encourage me. I was a high school player coming out of San Pedro High School. My grades were not that great, and I was coming off a rough time as a teenager. My dad was constantly motivating me because he believed I could accomplish something in my life. It came down to a simple day, two weeks before school was to begin. Most of my buddies were not continuing their education after high school and were getting in the work force in the project area where I was brought up.

My father turned to me and asked if I was going to junior college. I had been recruited by other schools, but my grades were not good enough to attend them. I just assumed I was going to start working as a longshoreman. I had visions of going to junior college, but needed his motivation for me to achieve that goal.

I attended Los Angeles Harbor Junior College, earned all-America honors for two years, and played at UCLA, where I had a great time. I was the captain of the squad my senior year, was drafted in the ninth round, and eventually was selected to the UCLA Hall of Fame.

The true starting point was my dad motivating me from a positive image of what he wanted me to do—to continue my education. I had that vision, but mine was not as strong as his. That day, it just kicked in that he believed in me. I was going to give it a shot. I still do not know what I would be doing if my dad did not have that positive vision for his son.

Administering Discipline

Along with positive motivation, I believe you must provide discipline. I do not believe you can be successful without some kind of discipline. I use discipline with love. Earlier in my career I used discipline because I felt it was needed at the time. I did not do it in love.

What do I mean by discipline with love? You should discipline with the vision of making a particular player better or making the program better. You should not use discipline simply because you are the head coach. Use it to respond to weaknesses you see in character or the team's character. We as a group will reap the benefits down the road.

Two scriptures in Ecclesiastes come to mind about discipline. One is very powerful for me when I think about my program day-in and day-out. It says, "The end of a matter is better than its beginning." The second says, "Because a matter is not dealt with quickly, the heart of man is inclined to do it over and over again."

If you don't discipline your guys right away, they are going to be inclined to continue on that path. Take not covering a particular area in practice. If you don't get on it right away, that area is going to get wider. I see it happen a lot in base running by not staying on your guys about the small details like, for example, reading pitchouts. If you don't have that type of discipline in your program, the small details are going to turn into huge mistakes in a crucial game setting.

I do not enjoy dispensing discipline. I do not get enjoyment out of disciplining my children, anyone in my program, or my coaching staff. I don't enjoy disciplining myself. I know that when I do it with myself, my children, or my players and coaches, we will receive the fruits of success. The mother of success is discipline.

Coach Wooden once said, "If you have self-discipline, you won't need anybody to discipline you." It is one of the secrets to teach your people. Discipline yourself on the field and off the field, daily. Use self-discipline in every area of your life, a constant reminder that you can get better.

The Result

The result of walking the tight rope toward building character is a group of tough young men who are game ready and life ready. They will have a loyalty not only to their teammates but also to their program and school. They will be loyal because over the season each one has had to confront a weakness or help a teammate confront a weakness. From the head coach to the players, they have seen individuals confront weaknesses, challenge them, and grow within those weaknesses. It builds an all-for-one mentality. They have been down the tough back alley of character development. They have set high standards. They have disciplined themselves. They have had some tough times. In the end, they have battled together seeking the hidden treasure of becoming a stronger man.

Every player that comes into our program desires to become a better man when he leaves it. They want to become better people and better baseball players. It is our job to attempt to satisfy that hidden desire. They might not all say it. But I guarantee that if you pull each of them aside, each will say he wants to become a better player and a better man, with more character, self-discipline, organizational skill, and a higher standard than when he arrived in the program.

We all want to make these guys better baseball players. We all love to win. The underlying thought about coaching and educating is that every player will become a stronger man, a full man. He will not only play well in the ninth inning of a close game but also be a big-league human being when he leaves your program.

PART VI

Off-the-Field Opportunities, Challenges, and Pressures

CHAPTER TWENTY-THREE

Learning and Developing as a Professional

Glen Tuckett

> "I want my baseball players to win more than just championships. I try to motivate players not just for a game, but for life!"

This is a provocative title that provides plenty of latitude. It suggests that learning is a prerequisite to total development. Becoming a professional is not achieved by happenstance nor can it be bequeathed. It is a long, arduous process. The consummate professional reaches that lofty stature by personal participation, study, work, dedication, and good old stick-to-itiveness.

I assume that the reader has a sincere interest in baseball and the people who play the game. I likewise assume that the reader wants to become a better coach and in some cases improve his coaching situation by getting a better job.

There is not a more rewarding experience in the world than being a baseball coach. Friends used to ask my oldest daughter, "What does your daddy do?" She answered, "Oh, nothing. He just goes down to school and plays ball with the boys."

The purpose of this chapter is to help coaches improve, to offer insights into the art of learning and acquiring coaching skills and a philosophy that will help the coach develop and become more proficient.

Painting Your Self–Portrait

Mahatma Ghandi once said, "My life is my message." I always felt that Brigham Young University baseball was my self-portrait. It was me, my strengths, my weaknesses. It was my philosophy in action. It encompassed the things that were important to me. BYU baseball (along with family and church) was my life.

If you don't like and appreciate kids, you shouldn't be in coaching. A very successful high school coach has recently stated, "I want my baseball players to win more than just championships. I try to motivate players not just for a game, but for life!" Thanks, Coach. The profession needs more men like you.

The coach should conduct himself with class. Correct, yes. Criticize, yes. But never strip a young man of his dignity. Players should be able to look back on their playing experience (no matter how many years have passed) as the most significant, memorable, enjoyable time of their lives. This can only happen if the coach is the impeccable leader—a man who is principled and weaves those principles into his personal life and into his daily interaction with his team.

There is no stereotype or prototype for a successful baseball coach. Successful leaders come in a variety of packages and bring with them a variety of skills and personal attributes.

The history of professional baseball clearly demonstrates that there is no foolproof method for becoming a successful manager. John McGraw was an absolute tyrant. Casey Stengel played the role of comedian. Sparky Anderson was blessed with an abundance of energy and enthusiasm. Tommy Lasorda was a cheerleader, the consummate psychologist. Regardless of their apparent differences in leadership style, each of the those managers (along with dozens of others) were predictable winners. Their distinct personalities, their charisma, and their thorough preparation were hallmarks of their success as managers.

College baseball has been blessed with coaches who possess tremendous knowledge of the game. They have been teachers primarily. Positive results were, and are, obtained in a variety of ways. John Scolinos (Pepperdine and Cal Poly) was uncommonly skilled in the art of making mediocre players good and average players great. Rod Dedeaux (University of Southern California) was the master psychologist. Bobby Winkles (Arizona State University) coached teams that redefined the word *hustle.* John Winkin (University of Maine) defied climate and created a nationally recognized program. Ron Fraser (University of Miami) demonstrated the value of promoting the grand old game. Currently, Skip Bertman (Louisiana State University) has proven that dynasties can still be built despite scholarship limitations.

As a coach, you almost have to be a dictator. Democracy goes out the window on game day. You don't hold a team meeting when you have men on first and third and one out. Show me a coach who isn't part dictator, and I'll show you a guy who is out of work.

Self-confidence is critical to decision making and decisiveness. Without it, the coach loses his team's confidence in challenging situations. Paul the Apostle said it best in his epistle to the Corinthians: "For if the trumpet give an uncertain sound, who shall prepare himself to the battle." (1 Corinthians 14:8)

To be successful, a coach soon realizes that it is performance that counts. Good teams perform well. Bad teams perform poorly. It doesn't matter how much the coach knows or how well he performed as a player. The thing that matters is how much the players know and how well they perform.

Here are some tips for the coach about professional and personal development:

- The greatest gift we can bestow upon others is a good example.
- A confused player cannot be aggressive. Prepare your players.
- Make a conscious effort to praise a player's positive performance in words rather than assuming he is aware of how you feel.
- Don't be reluctant to put your arm around his neck. Let him know you like him.
- Instruct. Don't punish. Express displeasure in a positive, impersonal manner.
- Few players have become poorer players because of compliments from a coach, but many players are driven to self-doubt by a coach's sarcastic criticism.
- Help the player develop a positive self-image built by repeated (sometimes small) successes.
- Shine up or polish your players' halos.
- Hold the mirror at the most flattering angle.
- Reenshrine the nobility of work. The work ethic can be taught. Baseball is a year-round game, a way of life, not just a spring pastime. Hard work is a foolproof confidence builder. Those who have worked the hardest are the last to surrender

The sensitive, successful coach makes his players better by getting them to think they are better players. The best example of this phenomenon is the methods used by the legendary Dr. Harold Hill in the popular musical *The Music Man*. If Harold Hill can play mind games and enjoy success, just imagine what an innovative baseball coach can do.

Young players need role models more than they need critics. The coach is first an educator, and he should be proud of it! I always tried to teach manhood, honesty, dedication, and decency through baseball. The young athlete wants a coach whom he can admire as a man. Long after your ballplayers have forgotten the signs or your method of executing the delayed steal, they will remember your example and the things you stood for.

The neophyte will learn early in his career not to overcoach. Can't you just imagine an overzealous hitting coach saying to a young Mark McGwire, "To generate power, you must hold on to the bat with your right hand until you have completed your follow-through!"

Some youngsters are gifted with unique skills. I once heard Coach John Wooden recite the following poem:

There once was a .400 hitter named Krantz
Who had a most unusual stance.

But with the coach's correction
His swing was perfection
And now he can't hit the seat of his pants.

Don't overcoach. Enough said.

The coach regulates the emotional climate of the players and the team. He finds their motivator button and then pushes it to activate the desired response. Motivator buttons are hard to locate. I have always wished that motivator buttons were anatomically exact like noses, ears, or elbows. They are not, so coaches must continue to search and to probe. Once the coach activates a player's motivator button he should get out of the way and let the young man perform. My holy grail, the thing for which I have searched all of my life as a coach, is to be able to locate the motivator button on young men.

Twenty-Five Gobs of Protoplasm

Each year I surrounded myself with 25 amoeba-like gobs of protoplasm. Many of them were like a ship without a rudder. They liked the game, they had a destination, but they didn't know how to get there. It was my job as the coach to mold and sculpt them into the traditional Brigham Young University baseball player.

Eddie Kimball (former athletic director at BYU) once stated concerning recruiting, "You'll find that it is easier to coach good players than it is poor players." Lester Maddox (former governor of Georgia) said, "Prison conditions will never improve until the state gets a higher class inmate." The point is that there is a correlation between skill level and success.

The coach who directs all his thoughts toward winning and building men makes it a point to know his players and knows how to arouse them emotionally. Players are different; they respond to different stimuli. A coach cannot turn players into robots, all alike and all doing the same things with the same level of skill. I have found by experience that we were successful when we had the bunters bunting and the hitters hitting. We always came up short when we had the bunters hitting and the hitters bunting! Discover each player's strength and capitalize on it.

Help your players eliminate the fear of failure. Fear is paralyzing. Fear of failure is the greatest demotivator in the world. Failure is the ignition to all greatness. In 1974 Lou Brock of the St. Louis Cardinals had 118 stolen bases and 33 failures. He was thrown out more than any player in the history of the National League yet set a record for stolen bases.

I tried never to be openly critical of physical errors. I knew they were part of the game. Billy Ripken (major-league infielder) recently stated, "Errors are a part of the game, but Abner Doubleday was a jerk for inventing them." Errors, mistakes, and misfortune provide feedback. In my opinion, feedback is the breakfast of champions. Successful players and coaches learn from mistakes. Mistakes are the difference between winning or losing. The team that makes the fewest number of mistakes (not errors) will normally be the team that wins the game. The objective is to eliminate mistakes and keep errors at a minimum. Little things don't mean a lot; they mean everything.

We need to teach kids that it is not a crime to hustle. It takes no talent whatsoever to run hard, to hustle. The nonhustler thinks he is sophisticated, but really all he is doing is creating a defense for his ego if he proves to be unsuccessful. Try hard. The game is fun. Smile and enjoy it.

Some people try to say that morale is almost an accident, that either a team has morale or it hasn't, and that's that! It is difficult to believe that something as important as team morale occurs because of some quirk of fate. A group of young men and their coach can band together in a harmonious and closely knit unit if they believe in themselves. In practically all instances, player morale is proportionate to the coach's interest in their morale.

The coach who disregards discipline, manners, respect, and gentlemanly behavior is not really a coach. The baseball diamond is the greatest laboratory in the world. Coaches who only concentrate on the skills, techniques, and strategies of the game are doing the great sport of baseball, and the young men whom they coach, a terrible injustice.

Many young people come from homes and programs that lack discipline and gentlemanly conduct. I have always maintained that if a youngster came to my program and had never been taught these important lessons, I would teach them to him. Discipline is much more than "Yes, sir" and "No, sir." The discipline to which I refer means deeper concentration, extra effort, and personal subordination for the betterment of the team. It means complete and unwavering self-control. It is a shame that the word *discipline* has taken on the narrow meaning of punishment.

Trial and (Excuse the Term) Error

Under normal conditions, experience has proven to be an effective teacher. A sage once stated, "Although he has coached for 17 years, he really does not have 17 years of experience. He has one year's experience 17 times." Experience is of greatest value when the coach is inquisitive, inventive, ambitious, and, most of all, flexible. The ability to learn from failure (and yes, even success) is the mark of the successful coach.

As a player and a coach, I improved my performance by trial and error. I will list a few skills I learned by personal experience:

- The underhand feed by the shortstop to the second baseman in a double-play attempt (and the feed from the first baseman to the pitcher covering first base) should be stiff wristed, not a flip.
- When executing the hit-and-run, the hitter should just hit the ball on the ground. It does not have to be hit to the right side of the infield.
- With a runner on first, or runners on first and second base, infielders retrieve all fumbled ground balls with their bare hand and always throw to first base.
- If offensive linemen in football can have and learn blocking rules, in baseball we can certainly have base-running rules. Here are just a few of them:
  - Every single is a double until the opponents prove it is a single, and so forth.
  - With a left-handed-throwing left fielder, a ball hit between the third baseman and the third-base line is a double. No decision; it's a double. The same rule works for the first-base line.
  - The base runner on second base (regardless of the number of outs) always scores on a ground-ball base hit to the right side that gets through the infield.

We had dozens of rules. I didn't want to have players who were uncertain. In short, we took the guesswork out of the game for the players. Much of the information conveyed and taught to the players was the result of my personal experiences.

The Sincerest Form of Flattery

Some of the most effective strategies and techniques I employed as a coach were borrowed or gleaned from others. I had very few original thoughts; therefore, I became an extremely skilled borrower. Find a new idea or technique, massage it, modify it, and make it yours. As Yogi Berra once said, "You can see a lot just by observing." It is not plagiarism for a coach to observe or to be taught a strategy and then use it as a part of his coaching arsenal. Imitation is the sincerest form of flattery.

Personal playing experiences have proven to be very helpful. As a player I learned a lot from managers who had been very good players and were able to convey their knowledge to me so that I did not have to reinvent the wheel. Three stand out in my mind. They taught indelible lessons by the way they played and the way they managed. Rupert Thompson had three rules: (1) hustle, (2) don't miss any signs, and (3) always be a gentleman. Hugh Luby, a real bear-down guy, smiled once every season just to stay in practice. Bill Brenner didn't overmanage. His motto: "Shake it off—you'll be up there again with men on base." I also studied opposing managers and players. I engaged in conversation and discussions with anyone who could help me gain useful knowledge about the intricacies of the game.

As I finally reached my goal (a goal is a dream with a deadline, according to Harvey Mackay) and assumed a baseball head coaching position, I found myself trying to act, behave, and coach like my coaching heroes. One day I would be Walter Alston, the next day I would try to imitate Rod Dedeaux, and the next day, Gene Mauch. It had to be confusing to the players, and it was certainly frustrating to me. There seems to be a subtle skill, a touch of chemistry, a charisma, a distinct personality about a successful coach that cannot be copied. I soon realized this, and I was convinced that to be successful, I would have to discard the borrowed persona and just be myself. Immediately, my comfort zone broadened and my effectiveness improved.

Many of the coaches against whom you compete may be doing a better job of coaching in particular areas than you are. Learn to consider them teachers, examples, not just competitors. Thinking differently about opposing coaches may eventually lead to a close, synergistic, mutually beneficial relationship. By sharing knowledge, both coaches become better. They can exchange ideas, techniques, and strategies in a non-threatening way and find that both of them will benefit.

Coaches should attend clinics, read books, view films and videos, subscribe to periodicals, obtain a copy of the coaching syllabus of successful coaches, attend coaching methods seminars, and so forth. The status quo is stagnating. Branch out.

Learn from other vocations and disciplines. Much of the information I adapted in my coaching career was obtained from books written about subjects unrelated to sport in general or to baseball in particular. As the poet Shelley remarked, "Some things through time and change are unquenchably the same." It is apparent to me that many common threads run through all successful endeavors.

Philosophy—the Coach's Personal Ground Rules

A workable, realistic philosophy is much more than a few trite words displayed on a bumper sticker. It is a system of principles by which a coach conducts his life. It is a creed. It is a set of guidelines. A coach's philosophy is the extension of his inner self. A philosophy has to do with (1) attitude, (2) goals, (3) dedication, and (4) a set of workable ground rules.

The coach striving to be recognized as a true professional will find a distinct difference between "funsies" and "keepsies." He is now playing hardball. He must be prepared and ready for the real world. A realistic coaching philosophy will help him in the preparation process.

Some points to consider in formulating a successful coaching philosophy are these:

- Increase the constants and decrease the variables. The ratio of constants to variables determines the probability of success. Coin flipping has never been a reliable way to make a decision.

- Accentuate the positive and eliminate the negative (and don't mess with Mr. In-Between).

- Be optimistic. Be upbeat. Pessimism is self-defeating.

- Go with your best pitch! Have your team and your players do the things they do best.

- Act—don't react. Be aggressive. Go on the attack. Set the tempo.

- Prepare—don't repair. If the team is prepared, the need for repair is dramatically reduced.

- Avoid playing catch-up baseball as much as possible. Don't get too far behind. The successful coach knows where to find the off button. Catch-up baseball is the hardest kind to play. It takes all the strategy out of the game—no sacrifice, no hit-and-run, and so on. Just sit back, keep your fingers crossed, and play for the big inning.

There is no foolproof method of handling players. What works for one may be the worst possible approach for another. As I matured as a coach, I adapted an amended version of Coach Paul Bryant's plan, which evolved to be the following:

- Have a game plan and believe in it.
- Learn to recognize a winner. It is easy to recognize winners who have ability. The tough job is being able to recognize winners who

don't have ability. One thing I have always noticed about winners—their eyes dance, they are inquisitive, they are ambitious. They refuse to quit.

- Get the winner in the ballgame. He can't do the team any good on the bench.
- Have the team ready to play at game time.

When it comes to championships, philosophy doesn't mean a whole lot if you don't have the personnel, but similarly, personnel doesn't mean a thing unless you get each player to do the best job he can. I learned a valuable lesson at Sea World in San Diego, California. I recognized that the most effective teachers in the world are animal trainers. After Shamu did a trick, the trainer gave him a fish—right then. Why are animal trainers such effective teachers? They give immediate rewards. That's the key! Coaches, give more fish!

There are many ways to win in baseball other than on the scoreboard. To me, success on the baseball diamond is never considered the ultimate goal. If we evaluate our program by the yardstick of winning and winning only, what if we lose? Wrist? Gas? Jugular vein? There have to be some positive residuals, some spin-offs. Many things are more important, in the long run, than winning. The successful coach promotes the other virtues but still leads his young men to victory. Nothing is as transparent as a hollow victory. Most people don't like to lose, but if one hasn't done his best and played his hardest, winning isn't much fun either.

Many coaches and players talk endlessly about how they hate to lose, what poor losers they are, how it grates on them, how much they despise ending up on the short end of the score. To me, the players and coaches who hate to lose dislike it so much they figure out a way to win!

When it comes to behavior, we don't need rules; we need principles. Too many rules and policies take all the juice out of life. As a coach, I had only one rule: If I do it, you do it, or you are permitted to do it! This is how it worked:

- If I hustle, you hustle.
- If I shine my shoes, you shine your shoes.
- If I don't show up to teach my classes, you don't have to attend your classes.
- If I am not respectful, you don't have to be respectful.
- If I swear, you can swear.

- If I tell a smutty story, you can tell a smutty story, and so forth.

The rule worked very well.

The coach interested in his personal growth and professional development should never tolerate vulgarity, pornography, smutty stories and jokes, lying, cheating, or dishonesty. Society is rapidly becoming immune to old-fashioned decency. We are going downhill at breakneck speed. It is disgusting to see how supposed leaders tolerate the filth about them. Some not only tolerate it, they sanction it. The coach must create a wholesome oasis in this desert of deception, vulgarity, and filth.

Society has changed dramatically during the past quarter of a century. The change in attitude is poignantly illustrated in a poem titled "An Essay on Man" by Alexander Pope.

> Vice is a monster of so fruitful mien
> As to be hated needs but to be seen.
> Yet seen too oft, familiar with her face
> We first endure, then pity, then embrace.

A final thought regarding the formulation of a realistic philosophy is that nothing dies such a tragic death as does success unattended.

A Legitimate Love Affair

The modern-day coach should pattern himself after the icons who have influenced the game in a positive manner. It seems that the old-time coaches had an uncommon love of the game. It was a way of life. They loved the game, and they loved it unashamedly. They were the pioneers, the trailblazers. They fought the hard battles. They made the game what it is today. They dug the wells from which all of us drink.

All the great coaches of the past have had a sincere appreciation, even a reverence, for the game. It was much more than a game! I have had an unashamed, lifelong love affair with baseball. It has served as my north star, my Polaris, my point of reference. I had a field of dreams long before it became a catch phrase.

I can't remember when I didn't eat, sleep, and drink baseball. I never wanted to be a cowboy or a fireman. I always dreamed of being the shortstop for the New York Yankees. On one occasion when I was about eight years old (when I was in a rather serious mood), I asked my dad a very searching and, to me, important question, "Dad, do they play baseball in heaven?" If they didn't I wasn't sure I wanted to go there. My dad was a loving, caring, and wise parent. His answer indicated how wise he was. He suggested to me that he was sure they played baseball in heaven.

I was a confirmed hero worshiper as a youngster. At one stage of my life my hero was Les Scarsella of the Oakland Oaks of the old Pacific Coast League. He was an outstanding hitter. Les walked pigeon-toed. Because he was my hero, I walked pigeon toed for two years, yet I never became a good hitter.

When I was playing professional baseball, I heard that Stan Musial, another one of my heroes, didn't eat lunch. I quit eating lunch—but I still hit .250.

Baseball may be one of the last bastions for goodness and decency. The professional game needs more men like Cal Ripken, Jr., Sammy Sosa, and Mark McGwire. We need heroes for today's youth.

Coach, your actions, your demeanor, and your life will be important to the future of the game and to the future of your players. Develop and display a reverence for the game!

The Journey Is Never Over

Acquiring and disseminating knowledge is a never ending process in the game of baseball. Strategy has evolved and changed almost as graphically as game uniforms. Some strategic moves never considered 30 years ago are now common practice. The wise coach stays on the forefront and refuses to let the game pass him by.

The young coach should ask himself this question: Am I willing to study and become a scholar, an expert, in the baseball coaching profession? Experiment, read, discuss, watch videos, attend games (both amateur and professional), and so on. Do everything you can to increase your knowledge of baseball. Exchange ideas, discuss situations, review the latest literature, experiment with the myriad teaching and coaching aids currently available.

Find mentors who will share their thoughts, their methods, and their secrets of success. They will describe to you the pitfalls and minefields that lie before you and possible ways to avoid them. They will relate to you what they might have done that would have improved their chances of being even more successful. It is one thing to have the knowledge; it is certainly another thing to be able to teach others and have them be able to perform at a high skill level.

Innovative, visionary, adventurous coaches often unbalance the homeostasis. They disrupt the status quo. They defy tradition. They are always looking for a better way. They have appreciation for "the book" by which the game has always been played, but they do not canonize it. Traditionally coaches coached by the book, but no one has ever proven that the author of the book was all knowing and infallible. The author of the book probably turns over in his grave when he hears of a coach bringing the infield in before the fifth inning or a coach purposely putting the winning run on base or a pitcher throwing a change-up when he has two strikes on the hitter. The game continues to change, and the successful coach must sift through the options and use the new (or recycled) strategies that fit his coaching style and philosophy.

Don't minimize coaching as a factor in team success. Coaching on the amateur level is from 50 to 75 percent responsible for winning programs. The competent coach galvanizes his team, and the players continually look to him for guidance and direction. Players come and go, but in the case of winning high school and college dynasties, the coach is permanent. He has put together a winning formula. By staying on the cutting edge of baseball knowledge, he amends his formula and perpetuates his winning tradition.

The successful and winning coach must abandon the status quo. The game will pass him by if he is not flexible and willing to make needed changes. He should

- attend clinics,
- read the published material,
- attend games and pick up pointers,
- exchange information with other successful coaches, and
- join (and be an active participant) in local, state, and national baseball coaches organizations.

The coach who perpetuates a successful program does it by study and application.

Many truly outstanding books have been written about baseball. A coach should read every book he can get his hands on. There is so much wisdom available. Besides the many how-to books written by the likes of Ted Williams, Bob Shaw, Charlie Lau, and others, I have found a wealth of knowledge about the intricacies and nuances of the game in the following books:

- *A Thinking Man's Guide to Baseball,* Leonard Koppett
- *All About Baseball,* Leonard Koppett
- *Percentage Baseball and the Computer,* Earnshaw Cook
- *The Complete Baseball Handbook,* Walter Alston

There are dozens more—read, evaluate, assimilate, facilitate! Coach Paul Bryant once said, "The price of victory is high, but so are the rewards." Coach, pay the price!

How to Climb the Coaching Ladder

The best and surest way to climb the coaching ladder, to be recognized as a professional, to attract the attention of people in the baseball world, is to win. It's that simple!

Society is obsessed with climbing the corporate ladder. The desire to improve one's performance and be recognized as a success seems to be a most effective motivational tool. If the desire to improve one's station in life were not inherent in most of us, we would always have far too many fiddlers and not enough conductors.

Many avenues lead to the top in one's profession. Literally hundreds of men in the country, however, have decided that their niche in life is to coach Little League, legion, or high school baseball. They are not interested in college coaching. Some of the most outstanding baseball minds in the country are coaching high school baseball, and they are content and fulfilled. Thank heaven for men such as this.

Years ago it was possible for an outstanding young high school coach to be identified and rewarded with a position as head coach at a college or university. During the past 15 or 20 years this type of advancement has seldom happened.

The young lion who has been the assistant in a successful program has a distinct advantage as he begins his climb up the coaching ladder. He has learned valuable lessons regarding handling players, teaching skills, patience, discipline, strategy, and so on. As he adds his unique style to the model to which he has been exposed, he begins to develop his persona and coaching philosophy. If he continues to improve and enjoy some coaching success, he becomes a very marketable commodity in the baseball coaching profession.

The best thing that can happen to an ambitious, young assistant coach is to have an advocate, a mentor, who is willing to help him secure a head coaching position. A graphic case in point follows. Many years ago Danny Litwhiler (Florida State and Michigan State) had a youngster in his program named Ron Fraser. Ron was a good player, a hard worker, and inquisitive. Eventually, Coach Litwhiler was able to help Ron secure the head coaching position at the University of Miami. Fraser was not only a thorough teacher and coach, he was a master promoter. Soon the Miami Hurricanes were the envy of everyone in college baseball.

Skip Bertman was the pitching coach at Miami. Because of his fine work and the endorsement of Ron Fraser, Skip became the head coach at Louisiana State University. During the '90s Louisiana State University has been the dominant baseball program in the country.

Jim Wells was an assistant at LSU. Jim is an extremely inquisitive person who learns rapidly. The University of Alabama was looking for a head baseball coach, and because of the endorsement of Skip Bertman, Jim is currently the head coach at Alabama and enjoying tremendous success.

Jim Wells has two outstanding young men serving as assistant coaches—Mitch Gaspard and Todd Butler. Both are destined to become successful head coaches at the college level. When this happens it will be because they have worked with Jim Wells and he has recommended them.

To paraphrase the Bible, "Litwhiler begat Fraser; Fraser begat Bertman; Bertman begat Wells; Wells will beget Gaspard and Butler."

It is apparent by this anecdote that the most effective way to obtain a head coaching position is to have worked successfully for a person who is respected and who will expend time and energy in helping his assistant get a head coaching position.

I conclude with the stirring words of Sir Winston Churchill, "To every man there comes in his lifetime that special moment when he is figuratively tapped on the shoulder and offered that chance to do a very special thing, unique to him and fitted to his talents. What a tragedy if that moment finds him unprepared or unqualified for that work."

Hitting the Clinic Circuit

Richard "Itch" Jones

When I accepted my first baseball coaching position at MacMurray College, I knew that baseball clinics would be beneficial. Roy Lee, baseball coach at Southern Illinois University at Edwardsville, invited me to attend the National Baseball Clinic in Houston, Texas, in 1966. I was amazed at the knowledge of the speakers and how well they presented the techniques and theories of baseball.

When I left the clinic I hoped that someday I would understand the game well enough to be asked to speak at a clinic. In 1972 I was asked to speak at the ABCA clinic in San Francisco. Since that day I have had the opportunity to speak at numerous clinics throughout the United States, Canada, and Taiwan. I have found these clinics to be a valuable avenue for exchanging the latest theories, techniques, and philosophies of the great game of baseball. By attending clinics, a coach is able to enhance his baseball knowledge and keep abreast of the game.

Speaking Opportunities

I have always considered it a privilege and honor when I have been asked to speak at a baseball clinic. Usually the person who asks you to speak has heard you speak or your name was referred to him as a clinician whom coaches would like to hear. He has been told that you will attract coaches and present them with ideas that will improve their baseball programs. Once the clinic coordinator makes contact, you and he will decide the dates of the clinic, the number of times you will speak, and the amount of time allotted for each talk.

Normally a contract is sent to you stating the dates, times, and subjects to be covered. Once you return the contract, an agreement has been made between you and the clinic coordinator.

Preparation

You and the clinic coordinator have chosen the topics that will be covered, the length of time for each talk, the time of day, and the date of the clinic. It is important for you to know the audience and the approximate number that will be present. To prepare, you need to know whether the clinic will be for coaches, players, or a combination. If only players attend, it is important to know the age level. It is the speaker's responsibility to gear his presentation to the knowledge level of the audience.

You should inform the coordinator of any additional equipment that you might need, such as an overhead projector, chalkboard, bases, bats, balls, or screens. Check to see how much room you have if you use live demonstrations to complement your presentation.

You should forward an outline of your presentation early enough so the coordinator can have copies available for each coach or player in attendance. The outline should be well organized and detailed enough to cover the time allotted for the talk. You should leave time at the end of the presentation to entertain any questions that the coaches might have concerning the subject that you covered.

Travel Arrangements

Some clinic coordinators want to make the travel arrangements for their speakers. Others want the speaker to make his own travel arrangements. You need to clarify the date and times of your departure and arrival. The clinic coordinator will usually encourage you to stay over on a Saturday night because airline tickets are usually less expensive that way. Buying tickets 21 days before departure will often reduce the price of the ticket. Due to airline flight schedules and connections, you may find it to be more convenient to drive to a larger city rather than depart from a smaller airport.

Because many speaking engagements are in the winter months, it is important for you to be prepared for flight cancellations. If this occurs, know the flight times and flight numbers of the next few flights leaving for your destination. When delays occur call the clinic coordinator and keep him informed of your approximate arrival time so that he can make any necessary changes in the program.

It is a good policy to arrive at your speaking engagement the night before, or at least four hours before, your presentation. This takes the worry off the clinic coordinator and enables him to keep the program on schedule.

Presentation

You should be in the area where you are to speak at least 10 minutes early so the program can stay on schedule. This will enable the clinic coordinator to introduce you when he is ready to start the next session. You will have an opportunity to get any equipment that you might need in place for the presentation, which will keep confusion to a minimum when you are introduced.

While waiting to speak, you may want to mingle with the coaches and listen to the other speakers. This will give you a feel for what the coaches in the audience are expecting from speakers at the clinic.

341

With your material organized and a feel for the audience, you are ready to make your presentation. Because each coach has an outline of the talk, it is important that you follow your outline.

Good speakers are confident, enthusiastic, make eye contact with the audience, and make each person feel important and realize that he can teach to his team what you are presenting. When you finish the presentation, you want to have inspired the audience to put these new techniques to use with their teams. You want the coaches to feel that they learned more about the game of baseball, that the time they spent at your session was educational and worthwhile. As a speaker, remember that the coaches pay for the clinic and it is the speaker's responsibility to make it a useful learning experience.

Visual aids or demonstrations are usually helpful because the coaches can both listen and see the techniques. If you need an assistant with the talk, you should rehearse to ensure that the demonstration goes smoothly.

Start your talk on time and finish on time so that the clinic can stay on schedule. When a speaker goes past his scheduled time, it creates a problem for the coordinator and the remaining speakers. To prevent this from happening, the coordinator should signal to the speaker when he has approximately 10 minutes to go, then 5 minutes, and then every minute until he signals "cut." This will keep the program on schedule, and the next speaker will not have to cut short his talk. The coaches in the audience appreciate a program that stays on schedule because they will know when to move from one session to the next.

Leave approximately five minutes to entertain questions and answers at the end of each talk. This will give the coaches in the audience an opportunity to get clarification on something that you may not have stated clearly. Once this five minutes is up, leave the area so the next speaker can begin speaking. In many clinics the coordinator will have a room or area to go to if coaches have further questions. During this time you may entertain questions related to your talk or answer any questions that a coach might have concerning any aspect of the game. Clinic coordinators appreciate clinicians who are available following their presentations to discuss baseball with audience members.

Humor

A little humor is helpful to loosen up both the audience and you. A speaker often includes some experiences that illustrate a point that he is trying to make. Humorous anecdotes can be a good idea or approach as long as it does not detract from the presentation or take up too much time. Keep in mind that the jokes should be appropriate to the situation and not embarrass anyone. It has happened that clinicians have told off-color stories or jokes and offended some listeners. If you use humor, be sure that it is acceptable to the entire audience. If one person is offended, then the jokes or off-color stories were not appropriate. Speak to the audience as you would want a speaker to speak in front of your wife and children.

Sometimes a speaker may have an embarrassing moment during a presentation. I have had my share, but there is one that sticks out. I was speaking at "Be the Best You Are" in the Hyatt Hotel at Cherry Hill, New Jersey, and I had been assigned back-to-back sessions. Following the first session, I left the podium to go to the rest room. When I reentered the auditorium, 1,200 people stood and gave me a standing ovation. I quietly said, "Thank you," and then I heard it over the speaker. I had forgotten to take off or turn off the cordless microphone. I was embarrassed but happy to know that I had not said anything to upset the audience.

Exhibitors

If you have borrowed a bat, ball, or some other equipment from one of the exhibitors, the vendor will surely appreciate being recognized. We often forget to acknowledge the vendors for the effort they put forth to make clinics successful. The vendors are congenial when it comes to lending the speaker equipment that will enhance a presentation. They pay to have their booths in the exhibit area, so it is important that the speakers suggest to the coaches that they visit the booths to see what is available for their programs or facilities.

Vendors will have on display the newest and most up-to-date equipment that a coach can buy for his program. Vendors enjoy having coaches stop by so that they can explain the changes, advantages, and cost of the equipment. By going through the exhibit area, a coach will see equipment that his program may need to meet safety precautions set forth by the rules, from Little League through professional baseball. A trip through the exhibit area can help coaches prepare for equipment purchases that may have to be made before the beginning of the season. Often a coach will find that he can buy large pieces of equipment like a pitching machine and extend his payments over time so that his school will not have to make one large payment. Thanks, vendors, for the great job you do at these clinics.

Coaches: Take Notes and Ask Questions

Coach, if you have selected a clinic that you think will help improve your baseball teaching skills, then go prepared to take notes and ask questions. A good way of getting the most out of any clinic is to write down specific questions before arriving. While at the clinic, you may add to your list of questions as you hear and talk to coaches. This way, you will be able to get your questions answered, whether by the speaker or someone else attending the clinic. You will get what is most important in the talk and will be able to get answers to the questions you brought. Besides, by taking notes you will concentrate more on what is being said.

At the clinic, find a coach from your area or conference or someone you respect who has had success. Sit and talk with him to learn what he has done to build and maintain a successful program. Coaches will be willing to discuss with you what it took for their programs to be successful. It might begin with their booster club or the summer program they set up in their city. Most coaches can pinpoint what occurred that was instrumental in getting their programs to the next level. You can learn a tremendous amount by standing in the hallway or meeting with a group of coaches in a room to discuss different topics of the game.

A good way to open a discussion between a number of coaches is to ask each coach what he believes is his strongest area in the game. Follow that up by having each coach mention the areas in which he is least competent. Once each coach states his strengths and weaknesses, you will have an opportunity to help each other. By doing this, a group of coaches may form a bond, make it a point to get together a few nights during the clinic, and look forward to meeting the next year to exchange ideas.

Coaches will soon find that these meetings are worthwhile and will discover ways to present the game. The danger of burnout will diminish. Once you develop this bond with your fellow coaches, the clinics become more exciting because the group can review what they heard from the clinicians. Through the years coaches will find that these meetings were the most educational part of the clinic. Because a coach comes from a high-powered program does not mean that he has complete knowledge of the game. Some of the best baseball teachers may be at the youth level, because they have to teach every fundamental of the game—getting dressed, throwing, hitting, fielding, and so on.

Speaking Opportunities

Advantages and disadvantages come with accepting speaking engagements at baseball clinics. Accepting will give you an opportunity to share your knowledge with coaches at all levels, in different areas of the country. In return you will gain further knowledge of the game because you will learn from the questions the audience asks as well as from your conversations with the coaches who attend the clinics. If you are a college coach, it will keep your name and the college or university you represent in front of the coaches whose players you may be recruiting. Speaking will also give you an opportunity to broaden your recruiting territory as you speak in different cities throughout the United States.

To most, the advantages outweigh the disadvantages, but a few of the disadvantages for a college coach include missing practice and spending more days on the road and away from campus. Once practice begins in the winter months, a college coach must arrange his practice and speaking arrangements to minimize conflicts. Every time a coach accepts a speaking engagement, he will be away from his team another day or two during preseason practice and conditioning.

Collegiate coaching requires many days on the road recruiting. During the regular season, a coach may choose not to speak so that he can reduce his days on the road—days away from school, home, and family.

Winter clinics are sometimes a problem because the weather can cancel flights. Rescheduled return times may cause the coach to miss a practice session that he had arranged before leaving campus. Once the coach accepts a speaking engagement, it is important that he arrange with his staff to cover all details of practice, office operations, and any other contingencies that may occur while he is away.

I have enjoyed my 28 years as a baseball clinician for many reasons: first for the people I have met, second for the sponsors, and third for the opportunity to share new ideas with coaches who have dedicated themselves to the great game of baseball.

Clinics That I'll Remember

"Be the Best That You Are," sponsored by Jack and Ty Hawkins in Cherry Hill, New Jersey, is a great clinic. Jack and Ty have given me the opportunity to speak in 23 of the last 25 years of their clinic. This clinic has brought in some outstanding professional and college coaches. From the professional ranks the clinic has featured Bob Shaw, Ted Williams,

Hank Aaron, Charlie Lau, Earl Weaver, Tom Seaver, Bob Boone, Tom House, Ben Hines, and Johnny Oates. Table 24.1 shows some current clinics of note.

From the college ranks, I want to thank the following coaches for the many ideas they have shared. Their suggestions have improved my coaching and surely the coaching of many others who have heard them speak. Thank you, Ron Polk, Gary Ward, Bobby Winkles, Duane Banks, John Scolinos (my favorite clinician), Bobby Randall, John Winkin, Mark Johnson, Skip Bertman, Jerry Kindall, Pat McMahon, Keith Madison, Rod Delmonico, and Gordon Gillespie. Thanks, coaches, from high school, college, and the professional ranks, for sharing your baseball expertise to help all of us to broaden our knowledge of the game. I apologize to the many great coaches and speakers whose names I have omitted.

TABLE 24.1

Clinic name	City	Sponsor
The Bash	Richmond, VA	Bill Pelot
Best in the Midwest	Toledo, OH	Bruce Edwards
Westchester Sports Clinic	Westchester, NY	Pete Berland and Phil DiRuocco
Mid-Atlantic Baseball Clinic	Gaithersburg, MD	Joe Stolz and Dick Birmingham
Best In the West	Seattle, WA	Jim Harryman
Ontario Best Ever Coaching Clinic	Ontario, Canada	Sam Dempster and Jim Lutton
American Baseball Coaches Association	State high school clinics held in the majority of the states	

CHAPTER TWENTY-FIVE

Beating the Burnout Factor

Jerry Kindall

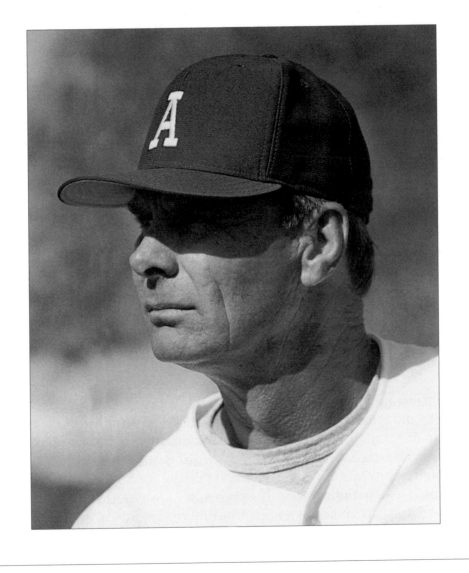

A longtime coaching friend of mine surprised me years ago with this statement:

> After my team won its first national championship and the postgame celebration at the field and hotel was finished, my wife and I were too excited to sleep. The next day, however, as we were returning home I broke into a cold sweat as I realized the never ending task of recruiting and preparing for next year demanded my immediate attention. I actually began to tremble.

I was baffled by that statement because, as a young head coach at the University of Arizona, I felt certain that when you reached the pinnacle of coaching success—a national championship—the pressure and anxiety I was feeling at that time would be gone. My friend and I continued to share our feelings over the years about this phenomenon of continuing and unrelenting pressure a coach feels in spite of ongoing success in terms of wins and losses. (He went on to lead his team to two more national titles, and our Arizona team subsequently won three NCAA championships.) He was right! I discovered that the high expectations created among fans, the student body, the administration, and your players when your team is successful can weigh heavily on the coach and his emotions. When the team is doing poorly and losing, the unrest and dissatisfaction among those same people seem to follow the coach to his pillow late into the night and stare out at him from the mirror in the morning.

I have been there! For 24 years as head coach at Arizona (1973–1996), 5 years as assistant coach at the University of Minnesota (1967–71), and 4 years of coaching USA national teams (1979, 1991, 1998, 1999), I have experienced the exaltation of victory, the resulting high, and often unrealistic expectations for immediate and uninterrupted repeats. I have also looked up from the bottom of the league and a losing record to read and hear the criticism and disgust at my performance as coach. Are the demands on the coach any different in these opposing situations? To the serious-minded coach who feels responsible to call forth the best in his players and team, the pressure is the same whether you are the defending champion or the last-place team.

Stress and tension try all of us. We feel it at home, in the office, on the field, in our community activities. Even at our leisure these unwelcome intruders accost us. The common catchword for these emotions is *burnout,* a fairly new word in the American lexicon, defined as "physical or emotional exhaustion especially as a result of long-term stress or dissipation." Burnout runs the gamut from mere weariness to blackout. A thesaurus offers 35 synonyms for burnout including jadedness, insensibility, rundown, along with more familiar symptoms of fatigue and lethargy.

Whatever we call it, I believe all of us in coaching have experienced burnout to some degree. Some, through sheer willpower, endure these crippling emotions and emerge after many years with scarcely an emotional scratch. Others suffer literally a mental and physical collapse. Most of us are somewhere in between. We all know friends and associates in the coaching fraternity who have quit prematurely because they simply couldn't take it. It pains me to count the tens of thousands of quality coaching hours lost to players and teams because dedicated, talented coaches felt unable to continue because of burnout.

But there is good news. Burnout can be countered and overcome in nearly every case by early recognition and acknowledgment of what is happening in and around us. We then need to take necessary steps to equip ourselves with emotional, physical, and, yes, spiritual tools to deal successfully with the threat of burnout.

Here are some checkmarks and principles to help us be at our best on behalf of our families, associates, and players.

Danger Signs

Irritability and short temper are among the first evidences of burnout. Regrettably, the early targets of these emotions are the ones dearest and closest to us—our wives and children. Correspondingly though, these loved ones can be the solution in short-circuiting the early stages of our irritation and poor temper. Early in my career as a pro baseball player, I resolved not to bring my 0 for 4s and other poor performances home to burden my wife and four children. It wasn't always easy to hear her loving rejoinders after a bad day at the yard, but it did soften my heart and brought me back to the priority of serving my family.

When I began coaching, the likelihood of my having a troubled mind after games and practices increased. No longer was I burdened merely by my personal performance. Now my concerns were multiplied by 25 or 30 or more. I found it imperative to renew my pact with my family and put them first whenever I was home. It took some effort to stop feeling selfish and sorry for myself at these times, but it resulted in a much happier "home plate" for me and, particularly, for my family. Instead of allowing my irritability to grow and gnaw at my coaching career, I was able to step back and enjoy the real blessing of life.

Irritability will also show quickly in our relationship with our coaching associates. The interplay with our coaches during the season is second only to that with our families. Harmony and understanding are essential for a successful staff and, by extension, a successful team. By building confidence and trust in one another, we can reach the point where each cares enough for the others to confront the edginess and shortness of temper that inevitably occur in coaching deliberations. Together, then, we can ward off the early signs of burnout. We should always have room for honest disagreement among the coaching staff, but we must have understanding and genuine concern for one another.

Fatigue is the next danger sign we must acknowledge. We cannot allow it to reach a point where it graduates from a simple physical symptom to an emotional problem. Common among all successful baseball coaches is the willingness to spend however many hours, days, and weeks are necessary to prepare a team fully. But in that noble commitment lies the not-so-subtle trap of physical exhaustion and a run-down body. Ignoring the symptom of chronic weariness leads rather quickly to a lowered resistance to infection, sleepless nights, inattentiveness to normal daily responsibilities, and a growing lack of confidence in coaching ability. Again, our loved ones can help us recognize the symptom of fatigue and cause us to pay closer attention to rest, proper nutrition, and generally taking better care of our bodies. For all of us, it remains necessary to have an annual medical checkup to guard our health and allow us to maximize our commitment and service to our team.

An outgrowth of unrelenting physical fatigue is more serious still—lack of interest in coaching. This insidious demon requires our honest introspection to subdue and conquer and return to our genuine love for coaching. Whereas others can help us identify and overcome the earlier danger signs of irritability, short temper, and fatigue, we detect lack of interest up close and personal. This danger sign of impending burnout can develop slowly over time or suddenly bring us to a sickening realization that we don't care anymore. We can measure our indifference to coaching if we no longer are interested in the academic and personal progress of our players, if we no longer care about the condition of our baseball fields, if our practices become poorly organized, if we lose confidence in and find fault with our coaching associates, if we no longer feel the excitement and privilege of coaching a baseball team, and, finally, if we no longer are interested in learning more about techniques of coaching and self-improvement.

Although these and other realizations that we are losing interest come to our minds first, others close to us—family, associates, players—will soon see that, "Coach is not the same." Overcoming mind and spirit fatigue is far more difficult than overcoming physical fatigue.

In my more than 30 years of coaching baseball, I confess to the murmuring of several of the above symptoms. I found the best way to quiet and dispel these unwelcome visitors was to attend one of the many coaching clinics offered across the country. Listening to outstanding baseball coaches lecture and demonstrate, taking part in the late night bull sessions in the hotel rooms and lobby, picking the brains of other coaches, perusing the new equipment and teaching aids, and simply absorbing the free-flowing excitement of the greatest game of all was enough to fire me up for another season of coaching and to remain forever grateful that God has allowed me to be a baseball coach! (I suggest that you strongly consider attending the annual coaching clinic held every January by the American Baseball Coaches Association [ABCA]. You will discover four days of outstanding clinic sessions, hundreds of baseball coaching exhibits, award luncheons and dinners, and several thousand baseball coaches of like mind. For over 30 years this has been my nourishment and refreshment for the baseball soul.)

Preventive Measures

Once we are aware of the danger signs leading to burnout, we can take care not only to avoid them but also to establish ways to solidify and strengthen our coaching attitudes. In short, we can ask, "What kind of coach do I want to become?" Surely we learn as we go along. Our coaching philosophy 10 years from now will be different from what it is today. But I believe it is helpful to establish early in our careers some foundational attitudes that will prevail until we hang 'em up. It took me much too long to put the following principles firmly in place when I became a head coach, and I struggled needlessly with anxiety and stress. When I discovered the wisdom of these principles I became a better coach—more self-assured, better organized, less uptight, and certainly a nicer person to be around. These are not the only cautionary principles helpful to coaches, but they do give us a starting point.

Have Realistic Expectations

Many of us are by nature optimists and positive thinkers. I believe that it is a gift in coaching to look at the bright side of things. But that attitude must be tempered by pragmatism and a realistic evaluation of the many variables we face each year with our teams. Most notable among these variables is talent—how good are the players? No team will year after year ride the crest of having the best talent in the league. Our expectations and goals for each year must be tied to that principle. It is unfair to the fans, our staff, and especially our players to proclaim blindly that we are the best team in the league when we know better. To impose unrealistic expectations on a young team, be it Little League, high school, or college, creates unnecessary pressure and tension on all involved—especially the coach!

In preseason workouts in 1985, our Arizona Wildcats looked good. We had strong arms on the pitching staff, speed defensively and on the base paths, and an impressive offensive attack. The coaching staff—pitching coach Jim Wing, hitting coach Jerry Stitt, and myself—gradually began setting our goals a bit higher each week, and we challenged our players accordingly. We made it to the College World Series in Omaha! Our expectations for the team were sound and realistic, and although we didn't win the NCAA title, we proved that our goals for that team could be attained. With many of those players returning in 1986, we immediately began planning for a return trip to Omaha. Our coaching strategy throughout fall practice and preseason workouts was to challenge and remind our players we were capable of winning it all that season. And we did! The players had the ability and the will to rise to the challenge. When they hoisted the NCAA championship trophy for all to see following the title game against an outstanding Florida State team, no Arizona player or coach was surprised. We had planned and expected and worked diligently for 12 months for exactly that to happen.

That two-year flush of success and victory misled me in 1987. Many of the players from the '86 team were now in pro ball or had completed their eligibility. Our '87 team was younger and simply not as talented. I unwisely placed goals and expectations on that team that were plainly out of our reach, which led to strain, tension, and erosion of self-confidence. Finally, I backed off and our staff reevaluated that team's strengths and weaknesses more accurately. The last two months of the season became much more fun for both players and coaches.

We must continue to accept no less than the best effort from our players. Encouragement should be the by-product of every practice and game we plan and coach. Our challenge to every player should be for him to strive for maximum output on behalf of the team. We must be at his side constantly to help and encourage that outcome. Our realistic expectations for that player and that team will free us up to be at our coaching best.

Recognize and Respect Authority

All of us live under some form of authority. Rich or poor, big or small, each of us is subject to the will and wishes of some person or group of persons. Even the wealthiest and most powerful CEOs of large corporations are under the authority of a board of directors. Those of us in coaching often find ourselves unhappy and bristling with our superiors for reasons real and imagined. This will cause an uneasy and sometimes adversarial relationship with that important person or persons. A college coaching friend I respect serves to remind me how difficult it must be to work with a constant chip on the shoulder. It seems whenever we speak, I hear a litany of problems and complaints about the athletic director, the grounds crew, recruiting, parents, academic standards, and so on. When we dwell in the negative aspects of any situation—and certainly coaching baseball presents enough of these—it makes that situation much more daunting and fearsome. At disappointment and discouragement, I suggest we form a habit of humming the tune to that old ditty, "Why don't you accentuate the positive, eliminate the negative, latch on to the affirmative, don't mess with misery in between." We must all deal with orders and authority from above in the hierarchy of coaching. Let's do the best we can with a happy heart and a smile on our face. Not only will we be more at peace with our jobs, we will gladden the hearts of our players, associates, and most important, our families.

Use and Trust Your Associates

My first head coaching job was at the University of Arizona. I reported on February 1, 1972, with a great deal of trepidation and uncertainty. The history of success had been firmly established by my predecessors, "Pop" McKale and Frank Sancet. My greatest fear was messing up a great 70-year tradition of winning baseball. I had been blessed with playing for and coaching under the legendary Dick Siebert at the University of Minnesota. I felt I knew the game well enough, but I was not very well prepared for the host of other responsibilities thrust upon me—budget construction and control, public relations, promotion of the program, recruiting, raising money, hiring a staff, alumni needs and concerns, and more. Further, I felt personally responsible to be the lead in every area of the game—pitching, hitting, base running, fielding, team offense and defense, team rules and requirements, and so on. Besides that, I handled all travel, meals, and hotel arrangements. In retrospect, I see now that I not only created a monster for myself but inadvertently overlooked the extraordinary talents and abilities of my assistant coaches, Jim Wing and Mark Johnson.

It took me the better part of two years to realize I was less a teacher of pitching and catching than Jim Wing and less a teacher of hitting, outfield play, and base running than Mark Johnson. When I gave them the responsibility and trust to teach and coach their areas of expertise, I became a more effective head coach and our team performance improved dramatically. I finally recognized, and maintain to this day, that these two men are among the best coaches in the country. Regrettably, I nearly wasted their talents early on. I learned in time to lean heavily on their judgment and entrust them more and more in helping me with all decisions about our baseball program. When Mark moved on to Mississippi State and then to Texas A&M, Jerry Stitt joined our staff and proved to be equally valuable to the welfare of our team.

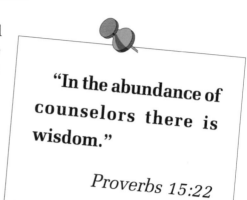

"In the abundance of counselors there is wisdom."

Proverbs 15:22

I learned also to turn to our graduate assistants for advice and to share responsibility for certain areas of coaching with them. Now, many years later, I find that many of those GAs are successful head coaches in college, junior college, and high school. I shudder to think of how much value and excellent coaching my Arizona teams would have missed had I not wised up and turned to my assistant coaches for counsel and advice. I strongly suggest you do the same. Free yourself of some of the myriad concerns and headaches that confront a baseball coach. In the process, you will lessen considerably the danger of experiencing burnout in your coaching. No less authority than King Solomon writes in the Bible (Proverbs 15:22), "In the abundance of counselors there is wisdom."

Priorities

Recently I heard an address from a leader in our community who for years has been responsible for tying together many loose ends in his organization to form a successful enterprise (no, he is not a baseball coach, but it does sound familiar). He titled his address, "Four Key Principles of Leadership" and spoke to his audience on the principles of organization, delegation, coordination, and prioritization.

Afterward, as I reviewed my notes, I saw the clear parallels of those principles to the ones used by successful baseball coaches. Further, I believe that the binding principle is prioritization. Those coaches who can acknowledge and perform the truly important things in life will, in turn, be better organizers, better delegators, and better coordinators. As

I planned this chapter on avoiding burnout in coaching baseball, I found it necessary to break down a list of many important life lessons learned in over 30 years of coaching and 10 more as a professional player. What emerged are these five critical priorities. Certainly there are others that many of you think equally or more important than the following, but I submit these as truly important priorities for you to consider.

Your Wife and Children Come First

A biblical principle repeated throughout the New Testament urges the husband-father to honor and esteem his wife above all other human endeavors and to model for his children unselfish love to their mother. (Acts 10:2; 1 Timothy 3:4, 5:8; Ephesians 5:25, 5:31, and 6:4 are several of these passages.) For many years a framed statement hung in my office with these words in bold letters: "The most important thing a father can do for his children is to love their mother." (author unknown) That served as a daily reminder to me where my first priority as a baseball coach lay—at home.

I happen to believe that George Steinbrenner has done a great deal for college and USA Baseball serving as chairman of the US Olympic Foundation of the United States Olympic Committee. I admire and appreciate his deep interest in, and generosity to, amateur baseball. But I feel Steinbrenner sent the wrong message to coaches when he was quoted in Hal Bodley's column of the March 19, 1993, edition of *USA Today*. It occurred during Buck Showalter's rookie spring training as Yankee manager.

> Clearwater, FL—Know when a man's doing a great job? New York Yankee's owner George Steinbrenner says it's when a man's wife is so angry with her husband she slams the phone down and tells him to . . . well, you know what she tells him. That's what happened to Yankee's Manager Buck Showalter the other day. "The way you can tell if a guy's doing the job is if his wife is unhappy with the hours he's spending on it," Steinbrenner said Thursday. "Then, you know you got the right guy." Steinbrenner says Showalter forgot his wife's birthday.

Surely and regretfully, many of us have forgotten important dates and special events in our wives' lives, but to make that seem like a requirement for a successful coach is badly missing the mark.

Rather, let us take as an example a well-known college coaching friend who, on Valentine's Day before an important game, delayed his appearance at home plate with the umpires and opposing coach, and presented his wife a dozen red roses along with a warm embrace and kiss. As he returned from the stands to the dugout, his entire team, who had watched this tender moment, stood and applauded. I dare say those players will soon forget the signs, team defenses, cutoffs, relays, and double steals that their coach had taught them so thoroughly. But they will never forget the day their coach honored and loved his wife above all others.

It grieves us all to see and hear of coaches' families breaking apart. And generally, not far behind will come a burned-out coach bearing the guilt and remorse of having put baseball and the team ahead of his family. When that happens, the tensions, stress, and anxiety already inherent in coaching will multiply. I can virtually guarantee that when your wife and children clearly know that you prize them above coaching, their support and love will free you up to enjoy your career even more.

Organize and Plan Your Responsibilities Beforehand

When I was an assistant coach under the late Dick Siebert at the University of Minnesota, I marveled at the time and energy he put into planning our practices. Every day Dick posted a detailed practice plan accounting for every minute, every drill, every group (pitchers, catchers, infielders, outfielders), every team defense and offense, and every practice location on the field or in the field house. Further, every player's name appeared on the plan at least once, noting when and where he was supposed to be. Coach Siebert conducted long practices, but they seemed to go quickly because we knew beforehand what was expected of us and how we were to meet those expectations. When game day came the lineups were up early, batting practice groups listed, pregame infield participants named, charters identified, bullpen players assigned, and the scouting report on our opponent posted. I knew Siebert did all those on Sunday afternoon for the coming week's practices and games. Not infrequently, I would think that if I became a head coach there would be no way I would waste all that time planning such detailed practices and games. And I would never do it so far ahead of the event.

When I became head coach at Arizona, I found I could do it no other way. Dick Siebert proved that careful preparation and advance planning resulted in productive practices and winning games. This philosophy also shows respect for the players' time and demonstrates a personal interest in them beyond run, throw, hit, and field. Over the quarter century I have been a head coach, I have been eager to get to the field and execute a well-prepared, comprehensive, goal-defined practice or game plan. This frees me up to be a confident leader on the field and removes the stress and anxiety of uncertainty. The players feel that energy from the coach and respond in kind. Conversely, when I approach the practice feeling unprepared and poorly organized, the players somehow pick up on that and lose some measure of confidence in their leader. Time drags. Boredom and early fatigue set in, followed by a poor practice or game.

A useful mental exercise for us coaches following a practice or game would be to think through and list why our team did well or poorly. Chances are the victories will show, in retrospect, that good planning and organization preceded the job well done.

Your Highest Calling Is to Serve

Most baseball coaches are Type A personalities—that is, we like to be center stage, a leader, aggressive, in the spotlight. This may also mean that we become opinionated, inflexible, controlling, hard to be around. I have already stated that when I first came to Arizona (my first head coaching job), I felt I had to be fully and unquestionably in control—a dictator of sorts. No wonder I felt undue pressure and lack of confidence. As I grew in my coaching, albeit painfully at times, I began to feel unburdened and more at ease when I recognized that a successful coach is more a servant than a master. Again, that lesson was sharpened by scriptural principles and ideals. Jesus' commands in Mark 9:35 and John 13:12–25 and the Apostle Paul's words in Romans 12:1-2 drove that home in my life when I decided what kind of coach, husband, father, and friend I wanted to become.

Deep down, when do we feel the best about ourselves? I suggest those feelings occur when we have done a good deed for someone, when we have put the other person or persons ahead of our selfish interests and acted in the role of a servant. Does it not ennoble a person to be kind rather than harsh, forgiving rather than vengeful, laudatory rather than critical? The leaders I wanted to follow and obey in my early life as a player demonstrated those positive values. I can't recall who said the following but I have seen it in the lives of coaches I admire most: "No man stands so tall as when he stoops to help."

Translating the concept of servanthood into our coaching could well ease those nagging and destructive symptoms of burnout and put our players and associates in an altogether different light. Try it. You'll like it!

Have Rules and Regulations for Your Team

Thoughtful young people today want the adult world to model and show the way as they begin to form their life values and ideals. Although a player may murmur and resist, I believe we are helping that person toward a clearer understanding of right and wrong. Much of today's society is reluctant to make value judgments and seems instead to recommend that young people do whatever feels good. I believe a baseball coach should establish policies and guidelines for his team that call for ethical and moral behaviors on and off the field. The players should have a higher code of conduct than that required of the rest of the student body. One of the outcomes of participation in a team sport should be the recognition that group goals supersede individual goals and that the welfare and success of the team may require individual sacrifice and selflessness. To be part of a group working together for a common goal is one of the earliest and best memories of the winning athlete. It is group dynamics at its best!

But that doesn't happen by accident. The coach creates that experience by offering guidelines and definitions of what it means to be a team player. We can help and encourage our players by setting down rules and regulations that hold them responsible to their teammates, coaches, their school or college and their families. It does not advocate oppressive policies for your team but rather what works for the welfare of the entire group. Teamwork is not some sort of mystical dream but a real dynamic that can empower a group of baseball players. Further, well-defined rules and regulations give needed discipline and structure to your team and fully clarify expectations and goals. Look no further than this book's chapter by Bobby Winkles and his list of rules for the champion Arizona State Sun Devils. Although Coach Winkles formed his rules in the mid-60s, they remain forever contemporary and foundational.

When the entire team and staff understand and accept the purpose of written rules, it gives you, the head coach, the confidence and well-being to handle other responsibilities of directing your program.

Attend Clinics—Keep Learning!

When I served as second vice president of the American Baseball Coaches Association, it was my responsibility to supervise the two and a half days of instructional clinics at our annual convention. It required introducing every one of our 20 or so distinguished clinicians. Along with several thousand other coaches in attendance, I listened thoughtfully and took careful notes. For the first time in my many years of attending the ABCA convention, I heard every word of these highly successful college, junior college, and high school coaches whom I admired and respected. I gained more coaching information in those few days than I had in any other single time during my lifetime of baseball. I could hardly wait to get back to my team at Arizona and implement some of those ideas and principles of winning baseball. I was overflowing with new and exciting challenges to be a better coach and felt more equipped than ever before in my career. And I was about to begin my 20th year as a college head coach! But perhaps the most significant result of faithful attendance at those clinic sessions was the renewed energy and enthusiasm I felt from learning and being with my peers. I daresay that the Wildcats' success that year and my enjoyment and gratitude at being their coach were largely fueled by what I experienced at those clinic sessions. I was virtually immune from any thought of burnout!

A Closing Note

Perhaps it is time to say again that none of us is above the symptoms and danger of burnout. Every coach I have spoken to concerning this phenomenon seems relieved to know others share the same feelings. Don't be ashamed or feel isolated when your life as a coach raises questions, doubts, and feelings of stress. Perhaps it is time for you to talk man to man with a trusted coach or friend and together evaluate your priorities. I suspect it will lead you, as it has me, to reaffirm this simple, yet profound truth from Ecclesiastes 2:24: "A man can do nothing better than to eat and drink and find satisfaction in his work."

ABOUT THE EDITORS

Jerry Kindall coached 24 years and posted a 860-580 record at the University of Arizona, where he was the winningest coach in the university's history. He led the Wildcats to three NCAA Division I National Championship titles (1976, '80, and '86), and was named National Coach of the Year after each of those seasons. He was inducted into the ABCA Hall of Fame in 1991. Kindall is currently USA Baseball's Senior Advisor to the National Team. Kindall played eight years in the major leagues with the Chicago Cubs, Cleveland Indians, and Minnesota Twins.

John Winkin coached for 42 years in Maine, first at Colby College (1954-1974) and then at the University of Maine (1974-1996). He amassed a 943-670 career record and appeared in 12 NCAA Regional Tournaments and 6 College World Series. Winkin received the College Division Coach of the Year award in 1965 and the prestigious Lefty Gomez award in 1986. He is a member of the ABCA Coaching Hall of Fame, Maine Baseball Hall of Fame, and the Maine Sports Hall of Fame. He currently has a fellowship in sports leadership at Husson College.

ABOUT THE CONTRIBUTORS

Bob Bennett has amassed a 1190-685 coaching record in his 31 years at Fresno State University. Coach Bennett has been selected conference coach of the year 13 times and Regional and National Coach of the Year once each. Bennett is a Lefty Gomez Award recipient (2000) and is a member of four halls of fame, including the ABCA Hall of Fame.

Skip Bertman, Louisiana State University's all-time winningest coach, has guided the Tigers to a 774-288-2 record in 16 seasons. He has won four NCAA Championships in the 1990s (1991, '93, '96, and '97) and made 10 College World Series appearances in 14 years. Under Bertman, LSU has compiled the highest all-time NCAA Tournament winning percentage (.733) with a 77-28 record. Coach Bertman has received five National Coach of the Year awards.

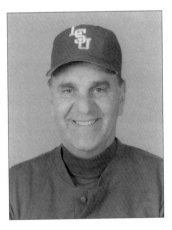

Chuck "Bobo" Brayton coached for 44 years at the collegiate level. At Washington State University (1962-1994) he racked up a 1162-523 record. Brayton received the Lefty Gomez Award in 1983 and is a member of the American Baseball Coaches Association (ABCA) and Washington State University halls of fame.

Ed Cheff has won 10 NAIA Championships (1984, '85, '87-'92, '96, and '99) in his 24 seasons at Lewis-Clark State College (ID). His success prompted *Collegiate Baseball* to name him NAIA Coach of the Decade of the 1980s, and he has been selected as the NAIA Coach of the Year five times. Altogether he has compiled a win-loss mark of 1153-316 (.784), and is only the third coach in NAIA history to win 1,000 baseball games.

Rod Dedeaux is widely regarded as the most successful college baseball coach ever, leading the Trojans to 11 national championships from 1948 to 1978. He posted an overall record of 1,332-571. Dedeaux was named Coach of the Year six times, was inducted into the ABCA Hall of Fame in 1970, and received the Lefty Gomez Award in 1980. Dedeaux was named Division I Coach of the Century by *Collegiate Baseball* in 1999, and head coach of the All-Time College World Series team in 1996.

Ron Fraser spent 29 of his 35-year coaching career at the University of Miami (1963-92), where he achieved a 1274-438 record and won two Division I National Championships (1982, 1985). Fraser was named National Coach of the Year three times, was named *Collegiate Baseball*'s Division I Coach of the Decade for the 1980s, won the Lefty Gomez Award in 1989, and was the second coach on *Baseball America's* list of the Greatest Coaches of the 20th Century.

Gordon Gillespie has been coaching college baseball for 46 years and is the winningest coach ever with a 1520-788 career record. His teams have won four NAIA Championships. He has received countless awards and honors, including the Lefty Gomez Award in 1991, membership in 13 halls of fame, and NAIA Coach of the Century. Gillespie is currently head baseball coach at Ripon College in Wisconsin.

Charlie Greene coached at Miami-Dade Community College from 1968 to 1997, leading the school to three state championship titles (1970, '78, and '81) and one NJCAA National Championship Title (1981), for which he received the National Coach of the Year Award. Coach Greene posted a career record of 1,047-548 and is a member of three halls of fame, including the ABCA Hall of Fame.

Cliff Gustafson coached 29 years at University of Texas, amassing a 1427-373 record, and becoming the all-time winningest coach in NCAA Division I baseball history. In addition, Gustafson took his teams to more College World Series than any other coach in history (17) and won two National Championships (1975, 1983). Coach Gus is a member of the ABCA Hall of Fame.

Tom House played at USC under Coach Rod Dedeaux, then advanced to the major leagues where he pitched for the Atlanta Braves (1967-75), Boston Red Sox (1976-77), and Seattle Mariners (1977-79). He has coached major league pitchers since 1980 for the Houston Astros, San Diego Padres, and Texas Rangers, where he helped pitching great Nolan Ryan add years to his career.

Richard "Itch" Jones has been coaching baseball for 33 years at the collegiate level, compiling a career record of 1056-600 at MacMurray College, Southern Illinois University, and currently the University of Illinois. He was named NCAA Division I Coach of the Year in 1990 and *Sporting News* Coach of the Year in 1978. Jones is a member of the ABCA, Southern Illinois University, and IHSA Coaches halls of fame.

Dave Keilitz is Executive Director of the American Baseball Coaches Association. Keilitz enjoyed a highly successful coaching career at Central Michigan University, leading the Chippewas to a 456-208 record in 14 seasons. He is a member of the ABCA Hall of Fame.

Danny Litwhiler coached for 36 years, 30 of which were spent at the collegiate level at Florida State (1955-1963) and Michigan State (1963-1982) universities. His career collegiate record of 677-444 included three College World Series appearances. He received the Lefty Gomez Award in 1976 and is a member of six halls of fame, including the ABCA Hall of Fame.

Andy Lopez has coached at the collegiate level for 16 years, amassing a record of 630-346 at California State University, Pepperdine University, and the University of Florida—his current post. Lopez guided his 1992 Pepperdine team to a NCAA Division I National Championship. Coach Lopez has twice been named National Coach of the Year (1992, 1996).

Mark Marquess has guided the Stanford baseball program for the past 22 years and posted an 853-453 record. His Stanford teams have captured two NCAA Championships and advanced to the College World Series eight times. The all-time winningest coach in Stanford history, Marquess has been selected NCAA Coach of the Year three times (1985, '87 and '88) and was the 1996 Lefty Gomez Award recipient.

Ron Polk has a career record of 1243-555 over 31 years, and is one of only three coaches to take three different schools to the College World Series: Arizona (1966), Georgia Southern (1973), and Mississippi State (1979, '81, '85, '90, and '97). Polk was selected as the sixth Greatest College Baseball Coach in History by *Baseball America* in 1999, has received the Lefty Gomez Award (1988), and is a member of four halls of fame, including the ABCA Hall of Fame. He is currently the head baseball coach at the University of Georgia.

Gary Pullins coached for 28 years at the collegiate level and compiled a 1014-524 career record. At Brigham Young University, Pullins led the Cougars to seven WAC Conference Championship titles. He was awarded nine conference, four division, and four regional coach of the year awards. Pullins is also a former president of the ABCA.

Ken Schreiber is one of four high school coaches to have won more than 1,000 games (1,010-217). In 39 years at LaPorte High School, Schreiber's teams have won a record seven Indiana state championships (1967, '71, '76, '82, '87, '90 and '92). He has been named Indiana Coach of the Year nine times and National Coach of the Year three times. He is a member of seven halls of fame and was selected as *Collegiate Baseball*'s High School Coach of the Century.

John Scolinos is a 45-year coaching veteran, famous for his performance at Cal Poly-Pomona University. His career record is 1198-949, which includes three NCAA Division II National Championships and three National Coach of the Year awards. Scolinos was named Division II Coach of the Century and Coach of the Decade (1970s) by *Collegiate Baseball*. He is a member of four halls of fame, including the ABCA Hall of Fame, and won the Lefty Gomez Award in 1987.

Hal Smeltzly coached for 34 years at the collegiate (391-166) and international (31-4) levels. Smeltzly piloted Florida Southern College to six NCAA South Regional Championships and three NCAA Division II National Titles (1971, 72 and 75). The ABCA recognized Smeltzly as National Coach of the Year in 1972. He is a member of four halls of fame, including the ABCA Hall of Fame.

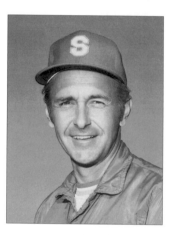

Bob Smith coached at Taylor University (Indiana) and Greenville College (Illinois) from 1958 to 1976, compiling a 243-149 record and capturing seven conference titles. Smith was president of the United States Baseball Federation from 1977 to 1990 and played an instrumental role in making baseball an Olympic sport. Smith won the Lefty Gomez Award in 1984 and is a member of four halls of fame, including the ABCA Hall of Fame.

Jack Stallings compiled a 1258-796 record in his 39 years as a collegiate coach. Stallings coached at Wake Forest (1960-68), Florida State (1969-1974), and Georgia Southern (1976-1999). He led GSU to five NCAA Regionals and one College World Series appearance (1990). Stallings received the Lefty Gomez Award in 1979 and was inducted into the ABCA Hall of Fame in 1988.

Glen Tuckett coached at Brigham Young University for 17 years (1960-1976), where he compiled a record of 498-251 and led the Cougars to two College World Series. Tuckett has served as president of the ABCA and as the Director of Athletics for BYU and the University of Alabama. He is a member of five halls of fame, including the ABCA Hall of Fame, and was a Lefty Gomez Award recipient in 1990.

Gary Ward coached for 19 seasons at Oklahoma State University, posting a 953-313 record. Ward led OSU to 10 College World Series appearances, including seven straight from 1981 to 1987. His teams dominated what was then the Big Eight Conference, winning 16 consecutive titles. Ward was named Conference Coach of the Year four times.

Bobby Winkles coached for 24 years at the collegiate, international, and professional levels. Thirteen of those years were spent at Arizona State University, where Winkles' teams played to a 524-173 record and won three NCAA Division I Championships (1965, '67 and '69). He was named National Coach of the Year twice. Winkles was inducted into the Collegiate Baseball Hall of Fame in 1995.

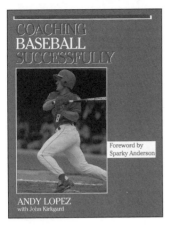

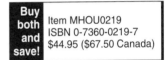
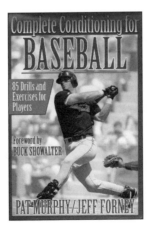

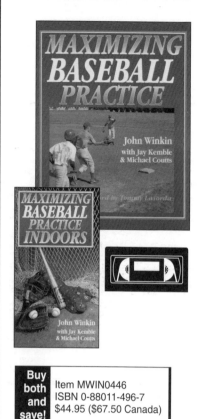

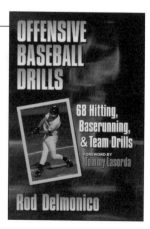